edited by

R. C. SLEIGH, JR.
University of Massachusetts

NECESSARY
TRUTH

Prentice-Hall, Inc., Englewood Cliffs, New Jersey

Library of Congress Catalog Card Number: 72–172063

Printed in the United States of America

ISBN: C 0–13–610766–4
ISBN: P 0–13–610758–3

10 9 8 7 6 5 4 3 2 1

PRENTICE-HALL INTERNATIONAL, INC., London
PRENTICE-HALL OF AUSTRALIA, PTY. LTD., Sydney
PRENTICE-HALL OF CANADA, LTD., Toronto
PRENTICE-HALL OF INDIA PRIVATE LIMITED, New Delhi
PRENTICE-HALL OF JAPAN, INC., Tokyo

CENTRAL ISSUES IN PHILOSOPHY SERIES

BARUCH A. BRODY
series editor

~~~~~~

Baruch A. Brody
MORAL RULES AND PARTICULAR CIRCUMSTANCES

Hugo A. Bedau
JUSTICE AND EQUALITY

Mark Levensky
HUMAN FACTUAL KNOWLEDGE

George I. Mavrodes
THE RATIONALITY OF BELIEF IN GOD

R. C. Sleigh, Jr.
NECESSARY TRUTH

David M. Rosenthal
MATERIALISM AND THE MIND-BODY PROBLEM

Richard Grandy
THEORIES AND OBSERVATIONS IN SCIENCE

Gerald Dworkin
*DETERMINISM, FREE WILL, AND MORAL
RESPONSIBILITY*

David P. Gauthier
MORALITY AND RATIONAL SELF-INTEREST

Charles Landesman
THE FOUNDATIONS OF KNOWLEDGE

Adrienne and Keith Lehrer
THEORY OF MEANING

Foreword

The Central Issues in Philosophy series is based upon the conviction that the best way to teach philosophy to introductory students is to experience or to *do* philosophy with them. The basic unit of philosophical investigation is the particular problem, and not the area or the historical figure. Therefore, this series consists of sets of readings organised around well-defined, manageable problems. All other things being equal, problems that are of interest and relevance to the student have been chosen.

Each volume contains an introduction that clearly defines the problem and sets out the alternative positions that have been taken. The selections are chosen and arranged in such a way as to take the student through the dialectic of the problem; each reading, besides presenting a particular point of view, criticizes the points of view set out earlier.

Although no attempt has been made to introduce the student in a systematic way to the history of philosophy, classical selections relevant to the development of the problem have been included. As a side benefit, the student will therefore come to see the continuity, as well as the breaks, between classical and contemporary thought. But in no case has a selection been included merely for its historical significance; clarity of expression and systematic significance are the main criteria for selection.

BARUCH A. BRODY

Contents

Introduction

Some things of a certain sort are true, and other things of that same sort are false. Some of the things of the sort that are true just happen to be true, and others are necessarily true. Two questions naturally arise here: What sort of thing is it that is true or false, and what is the difference between just happening to be true and being true of necessity? I shall assume rather dogmatically that it is propositions that are true or false in a nonderivative fashion and that a sentence is true (or false) derivatively just in case the proposition expressed by that sentence is true (or false). So that if I talk about a sentence being necessarily true, I mean that the proposition expressed by that sentence is necessarily true. The two sentences "It is raining" and "Il pleut," if uttered under the same circumstances, would seem to say the same thing, make the same assertion or statement. I put this somewhat pompously by saying that the two sentences (in these circumstances) express the same proposition. But I make no effort here to say what a proposition is. So having failed to say much that is illuminating with respect to our first question, let's try the more difficult one—What is the distinction that philosophers (and others) have in mind when they say that a proposition is not *only* true, but *necessarily* true. There seem to be two intuitions that lead to the relevant notion of necessity— one epistemological, having to do with two distinct (supposedly distinct) modes of knowledge; the other metaphysical or, perhaps, semantical, turning on the extent to which the truth of a proposition depends upon the meanings of the words in some sentence that expresses it. Very roughly, the first intuition comes to this: much of what we are justified in believing depends for its justification on the particular experiences we have had, for example, on what information we have gathered through the use of our senses. But some of the propositions we appear to be justified in believing do not depend for their justification on experience. Consider, for example, my beliefs that $7 + 5 = 12$, that red is a color, that all bachelors are unmarried. No doubt, some experience or other occasioned each of these beliefs, but the idea is that not one of these beliefs depends upon any experience for its justification. Propositions of this sort are thought of as necessary in an absolute sense.

Proceeding again in rough fashion, the second intuition seems to come to this: whether a sentence is true (*i.e.*, expresses a true proposition) is in every case partially determined by the meanings that are attached to the terms in the sentence. Now for some sentences truth (or falsity) seems to be *completely* determined by the meanings attached to the terms in the sentence. ("All bachelors are unmarried" will serve as an example.) Such sentences are said to express propositions that are necessary in the relevant absolute sense.

It is not unnatural to suppose that what we have here are two (rough) accounts of the same idea. If a proposition does not depend for its justification on experience, then what does it depend on? We might be inclined to say, "simply understanding the meaning of the terms in some sentence that expresses the proposition"; thus claiming that whatever is necessary by the first intuition is so by the second. Now if a sentence is determined as true simply in virtue of the meanings of its terms, then, we might argue that the proposition expressed by that sentence can be known without appeal to experience. This reasoning, were it sound, would show that whatever is necessary by the second intuition is so by the first.

Yet a third intuition deserves mention here. Some propositions seem to be true in virtue of the way the world is actually constituted. Others (*i.e.* the necessary ones) apparently would hold, regardless of how the world were constituted. This suggests the idea that a necessary truth is a proposition that is true in all possible worlds. Initially this concept may appear to be difficult to make precise. Indeed the next few paragraphs may suggest that an account of necessity in terms of possibility is no real clarification at all. Nonetheless, the concept of a necessary truth as a proposition true in all possible worlds has played a significant role in recent developments. (Something is said about this toward the end of this introduction.)

If some propositions just happen to be true, while others are necessarily true, then we would expect that some propositions just happen to be false, while others are necessarily false. Propositions that are necessarily false are said to be impossible. If a proposition is not impossible, then it is possible; and if a proposition is neither necessary nor impossible, then it is possibly true and possibly false, that is, contingent. Necessity, impossibility, possibility, and contingency comprise the modalities. Taking necessity as undefined, we may define the other modal notions as follows:

where p is any proposition:

'p is possible' means that the denial of p is not necessary,

'p is contingent' means that neither p nor its denial is necessary,

'p is impossible' means that the denial of p is necessary.

With those definitions in mind, we note that if p is necessary, then p is possible but not contingent. We also observe that some possible propositions are necessary, some contingent; but no contingent proposition is necessary, though every contingent proposition is possible. There is nothing sacred about necessity in this scheme; we might take possibility (or impossibility) as undefined and define the remaining modal notions with respect to it. Of course, an account of necessity in terms of possibility is not exactly what we are looking for. Such an account only clarifies the relations of the modal notions among themselves and provides a basis for a study of reasoning concerning the modalities.

What we have said so far is compatible with the idea that necessity (and the other modal notions) are primarily applied to propositions. But some of the things we want to say (especially when we are doing philosophy) suggest a different conception of necessity. Consider:

(1) It is necessary that 9 is greater than 7.

(2) It is not necessary that the number of planets is greater than 7.

(3) The number of planets is necessarily greater than 7.

In (1) necessity is affirmed of a proposition; it is denied of a proposition in the case of (2). But in (3) necessity seems to be affirmed not of a proposition but rather of the connection between a certain object—the number of planets (at present 9)—and a certain property—the property of being greater than 7. (Or perhaps we should read (3) as predicating the property of being necessarily greater than 7 of a certain object.) In any case, the notion of necessity employed in (3) seems to be different (or to be employed differently) from that notion as employed in (1) and (2). In the terminology of medieval logicians (1) and (2) are instances of modality *de dicto,* whereas (3) is an instance of modality *de re.* The last three essays in this book discuss the notion of *de re* modality. We will return to it toward the end of this introduction.

I hope these remarks provide the student beginning the study of philosophy with some understanding of what idea (or ideas) philosophers are concerned with when they discuss necessary truth. Obviously many questions remain. Can any of these intuitive accounts be made precise? Is there really any distinction to be made between truths that are necessary and truths that are not? Do the first two intuitive accounts outlined above really indicate the same concept as the argument of the preceding paragraph suggests? What exactly is the notion of meaning employed in outlining the second intuitive approach to necessity? Can any sense be made of the *de re* modalities? These and other questions are discussed in detail in the papers included in this volume.

Let us turn our attention now to the passages from Leibniz.

We might try to formulate the characterization of necessary truth to be found there in the following manner:

(i) Certain sentences express necessary truths in virtue of their form. These are the "identical propositions" of which two types are to be recognized—the affirmative and the negative. Examples of affirmative, identical sentence schemas mentioned by Leibniz are:

A is A.

Non-A is non-A.

Whatever is AB is A.

Examples of negative, identical sentence schemas are:

What is A is not non-A.

AB is not non-A.

The idea is that a sentence expresses an identical proposition (and, hence, a necessary truth) if it is an instance of one of those schemas.

(ii) However, there are, as Leibniz plainly recognized, many sentences that express necessary truths which are not instances of identities. Leibniz's basic idea here was this: If a sentence is not an identity, it may still express a necessary truth. It would if, by substitution of terms on the basis of acceptable definitions, it could be reduced to an identity. Or, proceeding in the other direction, from an identity by substituting on the basis of acceptable definitions, we may arrive at our sentence. Consider a fairly simple case formulated by Leibniz. We wish to show that "$2 + 2 = 4$" expresses a necessary truth. We employ the following definitions:

$D_f 1$: $2 = 1 + 1$
$D_f 2$: $3 = 2 + 1$
$D_f 3$: $4 = 3 + 1$

(a) $2 + 2 = 2 + 2$

This is the identity with which we begin. Then we subsitute for the last occurrence of "2" in (a) using $D_f 1$ and we have:

$$\text{(b) } 2 + 2 = 2 + (1 + 1)$$

We regroup our parentheses in (b) yielding:

$$\text{(c) } 2 + 2 = (2 + 1) + 1$$

Then, using D_f2, we substitute "3" for "2 + 1" in (c). So we have:

$$\text{(d) } 2 + 2 = 3 + 1$$

Lastly, we use D_f3 in the obvious way and get:

$$\text{(e) } 2 + 2 = 4$$

In summary then we might try to formulate Leibniz's account of necessary truth as

A sentence expresses a necessary truth just in case it is either an instance of an identity schema—such schemas to be defined by their form—or it is reducible to an instance of an identity schema (in a finite number of steps) by substitution on the basis of acceptable definitions.

Some comments:

(1) The above account of necessary truth attributed to Leibniz is close to the account of analytic truth found in the selection from Kant. In Kantian terms this account attributes to Leibniz the view that all *a priori* (*i.e.*, necessary) propositions are analytic. Now Kant rejects this view. In particular the student should note that the example $2 + 2 = 4$ is an instance of a kind of proposition that Kant regarded as necessary but not analytic (hence synthetic). So the student should concentrate on seeing just what it is Kant would reject in our purported proof of the analyticity of the proposition that $2 + 2 = 4$. No doubt attention will get focused on the "definitions" employed. This leads to another comment.

(2) Obviously Leibniz's account of necessary truth leans heavily on the notion of definition. For helpful and insightful comments on the use of this notion in explicating the idea of necessary truth see Quine's essay "Two Dogmas of Empiricism." Note that there is a lacuna in the proof above: by what right do we regroup parentheses in passing from step (b) to step (c)? The answer is obvious—by the principle of the associativity of addition. True enough, but then the question becomes whether this principle in turn can be shown to be necessary by substitution based on acceptable definitions applied to identities. I will not pursue this question here, but the student should.

(3) Let us assume that the truths of logic express necessary propositions. By "truths of logic" I mean sentences that are instances of valid schemas of first-order quantification theory with identity.

A rough account of the idea of a truth of logic is this. We may identify a certain list of terms as logical particles, for example, 'and', 'or', 'not', 'if··then··', 'some', 'any', 'is identical with'. A sentence is a truth of logic if it is true and every sentence which results from it by substituing uniformly and grammatically for its non-logical expressions is also true. [For more on this topic see Quine's essay "Truth by Convention" reprinted in THE WAYS OF PARADOX AND OTHER ESSAYS (Random House, 1966) and the first four chapters of Quine's PHILOSOPHY OF LOGIC (Prentice-Hall, 1970) and also R. Chisholm "The Truths of Reason," pp. 126–27 of this volume.]

It is appropriate to ask whether the account of necessary truth we are attributing to Leibniz has as a consequence that all the truths of logic are necessary truths. It seems doubtful that definitional replacement will be helpful in the case of many truths of logic. So presumably the vast bulk of these truths would have to fall into the first category, that is, be identities. But this too seems doubtful. Some truths of logic are identities, and perhaps all identities are truths of logic. If we assume, as Leibniz seems to suggest, that identities (at any rate those relevant to logical truth) may be recognized by some mechanical test, then we cannot identify the truths of logic with the identities. It is an important fact about the truths of logic that they cannot, in general, be singled out by a mechanical test. Indeed, if we take Leibniz's account of necessary truth and replace all references to identities by references to truths of logic, we obtain something very much like the usual contemporary understanding of analytic truth. Whether this notion of analytic truth can reasonably be identified with the notion of necessary truth is an important contemporary issue (see the Quinton and Chisholm essays for opposing views).

(4) The second passage from Leibniz will suggest to the reader that the account of Leibniz outlined above is inaccurate in at least one important respect. The class of negative identities seems to contain two non overlapping sub-classes—those that may be characterized in a purely formal way and "the disparates." Indeed, in the terminology employed in our preceding comments on Leibniz, we might say that "the disparates" appear to yield necessary propositions that are not analytic—that is, synthetic *a priori* propositions—and this notion takes us to Kant.

In the passages selected from Kant's CRITIQUE OF PURE REASON, we find an explicit development of the first two intuitions concerning the notion of absolute necessity with which our remarks began. *A priori* judgments are characterized by Kant as those that can be known independently of experience. "Independently of experience" is, of course, in need of clarification. Very roughly an *a priori* judgment is one whose justification does not require an appeal to what is known (or justified) by experience. This leaves us with the task of explaining what justification by experience comes to. In other words this leaves us with the task of explaining the *a priori* in terms of its opposite—the empirical (or *a posteriori*). Let us suppose we have some idea of what this comes to. Kant apparently identified that which is necessary (in the sense, that concerns us) with that which is *a priori*. So that for Kant the distinction between the necessary and the contingent appears to coincide with that between the *a priori* and the empirical. But Kant also develops the second of our intuitions concerning the notion of absolute necessity, in terms of a distinction between analytic and synthetic judgments, and he claims that this is a distinction not coextensive with the *a priori* versus the empirical. There is a trivial reason why they are not coextensive, which we should note. The distinction between *a priori* and empirical judgments is intended by Kant to be exhaustive of judgments, while the distinction between analytic and synthetic judgments, at least as formulated in the passages from Kant included here, applies only to judgments that are not compound and that are of subject-predicate form. The student should take note of extensions of Kant's analytic-synthetic distinction outlined by Chisholm. The nontrivial point which must be noted here is that within the class of judgments to which both distinctions apply, Kant wishes to insist that they are not coextensive. In particular his claim is that many important types of judgment are synthetic and *a priori*. Precisely what this claim comes to turns in part on how we understand Kant's elucidation of the analytic-synthetic distinction. His explanation of an analytic judgment as one in which the predicate is contained in the concept of the subject is notoriously metaphorical. The student will do well to mull over what Kant has to say here, perhaps using Leibniz's account of necessity as a guide. One way to get a grip on the problem of the synthetic *a priori* is to compare Kant's views concerning the status of simple truths of arithmetic—for example, that $7 + 5 = 12$—with those of Leibniz and with the Frege-Russell view outlined in Hempel's excellent expository essay "On the Nature of Mathematical Truth." The Frege-Russell view attempts to counter Kant's claim that truths of arithmetic are synthetic. It attempts to establish their analyticity by reducing them via definitions to truths of logic. One note of caution. Even if Kant's account is mistaken and the approach which Hempel outlines is acceptable, this approach does not constitute a definitional reduction of the truths of mathematics to truths of logic (in the sense of "truths of logic" outlined previously.) Conspicuous by its presence in the list of primitives which Hempel takes as belonging to "pure logic" is the predicate "is an element of." Thus he construes set theory along with first order quantification theory with identity as constituting pure logic. But there is much justification for drawing a line between first order quantification theory with identity and set theory and taking the former as pure logic, while relegating the latter either to mathematics or to a separate discipline. For an excellent discussion of the issues involved here the student should see the chapter entitled "The Scope of Logic" in Quine's PHILOSOPHY OF LOGIC (Prentice-Hall, 1970).

The synthetic *a priori* comes up for discussion again in the readings from Chisholm and Quinton. It will be seen that much hinges on getting a clear understanding of the intended contrasts—analytic-synthetic, *a priori*–empirical. One may read Quine's famous essay "Two Dogmas of Empiricism" as casting doubt on the ultimate tenability of either contrast: Sections 5 and 6 may be read as casting doubt on the *a priori*–empirical distinction; Sections 1 through 4, on the analytic-synthetic distinction. Quine argues that necessity, analyticity, definition, synonymity, semantic rule, and self-contradictoriness are technical concepts of a family such that given an understanding of some members of the family we may explain the others with respect to it (together with the notion of a truth of logic). The difficulty is that we appear to have no clear account of any member of the family in extra-familial terms. According to Quine that is exactly what we need to make sense of the distinctions based on these concepts. Bearing in mind the role of definitions in Leibniz's account of necessity, the reader will find Section 2 illuminating; here Quine argues that we need to understand the notion of synonymy in order to grasp the notion of a definition in the sense relevant to analyticity. Quine's attack on the analytic-synthetic distinction is attacked in turn in the reading by Grice and Strawson (pp. 73–78). The student will do well to set out their arguments and see whether he can formulate a reply that would be acceptable to Quine. After the student has had his crack at formulating a Quinian defense, he then ought to compare Quine's own rejoinders to be found in WORD AND OBJECT (pp. 206–207 for the first argument mentioned and pp. 63–65 for the second).[1] One may well come away from this encounter with the feeling that Quine's standards for any acceptable account of synonymy are unreasonably high. Before reaching this conclusion, however, it would be well to study WORD AND OBJECT in its entirety, where Quine spells out his views on synonymy, analyticity, and related matters in detail.

Let's suppose for the time being that necessity, analyticity, and the like still have life in them and consider the contrasting expositions of these notions offered by Quinton and Chisholm. Quinton introduces three concepts intimately related to our three intuitions concerning necessary truth. They are the *a priori,* the analytic, and necessity itself as what is "true in itself and independent of everything outside it." He

[1] W. V. O. Quine, *Word and Object* (New York: John Wiley & Sons, Inc., 1960), pp. 63–65, 206–207.

dissects the notion of analyticity into four different accounts and then argues that all four are accounts of the same concept; this in turn is identical with necessity pure and simple but perhaps not with the *a priori* as construed in a certain way. It should be obvious that various of these identifications are not accepted by Chisholm. The student will find it profitable, I believe, to concentrate on two:

(a) One may suspect that Chisholm would reject the identification of the necessary with what is analytic in any clear sense of the term. See in particular his discussion of our friends "the disparates."

(b) No doubt Chisholm would object to Quinton's identification of the necessary with the analytic in sense three (*i.e.*, that which is true in virtue of the conventions of language). This issue is an important one. The view that necessity is a matter of convention is tempting because, as Quinton says, it "makes necessity unmysterious by treating it, not as something objectively discoverable in the nature of things, but as a matter of human decision." (See p. 97.) Note carefully that Quinton rejects the view that necessary truths describe prevailing linguistic conventions; rather, his view is that necessary truths "are made necessary by convention not that they describe the conventions that prevail." (See p. 99.) But the notions of something's being true in virtue of linguistic conventions and the notion of something's being made true by linguistic convention are none too clear. "In virtue of," "made true by" are metaphorical; "linguistic convention" is not a whole lot better either. On these matters, see Chisholm's penetrating remarks on pages 122–24. Chisholm's positive suggestion might be put something like this: Perhaps it is a matter of convention that, as currently used by speakers of English, "red" means the property of being red and "colored" means the property of being colored. Thus, perhaps it is a matter of convention that the sentence "Everything red is colored" expresses the proposition that it does. But the necessity of the proposition so expressed is a consequence of the fact that the property of being red includes the property of being colored, and this fact is certainly not a matter of convention. The student should consider carefully Quinton's criticism of this type of view formulated on pages 99–101. Perhaps he will not find these criticisms convincing. I don't.

Are we out of the woods? Do we finally have an acceptable account of *de dicto* modality? Perhaps we should temper our enthusiasm with some consideration of the explanatory power of the notion of property inclusion as employed by Chisholm (see particularly pp. 111–13). The student should ponder what the prospects are for providing a general account of inclusion in the relevant sense without an appeal to the modal notions they are intended to explain.

So much for the modalities *de dicto;* let's look at the three papers that discuss the modalities *de re*. Quite frankly these are more difficult than their predecessors in this volume. But perhaps that is to be expected, since *de re* modalities are thought to be a befogged matter. Let's try to see in a rough and informal way what's going on here. Consider:

(1) It is necessary that 9 > (is greater than) 7.

(2) It is not necessary that the number of planets > 7.

(3) 9 has the property of exceeding 7 necessarily.

Let's read (3) as asserting that 9 has a certain property (that of exceeding 7) necessarily and as asserting (or entailing) that 9 has the property of necessarily exceeding 7. What account can we give of the idea that a certain object, 9, (the number of planets, as things now stand) has this modal property, that is, the property of necessarily (or essentially) exceeding 7? An obvious start would be to say that (3) is true in virtue of (1). More generally, where x is an object and F is a property we might try:

(4) x is necessarily F if and only if it is a necessary truth that x is F.

In this manner we would explain the *de re* modalities in terms of the suposedly clearer *de dicto* modalities. If we replace "x" in (4) by "9" and "is F" by "exceeds 7" then, in virtue of (1) we may derive (3). Suppose now we pick another name of 9, say "the number of planets" and replace "x" throughout in (4) by it and substitute for "is F" as before. Now in virtue of (2) we may derive:

(5) The number of planets does not have the property of exceeding 7 necessarily.

Recall:

(6) The number of planets = 9.

We note that (3) and (5) do not sit well together. Furthermore (4) has the probably unacceptable consequence that only things whose existence is necessary have necessary properties. We might try something like:

(7) x is necessarily F if and only if x is F, and there is *some* definite singular term, D, which refers to x such that the sentence that results from placing D in the blanks of "If there is such a thing as —————, then ————— is F" expresses a proposition that is necessarily true.

(7), unhappily, has the unacceptable consequence that whatever property our friend 9 has, it has necessarily—even the obviously accidental property of exceeding the number of left-handed ball players on the Mets, for just assign D as "the number which is both 9 and exceeds the number of left-handed ballplayers on the Mets." Let's now go to the other extreme and try:

(8) x is necessarily F if and only if x is F and, for *any* definite singular term D referring to x, the sentence that results from placing D in the blanks of "If there is such a thing as —————, then ————— is F" expresses a proposition that is necessarily true.

But this won't do either. Using (8) and (2) and an obvious choice of D, for example, "the number of planets," we may show that 9 does not have the property of exceeding 7 necessarily. If we follow the route suggested by (4), (7), and (8), we must practice discrimination in our choice of definite singular terms used to test whether an object has or lacks a given property necessarily.

About the metaphysics behind such discrimination and about the whole project of making sense of the *de re* modalities, Quine is thoroughly sceptical. Recent work of Montague, Kripke, Kanger, and Hintikka, among others, indicates that the logic of *de re* modalities may be made formally respectable in terms of a semantics which may be explained using the idea of possible worlds. Still, if we choose to use such a semantics in order to provide philosophical insight as well as formal respectability, we must take seriously the notions of possible but non-actual worlds, which contain possible but non-actual objects. We must also provide some acceptable account of how (in principle) we are to decide, given an object and a property, whether the object has or lacks the property of necessity. With respect to these problems persistent Plantinga presses on. In his first paper in this volume he sets out to counter the sceptical arguments of Quine and Kneale and then offers a positive account based on the idea of testing for the possession of *de re* modalities by using proper names of the objects under scrutiny. The notions he develops are ingenious and illuminating. One may well wonder, however, whether the notion of a proper name will bear the weight his account puts on it. Plantinga wonders himself.

In his second paper in this volume Plantinga provides an explanation of the notion of a possible world and then utilizes it to explain *de re* modalities and individual essences. This paper clearly demonstrates the philosophical importance and interest of the *de re* modalities.

part one

DE DICTO

GOTTFRIED WILHELM LEIBNIZ

Necessary and Contingent Truths

A true affirmation is one, the predicate of which is present in
the subject. Thus in every true affirmative proposition, necessary or
contingent, universal or singular, the concept of the predicate is in
some way contained in the concept of the subject, so that he who perfectly understood each concept as *God* understands it, would by that
very fact perceive that the predicate is present in the subject. Hence it
follows that all the knowledge of propositions which is in *God*,
whether it be of simple understanding about the essences of things, or
of vision about the existences of things, or mediate knowledge about
conditioned existences, results immediately from the perfect intellec-
tion of each term, which can be subject or predicate of any proposition; or that the *a priori* knowledge of complex things springs from the
understanding of those that are incomplex.

An absolutely necessary proposition is one which can be resolved
into identical propositions, or the opposite of which implies a contradiction. Let me show this by an example in numbers. I shall call
binary every number which can be exactly divided by two, and ternary or quaternary—every one that can be exactly divided by three
or four, and so on. For we understand every number to be resolved
into those which exactly divide it. I say therefore that this proposition:
that a duodenary number is quaternary, is absolutely necessary, since
it can be resolved into identical propositions in the following way. A

* Translated from *Opuscules et fragments inédits de Leibniz,* ed. Couturat (Paris:
Félix Alcan, 1903), pp. 16–22. By permission of the publishers. (The concluding por-
tion is omitted.) Reprinted here from *Philosophers Speak for Themselves—From
Descartes to Locke,* eds. T. V. Smith and Marjorie Greene (Chicago: University of
Chicago Press, 1957), pp. 306–12. By permission of The University of Chicago Press.

duodenary number is binary-senary (by definition); senary is binary ternary (by definition). Therefore a duodenary number is binary binary ternary. Further binary binary is quaternary (by definition). Therefore a duodenary number is quarternary ternary. Therefore a duodenary number is quarternary. Q.E.D. But even if other definitions had been given, it could always have been shown that it comes to the same thing. Therefore I call this necessity metaphysical or geometrical. What lacks such necessity, I call contingent; but what implies a contradiction, or that the opposite of which is necessary, is called *impossible*. Other things are called *possible*. In contingent truth, even though the predicate is really present in the subject, nevertheless by whatever revolution you please of either term, indefinitely continued, you will never arrive at demonstration or identity. And it is for *God* alone, comprehending the infinite all at once, to perceive how one is present in the other, and to understand *a priori* the perfect reason of contingency, which in creatures is furnished (*a posteriori*) by experience. Thus contingent truths are related to necessary as *surd roots,* that is, the roots of incommensurable numbers, to the expressible roots of commensurable numbers. For just as it can be shown that a small number is present in another greater number, by reducing both to the greatest common measure, so too essential propositions or truths are demonstrated: that is, a resolution is carried on until it arrives at terms which it is established by the definitions are common to either term. But as a greater number contains a certain other incommensurable number, and let whatever resolution you please be continued to infinity, it never arrives at a common measure—so in contingent truth, it never arrives at demonstration however much you may resolve the concepts. There is only this difference, that in surd roots we can nevertheless carry out demonstrations, by showing that the error is less than any assignable number, but in contingent truths not even this is conceded to a created mind. And so I consider that I have unfolded something secret, which has long perplexed even myself—while I did not understand how the predicate could be in the subject, and yet the proposition not be necessary. But the knowledge of things geometrical and the analysis of infinites kindled this light for me, so that I understood that concepts too are resoluable to infinity.

Hence we now learn that propositions which pertain to the essences and those which pertain to the existences of things are different. Essential surely are those which can be demonstrated from the resolution of terms, that is, which are necessary, or virtually identical, and the opposite of which, moreover, is impossible or virtually contradictory. And these are the eternal truths. They did not obtain only while the world existed, but they would also obtain if *God* had created a world with a different plan. But from these, existential or contingent truths differ entirely. Their truth is understood *a priori* by the infinite mind alone, and they cannot be demonstrated by any resolution. They are of the sort that are true at a certain time, and they do not only express what pertains to the possibility of things, but also what actually does exist, or would exist contingently if certain things were supposed. For example, take the proposition, I am now living, the sun is shining. For suppose I say that the sun is shining in our hemisphere at this hour, because up to now its motion has been such that, granted its continuation, this certainly follows. Even then (not to mention the nonnecessary obligation of its continuing) that its motion even before this was so much and of this kind is similarly a contingent truth, for which again the reason should be inquired—nor could it be fully produced except from the perfect knowledge of all parts of the universe. This, however, exceeds all created powers. For there is no portion of matter, which is not actually subdivided into other parts; hence the parts of any body whatsoever are actually infinite. Thus neither the sun nor any other body can be perfectly known by a creature. Much less can we arrive at the end of the analysis if we search for the mover causing the motion of any body whatsoever and again for the mover of this; for we shall always arrive at smaller bodies without end. But *God* is not in need of that transition from one contingent to another earlier or simpler contingent,—a transition which can never have an end (as also one contingent is in fact not the cause of another, even though it may seem so to us). But he perceives in any individual substance from its very concept the truth of all its accidents, calling in nothing extrinsic, since any one at all involves in its way all the others and the whole universe. Hence into all propositions into which existence and time enter, by that very fact the whole series of things enters, nor can the now or here be understood except in relation to other things. For this reason such propositions do not allow of a demonstration or terminable resolution by which their truth might appear. And the same holds of all accidents of individual created substances. Indeed even though some one were able to know the whole series of the universe, he still could not state the reason of it, except by having undertaken the comparison of it with all other possible universes. From this it is clear why a demonstration of no contingent proposition can be found, however far the resolution of concepts be continued.

It must not be thought, however, that only singular propositions are contingent, for these are (and can be inferred by induction) some propositions true for the most part; and there are also propositions almost always true at least naturally, so that an exception is ascribed to a miracle. Indeed, I think there are certain propositions most universally true in this series of things, and certainly never to be violated even by miracle, not that they could not be violated by *God,* but that when he himself chose this series of things, by that very fact he decided to observe them (as the specific properties of this very series chosen). And through these propositions set up once for all by the force of the divine decree, it is possible to state the reason for other universal propositions and also for many contingent propositions which can be observed in this universe. For from the first essential laws of the series, true without exception, which contain the whole aim of *God* in choosing the universe, and even include miracles as well, subaltern laws of nature can be derived, which have only physical necessity, and which are not modified except by miracle, by reason of an intuition of some more powerful final cause. And from these finally are inferred others the universality of which is still less; and *God* can also reveal to creatures this kind of demonstration of intermediate universals from one another, a part of which makes up physical science. But one could never by any analysis come to the most universal laws nor to the perfect reasons for individual things; for this knowledge is necessarily appropriate only to *God*. Nor indeed should it disturb any one, that I have said there are certain laws essential to this series of things, since we have nevertheless said above that these very laws are not necessary and essential, but contingent and existential. For since the fact that the series itself exists in contingent, and depends on a free decree of *God,* its laws too, considered absolutely, will be contingent; hypothetically, however, if the series is supposed, they are necessary and so far essential.

These things will now be of advantage to us in distinguishing free substances from others. The accidents of every individual substance if they are predicated of it constitute a contingent proposition, which does not have metaphysical necessity. And the fact that this stone tends downward when its support is removed, is not a necessary but a contingent proposition; nor can such an event be demonstrated from the concept of this stone with the help of the universal concepts which enter into it; and so *God* alone perceives this perfectly. For he alone knows, whether he himself is not going to suspend by a miracle that subaltern law of nature by which heavy things are driven downward. Nor do others understand the most universal laws, nor can they go through the infinite analysis which is necessary to connect the concept of this stone with the concept of the whole universe or with the most universal laws. However this at least can be foreknown from the subaltern laws of nature, that unless the law of gravity is suspended by a miracle, descent follows. But free or intelligent substances have in fact something greater and more marvellous in the direction of a certain imitation of *God;* so that they are bound by no definite subaltern laws of nature, but (as if it were a privation by a certain miracle), they act from the spontaneity of their own power alone, and by an intuition of some final cause they break the nexus and course of efficient causes according to their will. And so true is this, that there is no creature knowing of hearts, who could predict with certainty what another mind will choose according to the laws of nature,—as it can be predicted in another case, at least by an angel, how some body will act if the course of nature be not interrupted. For as the course of the universe is changed by the free will of *God,* so by the free will of the mind the course of its thoughts is changed; so that no subaltern universal laws sufficient for predicting their choice can be found in minds as they are in bodies. This does not, however, at all prevent the future actions of the mind, like his own future actions, from being fixed for *God,* as they are also fixed for the series of things which he chooses. And surely he knows perfectly the strength of his own decree, and also understands at the same time what is contained in the concept of this mind which he himself has admitted into the number of things that are to exist—in so much as it involves this very series of things and its most universal laws. And although this one thing is most true, that the mind never chooses what now appears worse, still it does not always choose what now appears better; since it can put off and suspend judgment till further deliberation and turn its attention to thinking of other things. As to the question whether this will be done, it is not sufficiently determined by any evidence or definite law; certainly not in those minds, which are not sufficiently confirmed in good or evil. For in the case of the blessed another statement must be made.

Hence also it can be understood, what that indifference is which attends liberty. Surely as contingency is opposed to metaphysical necessity, so indifference excludes not only metaphysical, but also physical necessity. It is, in a way, a matter of physical necessity, that *God* should do all things as well as possible (although it is not in the power of any creature to apply this universal rule to individuals, and thus to draw any certain consequences from the divine free actions). It is also a matter of physical necessity that those confirmed in good, angels or blessed, should act from virtue (in such a way, in fact, that it can be predicted with certainty even by a creature, how they will act). It is a matter of physical necessity, that what is heavy strives downward, that the angles of incidence and of reflection are equal, and other things of that kind. But it is not a matter of physical necessity that men should in this life choose some particular good, howsoever specious and apparent it may be, although that is sometimes emphatically to be presumed. For although it may never be possible for that complete metaphysical indifference to exist, such that the mind should be disposed in quite the same way to either one of two contradictories and, again, that anything should be in equilibrium as it were with all its nature, (for we have already observed that even a future predicate is really already present in the concept of the subject, and that therefore mind is not, metaphysically speaking, indifferent, since *God* from the perfect concept of it which he has already perceives all its future accidents, and since mind is not now indifferent to its everlasting concept), still the physical indifference of mind is great enough so that it is certainly not under physical necessity (nor yet metaphysical, *i.e.*, so that no universal reason or law of nature is assignable from which any Creature, however perfect and learned in the state of this mind, can infer with certainty, what the mind, at least naturally (without the extraordinary concourse of *God*) will choose. . . .

GOTTFRIED WILHELM LEIBNIZ

New Essays Concerning
Human Understanding

CHAPTER II

Of the Degrees of Our Knowledge

Th. Primitive truths, which are known by *intuition,* are of two kinds, like the *derivative.* They are truths of *reason* or truths of *fact.* Truths of reason are necessary, and those of fact are contingent. The primitive truths of reason are those which I call by the general name of *identical,* because they seem only to repeat the same thing without giving us any information. They are affirmative or negative. The *affirmative* are such as the following: *Each thing is what it is,* and in as many examples as you please, A is A, B is B. I shall be what I shall be. I have written what I have written. And *nothing* in verse as in prose, *is to be nothing* or a trifle. *The equilateral rectangle is a rectangle. The rational animal* is always *an animal.* And in the hypothetical: *If the regular figure of four sides is an equilateral rectangle, this figure is a rectangle.* Copulatives, disjunctives, and other propositions are also susceptible of this identicism, and I reckon indeed among the affirmatives: non-A is non-A. And this hypothetical: if A is non-B, it follows that A is non-B. Again, if non-A is BC, it follows that non-A is BC. *If a figure having no obtuse angle may be a regular triangle, a figure having no obtuse angle may be regular.* I come now to the identical *negatives* which belong either to the *principle of contradiction* or to the *disparates.* The principle of contradiction is in general: *a pro-*

* Reprinted from Gottfried Wilhelm Leibniz, *New Essays Concerning Human Understanding,* translated by Alfred Gideon Langley (La Salle, Illinois: The Open Court Publishing Co.), pp. 404–406; 472. Used by permission of The Open Court Publishing Co., La Salle, Illinois.

21

position is either true or false: this contains two true statements, one that the true and the false are not compatible in one and the same proposition, or *that a proposition cannot be true and false at once;* the other that the opposition or the negation of the true and the false are not compatible, or that there is no mean between the true and the false, or rather: *it is impossible for a proposition to be neither true nor false.* Now all this is also true in all imaginable propositions in particular, as *what is A cannot be non-A.* Again, AB cannot be non-A. An equilateral rectangle cannot be non-rectangle. Again, *it is true that* every man is an animal, then it is false that *any man is found who is not an animal.* We may vary these statements in many ways, and apply them to copulatives, disjunctives, and others. As for the *disparates,* they are the propositions which state that the object of one idea is not the object of another idea; as, *that heat is not the same thing as color;* again, *man and animal are not the same,* although every man is an animal. All this may be asserted independently of all proof or of reduction to opposition, or to the principle of contradiction, when these ideas are sufficiently understood not to require here analysis; otherwise they are liable to be misunderstood: for in saying, *the triangle and the trilateral are not the same,* we should be mistaken, since upon proper consideration we find that three sides and three angles always go together. In saying, *the quadrilateral rectangle and the rectangle are not the same,* we should also be mistaken. For it is found that the four-sided figure alone can have all the angles right angles. But we may also say in the abstract that *the triangle is not the trilateral,* or that *the formal causes* of the triangle and of the trilateral are not the same, as the philosophers express it. They are different relations of one and the same thing.

Some one after having heard with patience what we have just said up to this point, will lose it after all and will say that we are amusing ourselves with frivolous statements, and that all identical truths are useless. But he will make this judgment for want of having thought sufficiently upon these matters. The deductions of logic, for example, are demonstrated by identical principles; and geometers require the principle of contradiction in their demonstrations which reduce to the impossible.

. . . .

That two and two are four is not a truth at once immediate, supposing that *four* signifies three and one. We can then demonstrate it, and in this way:—

Definitions.—	(1) *Two* is one and one.
	(2) *Three* is two and one.
	(3) *Four* is three and one.

Axiom.—Putting equal things in their place, the equality remains.

Demonstration.—2 and 2 is 2 and 1 and 1 (by def. 1)..........$2 + 2$

2 and 1 and 1 is 3 and 1 (by def. 2).........$2 + \overbrace{1 + 1}$

3 and 1 is 4 (by def. 3).....................$\underbrace{3 + 1}_{4}$

Then (by the axiom) 2 and 2 is 4. Which was to be demonstrated.

I might, instead of saying that 2 and 2 is 2 and 1 and 1, say that 2 and 2 is equal to 2 and 1 and 1, and thus with the others. But it may be understood throughout in order to shorten the process; and that, in virtue of another axiom which states that a thing is equal to itself, or that what is the same, is equal.

Introduction to the Critique of Pure Reason

1. THE DISTINCTION BETWEEN PURE AND EMPIRICAL KNOWLEDGE

There can be no doubt that all our knowledge begins with experience. For how should our faculty of knowledge be awakened into action did not objects affecting our senses partly of themselves produce representations, partly arouse the activity of our understanding to compare these representations, and, by combining or separating them, work up the raw material of the sensible impressions into that knowledge of objects which is entitled experience? In the order of time, therefore, we have no knowledge antecedent to experience, and with experience all our knowledge begins.

But though all our knowledge begins with experience, it does not follow that it all arises out of experience. For it may well be that even our empirical knowledge is made up of what we receive through impressions and of what our own faculty of knowledge (sensible impressions serving merely as the occasion) supplies from itself. If our faculty of knowledge makes any such addition, it may be that we are not in a position to distinguish it from the raw material, until with long practice of attention we have become skilled in separating it.

This, then, is a question which at least calls for closer examination, and does not allow of any off-hand answer:—whether there is any knowledge that is thus independent of experience and even of all impressions of the senses. Such knowledge is entitled *a priori*, and dis-

* Reprinted from Immanuel Kant, *Critique of Pure Reason*, translated by Norman Kemp Smith (London: Macmillan and Company Limited, 1953, pp. 41–55. Used by permission of Macmillan and Company Limited, London; St. Martin's Press, Inc., New York; and the Macmillan Company of Canada.

tinguished from the *empirical*, which has its sources a *posteriori*, that is, in experience.

The expression '*a priori*' does not, however, indicate with sufficient precision the full meaning of our question. For it has been customary to say, even of much knowledge that is derived from empirical sources, that we have it or are capable of having it a *priori*, meaning thereby that we do not derive it immediately from experience, but from a universal rule—a rule which is itself, however, borrowed by us from experience. Thus we would say of a man who undermined the foundations of his house, that he might have known a *priori* that it would fall, that is, that he need not have waited for the experience of its actual falling. But still he could not know this completely a *priori*. For he had first to learn through experience that bodies are heavy, and therefore fall when their supports are withdrawn.

In what follows, therefore, we shall understand by a *priori* knowledge, not knowledge independent of this or that experience, but knowledge absolutely independent of all experience. Opposed to it is empirical knowledge, which is knowledge possible only a *posteriori*, that is, through experience. *A priori* modes of knowledge are entitled pure when there is no admixture of anything empirical. Thus, for instance, the proposition, 'every alteration has its cause', while an *a priori* proposition, is not a pure proposition, because alteration is a concept which can be derived only from experience.

II. WE ARE IN POSSESSION OF CERTAIN MODES OF A PRIORI KNOWLEDGE, AND EVEN THE COMMON UNDERSTANDING IS NEVER WITHOUT THEM

What we here require is a criterion by which to distinguish with certainty between pure and empirical knowledge. Experience teaches us that a thing is so and so, but not that it cannot be otherwise. First, then, if we have a proposition which in being thought is thought as *necessary*, it is an *a priori* judgment; and if, besides, it is not derived from any proposition except one which also has the validity of a necessary judgment, it is an absolutely a *priori* judgment. Secondly, experience never confers on its judgments true or strict, but only assumed and comparative *univerality*, through induction. We can properly only say, therefore, that, so far as we have hitherto observed, there is no exception to this or that rule. If, then, a judgment is thought with strict universality, that is, in such manner that no exception is allowed as possible, it is not derived from experience, but is valid absolutely a *priori*. Empirical universality is only an arbitrary extension of a validity holding in most cases to one which holds in all, for instance, in the proposition, "all bodies are heavy." When, on the other hand, strict universality is essential to a judgment, this indicates a special source of knowledge, namely, a faculty of *a priori* knowledge. Necessity and strict universality are thus sure criteria of *a priori* knowledge, and are inseparable from one another. But since in the employment of these criteria the contingency of judgments is sometimes more easily shown than their empirical limitation, or, as sometimes also happens, their unlimited universality can be more convincingly proved than their necessity, it is advisable to use the two criteria separately, each by itself being infallible.

Now it is easy to show that there actually are in human knoweledge judgments which are necessary and in the strictest sense universal, and which are therefore pure *a priori* judgments. If an example from the sciences be desired, we have only to look to any of the propositions of mathematics; if we seek an example from the understanding in its quite ordinary employment, the proposition, "every alteration must have a cause", will serve our purpose. In the latter case, indeed, the very concept of a cause so manifestly contains the concept of a necessity of connection with an effect and of the strict universality of the rule, that the concept would be altogether lost if we attempted to derive it, as Hume has done, from a repeated association of that which happens with that which precedes, and from a custom of connecting representations, a custom originating in this repeated association, and constituting therefore a merely subjective necessity. Even without appealing to such examples, it is possible to show that pure *a priori* principles are indispensable for the possibility of experience, and so to prove their existence *a priori*. For whence could experience derive its certainty, if all the rules, according to which it proceeds, were always themselves empirical, and therefore contingent? Such rules could hardly be regarded as first principles. At present, however, we may be content to have established the fact that our faculty of knowledge does have a pure employment, and to have shown what are the criteria of such an employment.

Such *a priori* origin is manifest in certain concepts, no less than in judgments. If we remove from our empirical concept of a body, one by one, every feature in it which is [merely] empirical, the colour, the hardness or softness, the weight, even the impenetrability, there still remains the space which the body (now entirely vanished) occupied, and this cannot be removed. Again, if we remove from our empirical concept of any object, corporeal or incorporeal, all properties which experience has taught us, we yet cannot take away that property through which the object is thought as substance or as inhering in a substance (although this concept of substance is more determinate than that of an object in general). Owing, therefore, to the necessity with which this concept of substance forces itself upon us, we have no option save to admit that it has its seat in our faculty of *a priori* knowledge.

III. PHILOSOPHY STANDS IN NEED OF A SCIENCE WHICH SHALL DETERMINE THE POSSIBILITY, THE PRINCIPLES, AND THE EXTENT OF ALL A PRIORI KNOWLEDGE

But what is still more extraordinary than all the preceding is this, that certain modes of knowledge leave the field of all possible experiences and have the appearance of extending the scope of our judgments beyond all limits of experience, and this by means of concepts to which no corresponding object can ever be given in experience.

It is precisely by means of the latter modes of knowledge, in a realm beyond the world of the senses, where experience can yield neither guidance nor correction, that our reason carries on those enquiries which owing to their importance we consider to be far more excellent, and in their purpose far more lofty, than all that the understanding can learn in the field of appearances. Indeed we prefer to run every risk of error rather than desist from such urgent enquiries, on the ground of their dubious character, or from disdain and indifference. These unavoidable problems set by pure reason itself are *God, freedom,* and *immortality.* The science which, with all its preparations, is in its final intention directed solely to their solution is metaphysics; and its procedure is at first dogmatic, that is, it confidently sets itself to this task without any previous examination of the capacity or incapacity of reason for so great an undertaking.

Now it does indeed seem natural that, as soon as we have left the ground of experience, we should, through careful enquiries, assure ourselves as to the foundations of any building that we propose to erect, not making use of any knowledge that we possess without first determining whence it has come, and not trusting to principles without knowing their origin. It is natural, that is to say, that the question should first be considered, how the understanding can arrive at all this knowledge *a priori,* and what extent, validity, and worth it may have. Nothing, indeed, could be more natural, if by the term "natural" we signify what fittingly and reasonably ought to happen. But if we mean by "natural" what ordinarily happens, then on the contrary nothing is more natural and more intelligible than the fact that this enquiry has been so long neglected. For one part of this knowledge, the mathematical, has long been of established reliability, and so gives rise to a favourable presumption as regards the other part, which may yet be of quite different nature. Besides, once we are outside the circle of experience, we can be sure of not being *contradicted* by experience. The charm of extending our knowledge is so great that nothing short of encountering a direct contradiction can suffice to arrest us in our course; and this can be avoided, if we are careful in our fabrications—which none the less will still remain fabrications. Mathematics gives us a shining example of how far, independently of experience, we can progress in *a priori* knowledge. It does, indeed, occupy itself with objects and with knowledge solely in so far as they allow of being exhibited in intuition. But this circumstance is easily overlooked, since this intuition can itself be given *a priori*, and is therefore hardly to be distinguished from a bare and pure concept. Misled by such a proof of the power of reason, the demand for the extension of knowledge recognises no limits. The light dove, cleaving the air in her free flight, and feeling its resistance, might imagine that its flight would be still easier in empty space. It was thus that Plato left the world of the senses, as setting too narrow limits to the understanding, and ventured out beyond it on the wings of the ideas, in the empty space of the pure understanding. He did not observe that with all his efforts he made no advance—meeting no resistance that might, as it were, serve as a support upon which he could take a stand, to which he could apply his powers, and so set his understanding in motion. It is, indeed, the common fate of human reason to complete its speculative structures as speedily as may be, and only afterwards to enquire whether the foundations are reliable. All sorts of excuses will then be appealed to, in order to reassure us of their solidity, or rather indeed to enable us to dispense altogether with so late and so dangerous an enquiry. But what keeps us, during the actual building, free from all apprehension and suspicion, and flatters us with a seeming thoroughness, is this other circumstance, namely, that a great, perhaps the greatest, part of the business of our reason consists in analysis of the concepts which we already have of objects. This analysis supplies us with a considerable body of knowledge, which, while nothing but explanation or elucidation of what has already been thought in our concepts, though in a confused manner, is yet prized as being, at least as regards its form, new insight. But so far as the matter or content is concerned, there has been no extension of our previously possessed concepts, but only an analysis of them. Since this procedure yields real knowledge *a priori*, which progresses in an assured and useful fashion, reason is so far misled as surreptitiously to introduce, without itself being aware of so doing, assertions of an entirely different order, in which it attaches to given concepts others completely foreign to them, and moreover attaches them *a priori*. And yet it is not known how reason can be in position to do this. Such a question is never so much as thought of. I shall therefore at once proceed to deal with the difference between these two kinds of knowledge.

IV. THE DISTINCTION BETWEEN ANALYTIC AND SYNTHETIC JUDGMENTS

In all judgments in which the relation of a subject to the predicate is thought (I take into consideration affirmative judgments only, the subsequent application to negative judgments being easily made), this relation is possible in two different ways. Either the predicate B belongs to the subject A, as something which is (covertly) contained in this concept A; or B lies outside the concept A, although it does indeed stand in connection with it. In the one case I entitle the judgment analytic, in the other synthetic. Analytic judgments (affirmative) are therefore those in which the connection of the predicate with the subject is thought through identity; those in which this connection is thought without identity should be entitled synthetic. The former, as adding nothing through the predicate to the concept of the subject, but merely breaking it up into those constituent concepts that have all along been thought in it, although confusedly, can also be entitled explicative. The latter, on the other hand, add to the concept of the subject a predicate which has not been in any wise thought in it, and which no analysis could possibly extract from it; and they may therefore be entitled ampliative. If I say, for instance, "All bodies are extended," this is an analytic judgment. For I do not require to go beyond the concept which I connect with "body" in order to find extension as bound up with it. To meet with this predicate, I have merely to analyse the concept, that is, to become conscious to myself of the manifold which I always think in that concept. The judgment is therefore analytic. But when I say, "All bodies are heavy," the predicate is something quite different from anything that I think in the mere concept of body in general; and the addition of such a predicate therefore yields a synthetic judgment.

Judgments of experience, as such, are one and all synthetic. For it would be absurd to found an analytic judgment on experience. Since, in framing the judgment, I must not go outside my concept, there is no need to appeal to the testimony of experience in its support. That a body is extended is a proposition that holds *a priori* and is not empirical. For, before appealing to experience, I have already in the concept of body all the conditions required for my judgment. I have only to extract from it, in accordance with the principle of contradiction, the required predicate, and in so doing can at the same time become conscious of the necessity of the judgment—and that is what experience could never have taught me. On the other hand, though I do not include in the concept of a body in general the predicate "weight," none the less this concept indicates an object of experience through one of its parts, and I can add to that part other parts of this same experience, as in this way belonging together with the concept. From the start I can apprehend the concept of body analytically through the characters of extension, impenetrability, figure, and so forth, all of which are thought in the concept. Now, however, looking back on the experience from which I have derived this concept of body, and finding weight to be invariably connected with the above characters, I attach it as a predicate to the concept; and in doing so I attach it synthetically, and am therefore extending my knowledge. The possibility of the synthesis of the predicate "weight" with the concept of "body" thus rests upon experience. While the one concept is not contained in the other, they yet belong to one another, though only contingently, as parts of a whole, namely, of an experience which is itself a synthetic combination of intuitions.

But in *a priori* synthetic judgments this help is entirely lacking. [I do not here have the advantage of looking around in the field of experience.] Upon what, then, am I to rely, when I seek to go beyond the concept A, and to know that another concept B is connected with it? Through what is the synthesis made possible? Let us take the proposition, "Everything which happens has its cause." In the concept of "something which happens," I do indeed think an existence which is preceded by a time, and so forth, and from this concept analytic judgments may be obtained. But the concept of a "cause" lies entirely outside the other concept, and signifies something different from "that which happens," and is not therefore in any way contained in this latter representation. How come I then to predicate of that which happens something quite different, and to apprehend that the concept of cause, though not contained in it, yet belongs, and indeed necessarily belongs, to it? What is here the unknown = X which gives support to the understanding when it believes that it can discover outside the concept A a predicate B foreign to this concept, which it yet at the same time considers to be connected with it? It cannot be experience, because the suggested principle has connected the second representation with the first, not only with greater universality, but also with the character of necessity, and therefore completely *a priori* and on the basis of mere concepts. Upon such synthetic, that is, ampliative principles, all our *a priori* speculative knowledge must ultimately rest; analytic judgments are very important, and indeed necessary, but only for obtaining that clearness in the concepts which is requisite for such a sure and wide synthesis as will lead to a genuinely new addition to all previous knowledge.

V. IN ALL THEORETICAL SCIENCES OF REASON SYNTHETIC A PRIORI JUDGMENTS ARE CONTAINED AS PRINCIPLES

1. *All mathematical judgments, without exception, are synthetic.* This fact, though incontestably certain and in its consequences very important, has hitherto escaped the notice of those who are engaged in the analysis of human reason, and is, indeed, directly opposed to all their conjectures. For as it was found that all mathematical inferences proceed in accordance with the principle of contradiction (which the nature of all apodeictic certainty requires), it was supposed that the fundamental propositions of the science can themselves be known to be true through that principle. This is an erroneous view. For though a synthetic proposition can indeed be discerned in accordance with the principle of contradiction, this can only be if another synthetic proposition is presupposed, and if it can then be apprehended as following from this other proposition; it can never be so discerned in and by itself.

First of all, it has to be noted that mathematical propositions, strictly so called, are always judgments *a priori,* not empirical; because they carry with them necessity, which cannot be derived from experience. If this be demurred to, I am willing to limit my statement to *pure* mathematics, the very concept of which implies that it does not contain empirical, but only pure *a priori* knowledge.

We might, indeed, at first suppose that the proposition $7 + 5 = 12$ is a merely analytic proposition, and follows by the principle of contradiction from the concept of a sum of 7 and 5. But if we look more closely we find that the concept of the sum of 7 and 5 contains nothing save the union of the two numbers into one, and in this no thought is being taken as to what that single number may be which combines both. The concept of 12 is by no means already thought in merely thinking this union of 7 and 5; and I may analyse my concept of such a possible sum as long as I please, still I shall never find the 12 in it. We have to go outside these concepts, and call in the aid of the intuition which corresponds to one of them, our five fingers, for instance, or, as Segner does in his *Arithmetic,* five points, adding to the concept of 7, unit by unit, the five given in intuition. For starting with the number 7, and for the concept of 5 calling in the aid of the fingers of my hand as intuition, I now add one by one to the number 7 the units which I previously took together to form the number 5, and with the aid of that figure [the hand] see the number 12 come into being. That

5 should be added to 7, I have indeed already thought in the concept of a sum $= 7 + 5$, but not that this sum is equivalent to the number 12. Arithmetical propositions are therefore always synthetic. This is still more evident if we take larger numbers. For it is then obvious that, however we might turn and twist our concepts, we could never, by the mere analysis of them, and without the aid of intuition, discover what [the number is that] is the sum.

Just as little is any fundamental proposition of pure geometry analytic. That the straight line between two points is the shortest is a synthetic proposition. For my concept of *straight* contains nothing of quantity, but only of quality. The concept of the shortest is wholly an addition, and cannot be derived, through any process of analysis, from the concept of the straight line. Intuition, therefore, must here be called in; only by its aid is the synthesis possible. What here causes us commonly to believe that the predicate of such apodeictic judgments is already contained in our concept, and that the judgment is therefore analytic, is merely the ambiguous character of the terms used. We are required to join in thought a certain predicate to a given concept, and this necessity is inherent in the concepts themselves. But the question is not what we *ought* to join in thought to the given concept, but what we *actually* think in it, even if only obscurely; and it is then manifest that, while the predicate is indeed attached necessarily to the concept, it is so in virtue of an intuition which must be added to the concept, not as thought in the concept itself.

Some few fundamental propositions, presupposed by the geometrician, are, indeed, really analytic, and rest on the principle of contradiction. But, as identical propositions, they serve only as links in the chain of method and not as principles; for instance, $a = a$; the whole is equal to itself; or $(a + b) > a$, that is, the whole is greater than its part. And even these propositions, though they are valid according to pure concepts, are only admitted in mathematics because they can be exhibited in intuition.

2. *Natural science (physics) contains a priori synthetic judgments as principles.* I need cite only two such judgments: that in all changes of the material world the quantity of matter remains unchanged; and that in all communication of motion, action and reaction must always be equal. Both propositions, it is evident, are not only necessary, and therefore in their origin *a priori,* but also synthetic. For in the concept of matter I do not think its permanence, but only its presence in the space which it occupies. I go outside and beyond the concept of matter, joining to it *a priori* in thought something which I have not thought *in* it. The proposition is not, therefore, analytic, but synthetic, and yet is thought *a priori;* and so likewise are the other propositions of the pure part of natural science.

3. *Metaphysics,* even if we look upon it as having hitherto failed in all its endeavours, is yet, owing to the nature of human reason, a quite indispensable science, and *ought to contain* a priori *synthetic knowledge.* For its business is not merely to analyse concepts which we make for ourselves *a priori* of things, and thereby to clarify them analytically, but to extend our *a priori* knowledge. And for this purpose we must employ principles which add to the given concept something that was not contained in it, and through *a priori* synthetic judgments venture out so far that experience is quite unable to follow us, as, for instance, in the proposition, that the world must have a first beginning, and such like. Thus metaphysics consists, at least *in intention,* entirely of *a priori* synthetic propositions.

CARL G. HEMPEL

On the Nature of Mathematical Truth

1. THE PROBLEM

It is a basic principle of scientific inquiry that no proposition and no theory is to be accepted without adequate grounds. In empirical science, which includes both the natural and the social sciences, the grounds for the acceptance of a theory consist in the agreement of predictions based on the theory with empirical evidence obtained either by experiment or by systematic observation. But what are the grounds which sanction the acceptance of mathematics? That is the question I propose to discuss in the present paper. For reasons which will become clear subsequently, I shall use the term "mathematics" here to refer to arithmetic, algebra, and analysis—to the exclusion, in particular, of geometry.[1]

2. ARE THE PROPOSITIONS OF MATHEMATICS SELF-EVIDENT TRUTHS?

One of the several answers which have been given to our problem asserts that the truths of mathematics, in contradistinction to the hypotheses of empirical science, require neither factual evidence nor any other justification because they are "self-evident." This view, however, which ultimately relegates decisions as to mathematical truth

* Reprinted with revisions with the kind permission of the author and the editor from *The American Mathematical Monthly*, vol. 52 (1945), pp. 543–56.

[1] A discussion of the status of geometry is given in my article, "Geometry and Empirical Science," *American Mathematical Monthly*, vol. 52, pp. 7–17, 1945.

to a feeling of self-evidence, encounters various difficulties. First of all, many mathematical theorems are so hard to establish that even to the specialist in the particular field they appear as anything but self-evident. Secondly, it is well known that some of the most interesting results of mathematics—especially in such fields as abstract set theory and topology—run counter to deeply ingrained intuitions and the customary kind of feeling of self-evidence. Thirdly, the existence of mathematical conjectures such as those of Goldbach and of Fermat, which are quite elementary in content and yet undecided up to this day, certainly shows that not all mathematical truths can be self-evident. And finally, even if self-evidence were attributed only to the basic postulates of mathematics, from which all other mathematical propositions can be deduced, it would be pertinent to remark that judgments as to what may be considered as self-evident, are subjective; they may vary from person to person and certainly cannot constitute an adequate basis for decisions as to the objective validity of mathematical propositions.

3. IS MATHEMATICS THE MOST GENERAL EMPIRICAL SCIENCE?

According to another view, advocated especially by John Stuart Mill, mathematics is itself an empirical science which differs from the other branches, such as astronomy, physics, chemistry, and so forth, mainly in two respects: its subject matter is more general than that of any other field of scientific research, and its propositions have been tested and confirmed to a greater extent than those of even the most firmly established sections of astronomy or physics. Indeed, according to this view, the degree to which the laws of mathematics have been borne out by the past experiences of mankind is so overwhelming that—unjustifiably—we have come to think of mathematical theorems as qualitatively different from the well confirmed hypotheses or theories of other branches of science: we consider them as certain, while other theories are thought of as at best "very probable" or very highly confirmed.

But this view, too, is open to serious objections. From a hypothesis which is empirical in character—such as, for example, Newton's law of gravitation—it is possible to derive predictions to the effect that under certain specified conditions certain specified observable phenomena will occur. The actual occurrence of these phenomena constitutes confirming evidence, their non-occurrence disconfirming evidence for the hypothesis. It follows in particular that an empirical hypothesis is theoretically disconfirmable; that is, it is possible to indicate what kind of evidence, if actually encountered, would disconfirm the hypothesis. In the light of this remark, consider now a simple "hypothesis" from arithmetic: $3 + 2 = 5$. If this is actually an empirical generalization of past experiences, then it must be possible to state what kind of evidence would oblige us to concede the hypothesis was not generally true after all. If any disconfirming evidence for the given proposition can be thought of, the following illustration might well be typical of it: We place some microbes on a slide, putting down first three of them and then another two. Afterwards we count all the microbes to test whether in this instance 3 and 2 actually added up to 5. Suppose now that we counted 6 microbes altogether. Would we consider this as an empirical disconfirmation of the given proposition, or at least as a proof that it does not apply to microbes? Clearly not; rather, we would assume we had made a mistake in counting or that one of the microbes had split in two between the first and the second count. But under no circumstances could the phenomenon just described invalidate the arithmetical proposition in question; for the latter asserts nothing whatever about the behavior of microbes; it merely states that any set consisting of $3 + 2$ objects may also be said to consist of 5 objects. And this is so because the symbols "$3 + 2$" and "5" denote the same number: they are synonymous by virtue of the fact that the symbols "2," "3," "5," and "+" are *defined* (or tacitly understood) in such a way that the above identity holds as a consequence of the meaning attached to the concepts involved in it.

4. THE ANALYTIC CHARACTER OF MATHEMATICAL PROPOSITIONS

The statement that $3 + 2 = 5$, then, is true for similar reasons as, say, the assertion that no sexagenarian is 45 years of age. Both are true simply by virtue of definitions or of similar stipulations which determine the meaning of the key terms involved. Statements of this kind share certain important characteristics: Their validation naturally requires no empirical evidence; they can be shown to be true by a mere analysis of the meaning attached to the terms which occur in them. In the language of logic, sentences of this kind are called analytic or true *a priori*, which is to indicate that their truth is logically independent of, or logically prior to, any experiential evidence.[2] And while the

---

[2] The objection is sometimes raised that without certain types of experience, such as encountering several objects of the same kind, the integers and the arithmetical operations with them would never have been invented, and that therefore the propositions of arithmetic do have an empirical basis. This type of argument, however, involves a confusion of the logical and the psychological meaning of the term "basis." It may very well be the case that certain experiences occasion psychologically the formation of arithmetical ideas and in this sense form an empirical "basis" for them;

statements of empirical science, which are synthetic and can be validated only a posteriori, are constantly subject to revision in the light of new evidence, the truth of an analytic statement can be established definitely, once and for all. However, this characteristic "theoretical certainty" of analytic propositions has to be paid for at a high price: An analytic statement conveys no factual information. Our statement about sexagenarians, for example, asserts nothing that could possibly conflict with any factual evidence: it has no factual implications, no empirical content; and it is precisely for this reason that the statement can be validated without recourse to empirical evidence.

Let us illustrate this view of the nature of mathematical propositions by reference to another, frequently cited, example of a mathematical—or rather logical—truth, namely the proposition that whenever $a = b$ and $b = c$ then $a = c$. On what grounds can this so-called "transitivity of identity" be asserted? Is it of an empirical nature and hence at least theoretically disconfirmable by empirical evidence? Suppose, for example, that a, b, c are certain shades of green, and that as far as we can see, $a = b$ and $b = c$ but clearly $a \neq c$. This phenomenon actually occurs under certain conditions; do we consider it as disconfirming evidence for the proposition under consideration? Undoubtedly not; we would argue that if $a \neq c$, it is impossible that $a = b$ and also $b = c$; between the terms of at least one of these latter pairs, there must obtain a difference, though perhaps only a subliminal one. And we would dismiss the possibility of empirical disconfirmation, and indeed the idea that an empirical test should be relevant here, on the grounds that identity is a transitive relation by virtue of its definition or by virtue of the basic postulates governing it.[3] Hence the principle in question is true *a priori*.

5. MATHEMATICS AS AN AXIOMATIZED DEDUCTIVE SYSTEM

I have argued so far that the validity of mathematics rests neither on its alleged self-evidential character nor on any empirical basis, but derives from the stipulations which determine the meaning of the mathematical concepts, and that the propositions of mathematics are therefore essentially "true by definition." This latter statement, how-

---

but this point is entirely irrelevant for the logical questions as to the *grounds* on which the propositions of arithmetic may be accepted as true. The point made above is that no empirical "basis" or evidence whatever is needed to establish the truth of the propositions of arithmetic.

[3] A precise account of the definition and the essential characteristics of the identity relation may be found in A. Tarski, *Introduction to Logic*, New York, 1941, Ch. III.

ever, is obviously oversimplified and needs restatement and a more careful justification.

For the rigorous development of a mathematical theory proceeds not simply from a set of definitions but rather from a set of non-definitional propositions which are not proved within the theory; these are the postulates or axioms of the theory.[4] They are formulated in terms of certain basic or primitive concepts for which no definitions are provided within the theory. It is sometimes asserted that the postulates themselves represent "implicit definitions" of the primitive terms. Such a characterization of the postulates, however, is misleading. For while the postulates do limit, in a specific sense, the meanings that can possibly be ascribed to the primitives, any self-consistent postulate system admits, nevertheless, many different interpretations of the primitive terms (this will soon be illustrated), whereas a set of definitions in the strict sense of the word determines the meanings of the definienda in a unique fashion.

Once the primitive terms and the postulates have been laid down, the entire theory is completely determined; it is derivable from its postulational basis in the following sense: Every term of the theory is definable in terms of the primitives, and every proposition of the theory is logically deducible from the postulates. To be entirely precise, it is necessary also to specify the principles of logic which are to be used in the proof of the propositions, that is in their deduction from the postulates. These principles can be stated quite explicitly. They fall into two groups: Primitive sentences, or postulates, of logic (such as: If p and q is the case, then p is the case), and rules of deduction or inference (including, for example, the familiar modus ponens rule and the rules of substitution which make it possible to infer, from a general proposition, any one of its substitution instances). A more detailed discussion of the structure and content of logic would, however, lead too far afield in the context of this article.

6. PEANO'S AXIOM SYSTEM AS A BASIS FOR MATHEMATICS

Let us now consider a postulate system from which the entire arithmetic of the natural numbers can be derived. This system was devised by the Italian mathematician and logician G. Peano (1858–1932). The primitives of this system are the terms "0," "number," and "successor." While, of course, no definition of these terms is given within the theory, the symbol "0" is intended to designate the number 0 in its

---

[4] For a lucid and concise account of the axiomatic method, see A. Tarski, loc. cit., Ch. VI.

usual meaning, while the term "number" is meant to refer to the natural numbers 0, 1, 2, 3 $\cdots$ exclusively. By the successor of a natural number n, which will sometimes briefly be called n', is meant the natural number immediately following n in the natural order. Peano's system contains the following 5 postulates:

P1.   0 is a number

P2.   The successor of any number is a number

P3.   No two numbers have the same successor

P4.   0 is not the successor of any number.

P5.   If P is a property such that (a) 0 has the property P, and (b) whenever a number n has the property P, then the successor of n also has the property P, then every number has the property P.

The last postulate embodies the principle of mathematical induction and illustrates in a very obvious manner the enforcement of a mathematical "truth" by stipulation. The construction of elementary arithmetic on this basis begins with the definition of the various natural numbers. 1 is defined as the successor of 0, or briefly as $0'$; 2 as $1'$, 3 as $2'$, and so on. By virtue of P2, this process can be continued indefinitely; because of P3 (in combination with P5), it never leads back to one of the numbers previously defined, and in view of P4, it does not lead back to 0 either.

As the next step, we can set up a definition of addition which expresses in a precise form the idea that the addition of any natural number to some given number may be considered as a repeated addition of 1; the latter operation is readily expressible by means of the successor relation. This definition of addition runs as follows:

D1.   (a) $n + 0 = n;$ (b) $n + k' = (n + k)'.$

The two stipulations of this recursive definition completely determine the sum of any two integers. Consider, for example, the sum $3 + 2$. According to the definitions of the numbers 2 and 1, we have $3 + 2 = 3 + 1' = 3 + (0')'$; by D1 (b), $3 + (0')' = (3 + 0')' = ((3 + 0)')'$; but by D1 (a), and by the definitions of the numbers 4 and 5, $((3 + 0)')' = (3')'$ $= 4' = 5$. This proof also renders more explicit and precise the comments made earlier in this paper on the truth of the proposition that $3 + 2 = 5$: Within the Peano system of arithmetic, its truth flows not merely from the definition of the concepts involved, but also from the postulates that govern these various concepts. (In our specific example, the postulates P1 and P2 are presupposed to guarantee that 1, 2, 3, 4, 5 are numbers in Peano's system; the general proof that D1 determines the sum of any two numbers also makes use of P5.) If we call the postulates and definitions of an axiomatized theory the "stipulations" concerning the concepts of that theory, then we may say now that the propositions of the arithmetic of the natural numbers are true by virtue of the stipulations which have been laid down initially for the arithmetical concepts. (Note, incidentally, that our proof of the formula "3 + 2 = 5" repeatedly made use of the transitivity of identity; the latter is accepted here as one of the rules of logic which may be used in the proof of any arithmetical theorem; it is, therefore, included among Peano's postulates no more than any other principle of logic.)

Now, the multiplication of natural numbers may be defined by means of the following recursive definition, which expresses in a rigorous form the idea that a product nk of two integers may be considered as the sum of k terms each of which equals n.

D2.   (a) $n \cdot 0 = 0$;   (b) $n \cdot k' = n \cdot k + n$.

It now is possible to prove the familiar general laws governing addition and multiplication, such as the commutative, associative, and distributive laws $(n + k = k + n, \ n \cdot k = k \cdot n; \ n + (k + l) = (n + k) + l, \ n \cdot (k \cdot l) = (n \cdot k) \cdot l; \ n \cdot (k + l) = (n \cdot k) + (n \cdot l))$.—In terms of addition and multiplication, the inverse operations of subtraction and division can then be defined. But it turns out that these "cannot always be performed"; that is, in contradistinction to the sum and the product, the difference and the quotient are not defined for every couple of numbers; for example, $7 - 10$ and $7 \div 10$ are undefined. This situation suggests an enlargement of the number system by the introduction of negative and of rational numbers.

It is sometimes held that in order to effect this enlargement, we have to "assume" or else to "postulate" the existence of the desired additional kinds of numbers with properties that make them fit to fill the gaps of subtraction and division. This method of simply postulating what we want has its advantage; but, as Bertrand Russell [5] puts it, they are the same as the advantages of theft over honest toil; and it is a remarkable fact that the negative as well as the rational numbers can be obtained from Peano's primitives by the honest toil of constructing explicit definitions for them, without the introduction of any new postulates or assumptions whatsoever. Every positive and negative integer—in contradistinction to a natural number which has no sign—is definable as a certain set of ordered couples of natural numbers; thus, the integer + 2 is definable as the set of all ordered couples (m, n) of natural numbers where $m = n + 2$; the integer − 2 is the set of all ordered couples (m, n) of natural numbers with $n = m$

[5] Bertrand Russell, *Introduction to Mathematical Philosophy*, New York and London, 1919, p. 71.

$+ 2$.—Similarly, rational numbers are defined as classes of ordered couples of integers.—The various arithmetical operations can then be defined with reference to these new types of numbers, and the validity of all the arithmetical laws governing these operations can be proved by virtue of nothing more than Peano's postulates and the definitions of the various arithmetical concepts involved.

The much broader system thus obtained is still incomplete in the sense that not every number in it has a square root, and more generally, not every algebraic equation whose coefficients are all numbers of the system has a solution in the system. This suggests further expansions of the number system by the introduction of real and finally of complex numbers. Again, this enormous extension can be effected by mere definition, without the introduction of a single new postulate.[6] On the basis thus obtained, the various arithmetical and algebraic operations can be defined for the numbers of the new system, the concepts of function, of limit, of derivative and integral can be introduced, and the familiar theorems pertaining to these concepts can be proved, so that finally the huge system of mathematics as here delimited rests on the narrow basis of Peano's system: Every concept of mathematics can be defined by means of Peano's three primitives, and every proposition of mathematics can be deduced from the five postulates enriched by the definitions of the non-primitive terms.[7] These deductions

---

[6] For a more detailed account of the construction of the number system on Peano's basis, cf. Bertrand Russell, loc. cit., esp. Chs. I and VII.—A rigorous and concise presentation of that construction, beginning, however, with the set of all integers rather than that of the natural numbers, may be found in G. Birkhoff and S. MacLane. *A Survey of Modern Algebra*, New York, 1941, Chs. I, II, III, V.—For a general survey of the construction of the number system, cf. also J. W. Young, *Lectures on the Fundamental Concepts of Algebra and Geometry*, New York, 1911, esp. lectures X, XI, XII.

[7] As a result of very deep-reaching investigations carried out by K. Gödel it is known that arithmetic, and *a fortiori* mathematics, is an incomplete theory in the following sense: While all those propositions which belong to the classical systems of arithmetic, algebra, and analysis can indeed be derived, in the sense characterized above, from the Peano postulates, there exist nevertheless other propositions which can be expressed in purely arithmetical terms, and which are true, but which cannot be derived from the Peano system. And more generally: For any postulate system of arithmetic (or of mathematics for that matter) which is not self-contradictory, there exist propositions which are true, and which can be stated in purely arithmetical terms, but which cannot be derived from that postulate system. In other words, it is impossible to construct a postulate system which is not self-contradictory, and which contains among its consequences all true propositions which can be formulated within the language of arithmetic.

This fact does not, however, affect the result outlined above, namely, that it is possible to deduce, from the Peano postulates and the additional definitions of non-primitive terms, all those propositions which constitute the classical theory of arithmetic, algebra, and analysis; and it is to these propositions that I refer above and subsequently as the propositions of mathematics.

can be carried out, in most cases, by means of nothing more than the principles of formal logic; the proof of some theorems concerning real numbers, however, requires one assumption which is not usually included among the latter. This is the so-called axiom of choice. It asserts that given a class of mutually exclusive classes, none of which is empty, there exists at least one class which has exactly one element in common with each of the given classes. By virtue of this principle and the rules of formal logic, the content of all of mathematics can thus be derived from Peano's modest system—a remarkable achievement in systematizing the content of mathematics and clarifying the foundations of its validity.

7. INTERPRETATIONS OF PEANO'S PRIMITIVES

As a consequence of this result, the whole system of mathematics might be said to be true by virtue of mere definitions (namely, of the non-primitive mathematical terms) provided that the five Peano postulates are true. However, strictly speaking, we cannot, at this juncture, refer to the Peano postulates as propositions which are either true or false, for they contain three primitive terms which have not been assigned any specific meaning. All we can assert so far is that any specific interpretation of the primitives which satisfies the five postulates—i.e., turns them into true statements—will also satisfy all the theorems deduced from them. But for Peano's system, there are several—indeed, infinitely many—interpretations which will do this. For example, let us understand by 0 the origin of a half-line, by the successor of a point on that half-line the point 1 cm. behind it, counting from the origin, and by a number any point which is either the origin or can be reached from it by a finite succession of steps each of which leads from one point to its successor. It can then readily be seen that all the Peano postulates as well as the ensuing theorems turn into true propositions, although the interpretation given to the primitives is certainly not the customary one, which was mentioned earlier. More generally, it can be shown that every progression of elements of any kind provides a true interpretation, or a "model," of the Peano system. This example illustrates our earlier observation that a postulate system cannot be regarded as a set of "implicit definitions" for the primitive terms: The Peano system permits of many different interpretations, whereas in everyday as well as in scientific language, we attach one specific meaning to the concepts of arithmetic. Thus, for example, in scientific and in everyday discourse, the concept 2 is understood in such a way that from the statement "Mr. Brown as well as Mr. Cope, but no one else is in the office, and Mr. Brown is not the same person as Mr. Cope," the conclusion "Exactly two persons are in the office" may be validly inferred. But the stipulations laid down in Peano's system for the natural numbers, and for the number 2 in particular, do not enable us to draw this conclusion; they do not "implicitly determine" the customary meaning of the concept 2 or of the other arithmetical concepts. And the mathematician cannot acquiesce at this deficiency by arguing that he is not concerned with the customary meaning of the mathematical concepts; for in proving, say, that every positive real number has exactly two real square roots, he is himself using the concept 2 in its customary meaning, and his very theorem cannot be proved unless we presuppose more about the number 2 than is stipulated in the Peano system.

If therefore mathematics is to be a correct theory of the mathematical concepts in their intended meaning, it is not sufficient for its validation to have shown that the entire system is derivable from the Peano postulates plus suitable definitions; rather, we have to inquire further whether the Peano postulates are actually true when the primitives are understood in their customary meaning. This question, of course, can be answered only after the customary meaning of the terms "0," "natural number," and "successor" has been clearly defined. To this task we now turn.

8. DEFINITION OF THE CUSTOMARY MEANING OF THE CONCEPTS OF ARITHMETIC IN PURELY LOGICAL TERMS

At first blush, it might seem a hopeless undertaking to try to define these basic arithmetical concepts without presupposing other terms of arithmetic, which would involve us in a circular procedure. However, quite rigorous definitions of the desired kind can indeed be formulated, and it can be shown that for the concepts so defined, all Peano postulates turn into true statements. This important result is due to the research of the German logician G. Frege (1848–1925) and to the subsequent systematic and detailed work of the contemporary English logicians and philosophers B. Russell and A. N. Whitehead. Let us consider briefly the basic ideas underlying these definitions.[8]

[8] For a more detailed discussion, cf. Russell, loc. cit., Chs. II, III, IV. A complete technical development of the idea can be found in the great standard work in mathematical logic, A. N. Whitehead and B. Russell, *Principia Mathematica*, Cambridge, England, 1910–1913.—For a very precise recent development of the theory, see W. V. O. Quine, *Mathematical Logic*, New York, 1940.—A specific discussion of the Peano system and its interpretations from the viewpoint of semantics is included in R. Carnap, *Foundations of Logic and Mathematics, International Encyclopedia of Unified Science*, vol. I, no. 3, Chicago, 1939; especially sections 14, 17, 18.

A natural number—or, in Peano's term, a number—in its customary meaning can be considered as a characteristic of certain *classes* of objects. Thus, for example, the class of the apostles has the number 12, the class of the Dionne quintuplets the number 5, any couple the number 2, and so on. Let us now express precisely the meaning of the assertion that a certain class C has the number 2, or briefly, that $n(C) = 2$. Brief reflection will show that the following definiens is adequate in the sense of the customary meaning of the concept 2: There is some object x and some object y such that (1) $x \in C$ (i.e., x is an element of C) and $y \in C$, (2) $x \neq y$, and (3) if z is any object such that $z \in C$, then either $z = x$ or $z = y$. (Note that on the basis of this definition it becomes indeed possible to infer the statement "The number of persons in the office is 2" from "Mr. Brown as well as Mr. Cope, but no one else is in the office, and Mr. Brown is not identical with Mr. Cope"; C is here the class of persons in the office.) Analogously, the meaning of the statement that $n(C) = 1$ can be defined thus: There is some x such that $x \in C$, and any object y such that $y \in C$, is identical with x. Similarly, the customary meaning of the statement that $n(C) = 0$ is this: There is no object such that $x \in C$.

The general pattern of these definitions clearly lends itself to the definition of any natural number. Let us note especially that in the definitions thus obtained, the definiens never contains any arithmetical term, but merely expressions taken from the field of formal logic, including the signs of identity and difference. So far, we have defined only the meaning of such phrases as "$n(C) = 2$," but we have given no definition for the numbers 0, 1, 2, . . . apart from this context. This desideratum can be met on the basis of the consideration that 2 is that property which is common to all couples, that is, to all classes C such that $n(C) = 2$. This common property may be conceptually represented by the class of all those classes which share this property. Thus we arrive at the definition: 2 is the class of all couples, that is, the class of all classes C for which $n(C) = 2$.—This definition is by no means circular because the concept of couple—in other words, the meaning of "$n(C) = 2$"—has been previously defined without any reference to the number 2. Analogously, 1 is the class of all unit classes, that is, the class of all classes C for which $n(C) = 1$. Finally, 0 is the class of all null classes, that is, the class of all classes without elements. And as there is only one such class, 0 is simply the class whose only element is the null class. Clearly, the customary meaning of any given natural number can be defined in this fashion.[9] In order to characterize the

---

[9] The assertion that the definitions given above state the "customary" meaning of the arithmetical terms involved is to be understood in the logical, not the psy-

intended interpretation of Peano's primitives, we actually need, of all the definitions here referred to, only that of the number 0. It remains to define the terms "successor" and "integer."

The definition of "successor," whose precise formulation involves too many niceties to be stated here, is a careful expression of a simple idea which is illustrated by the following example: Consider the number 5, i.e., the class of all quintuplets. Let us select an arbitrary one of these quintuplets and add to it an object which is not yet one of its members. 5', the successor of 5, may then be defined as the number applying to the set thus obtained (which, of course, is a sextuplet). Finally, it is possible to formulate a definition of the customary meaning of the concept of natural number; this definition, which again cannot be given here, expresses, in a rigorous form, the idea that the class of the natural numbers consists of the number 0, its successor, the successor of that successor, and so on.

If the definitions here characterized are carefully written out—this is one of the cases where the techniques of symbolic, or mathematical, logic prove indispensable—it is seen that the definiens of every one of them contains exclusively terms from the field of pure logic. In fact, it is possible to state the customary interpretation of Peano's primitives, and thus also the meaning of every concept definable by means of them—and that includes every concept of mathematics—in terms of the following 7 expressions, in addition to variables such as "x" and "C": *not, and, if—then; for every object x it is the case that . . . ; there is some object x such that . . . ; x is an element of class C; the class of all things x such that. . . .* And it is even possible to reduce the number of logical concepts needed to a mere four: The first three of the concepts just mentioned are all definable in terms of "*neither— nor,*" and the fifth is definable by means of the fourth and "*neither —nor,*" Thus, all the concepts of mathematics prove definable in terms of four concepts of pure logic. (The definition of one of the more complex concepts of mathematics in terms of the four primitives just mentioned may well fill hundreds or even thousands of pages; but clearly this affects in no way the theoretical importance of the result just obtained; it does, however, show the great convenience and in-

---

chological sense of the term "meaning." It would obviously be absurd to claim that the above definitions express "what everybody has in mind" when talking about numbers and the various operations that can be performed with them. What is achieved by those definitions is rather a "logical reconstruction" of the concepts of arithmetic in the sense that if the definitions are accepted, then those statements in science and everyday discourse which involve arithmetical terms can be interpreted coherently and systematically in such a manner that they are capable of objective validation. The statement about the two persons in the office provides a very elementary illustration of what is meant here.

deed practical indispensability for mathematics of having a large system of highly complex defined concepts available.)

9. THE TRUTH OF PEANO'S POSTULATES IN THEIR CUSTOMARY INTERPRETATION

The definitions characterized in the preceding section may be said to render precise and explicit the customary meaning of the concepts of arithmetic. Moreover—and this is crucial for the question of the validity of mathematics—it can be shown that the Peano postulates all turn into true propositions if the primitives are construed in accordance with the definitions just considered.

Thus, P1 (0 is a number) is true because the class of all numbers—that is, natural numbers—was defined as consisting of 0 and all its successors. The truth of P2 (The successor of any number is a number) follows from the same definition. This is true also of P5, the principle of mathematical induction. To prove this, however, we would have to resort to the precise definition of "integer" rather than the loose description given of that definition above. P4 (0 is not the successor of any number) is seen to be true as follows: By virtue of the definition of "successor," a number which is a successor of some number can apply only to classes which contain at least one element; but the number 0, by definition, applies to a class if and only if that class is empty. —While the truth of P1, P2, P4, P5 can be inferred from the above definitions simply by means of the principles of logic, the proof of P3 (No two numbers have the same successor) presents a certain difficulty. As was mentioned in the preceding section, the definition of the successor of a number n is based on the process of adding, to a class of n elements, one element not yet contained in that class. Now if there should exist only a finite number of things altogether then this process could not be continued indefinitely, and P3, which (in conjunction with P1 and P2) implies that the integers form an infinite set, would be false. Russell's way of meeting this difficulty[10] was to introduce a special "axiom of infinity," which stipulates, in effect, the existence of infinitely many objects and thus makes P3 demonstrable. The axiom of infinity does not belong to the generally recognized laws of logic; but it is capable of expression in purely logical terms and may be treated as an additional postulate of logic.

[10] Cf. Bertrand Russell, loc. cit., p. 24 and Ch. XIII.

10. MATHEMATICS AS A BRANCH OF LOGIC

As was pointed out earlier, all the theorems of arithmetic, algebra, and analysis can be deduced from the Peano postulates and the definitions of those mathematical terms which are not primitives in Peano's system. This deduction requires only the principles of logic plus, in certain cases, the axiom of choice, which asserts that for any set of mutually exclusive non-empty sets α, β, . . . , there exists at least one set which contains exactly one element from each of the sets α, β, . . . , and which contains no other elements.[11] By combining this result with what has just been said about the Peano system, the following conclusion is obtained, which is also known as *the thesis of logicism concerning the nature of mathematics:*

Mathematics is a branch of logic. It can be derived from logic in the following sense:

> **a.** All the concepts of mathematics, that is of arithmetic, algebra, and analysis, can be defined in terms of four concepts of pure logic.
> **b.** All the theorems of mathematics can be deduced from those definitions by means of the principles of logic (including the axioms of infinity and choice).[12]

In this sense it can be said that the propositions of the system of mathematics as here delimited are true by virtue of the definitions of the mathematical concepts involved, or that they make explicit certain characteristics with which we have endowed our mathematical concepts by definition. The propositions of mathematics have, therefore, the same unquestionable certainty which is typical of such propositions as "All bachelors are unmarried," but they also share the complete lack of empirical content which is associated with that certainty:

---

[11] This only apparently self-evident postulate is used in proving certain theorems of set theory and of real and complex analysis; for a discussion of its significance and of its problematic aspects, see Russell, loc. cit., Ch. XII (where it is called the multiplicative axiom), and A. Fraenkel, *Einleitung in die Mengenlehre*, Dover Publications, New York, 1946, §16, sections 7 and 8.

[12] The principles of logic developed in Quine's work and in similar modern systems of formal logic embody certain restrictions as compared with those logical rules which had been rather generally accepted as sound until about the turn of the 20th century. At that time, the discovery of the famous paradoxes of logic, especially of Russell's paradox (*cf.* Russell, loc. cit., Ch. XIII) revealed the fact that the logical principles implicit in customary mathematical reasoning involved contradictions and therefore had to be curtailed in one manner or another.

The propositions of mathematics are devoid of all factual content; they convey no information whatever on any empirical subject matter.

11. ON THE APPLICABILITY OF MATHEMATICS TO EMPIRICAL SUBJECT MATTER

This result seems to be irreconcilable with the fact that after all mathematics has proved to be eminently applicable to empirical subject matter, and that indeed the greater part of present-day scientific knowledge has been reached only through continual reliance on and application of the propositions of mathematics.—Let us try to clarify this apparent paradox by reference to some examples.

Suppose that we are examining a certain amount of some gas, whose volume v, at a certain fixed temperature, is found to be 9 cubic feet when the pressure p is 4 atmospheres. And let us assume further that the volume of the gas for the same temperature and $p = 6$ at., is predicted by means of Boyle's law. Using elementary arithmetic we reason thus: For corresponding values of v and p, $vp = c$, and $v = 9$ when $p = 4$; hence $c = 36$: Therefore, when $p = 6$, then $v = 6$. Suppose that this prediction is borne out by subsequent test. Does that show that the arithmetic used has a predictive power of its own, that its propositions have factual implications? Certainly not. All the predictive power here deployed, all the empirical content exhibited stems from the initial data and from Boyle's law, which asserts that $vp = c$ for *any* two corresponding values of v and p, hence also for $v = 9$, $p = 4$, and for $p = 6$ and the corresponding value of v.[13] The function of the mathematics here applied is not predictive at all; rather, it is analytic or explicative: it renders explicit certain assumptions or assertions which are included in the content of the premises of the argument (in our case, these consist of Boyle's law plus the additional data); mathematical reasoning reveals that those premises contain—hidden in them, as it were—an assertion about the case as yet unobserved. In accepting our premises—so arithmetic reveals—we have—knowingly or unknowingly—already accepted the implication that the p-value in question is 6. Mathematical as well as logical reasoning is a conceptual technique of making explicit what is implicitly contained in a set of premises. The conclusions to which this technique leads assert nothing that is *theoretically new* in the sense of not being contained in the content of the premises. But the results obtained may well be *psychologically new:*

---

[13] Note that we may say "hence" by virtue of the rule of substitution, which is one of the rules of logical inference.

we may not have been aware, before using the techniques of logic and mathematics, what we committed ourselves to in accepting a certain set of assumptions or assertions.

A similar analysis is possible in all other cases of applied mathematics, including those involving, say, the calculus. Consider, for example, the hypothesis that a certain object, moving in a specified electric field, will undergo a constant acceleration of 5 feet/sec². For the purpose of testing this hypothesis, we might derive from it, by means of two successive integrations, the prediction that if the object is at rest at the beginning of the motion, then the distance covered by it at any time t is $\frac{5}{2}t^2$ feet. This conclusion may clearly be psychologically new to a person not acquainted with the subject, but it is not theoretically new; the content of the conclusion is already contained in that of the hypothesis about the constant acceleration. And indeed, here as well as in the case of the compression of a gas, a failure of the prediction to come true would be considered as indicative of the factual incorrectness of at least one of the premises involved (*f.ex.*, of Boyle's law in its application to the particular gas), but never as a sign that the logical and mathematical principles involved might be unsound.

Thus, in the establishment of empirical knowledge, mathematics (as well as logic) has, so to speak, the function of a theoretical juice extractor: the techniques of mathematical and logical theory can produce no more juice of factual information than is contained in the assumptions to which they are applied; but they may produce a great deal more juice of this kind than might have been anticipated upon a first intuitive inspection of those assumptions which form the raw material for the extractor.

At this point, it may be well to consider briefly the status of those mathematical disciplines which are not outgrowths of arithmetic and thus of logic; these include in particular topology, geometry, and the various branches of abstract algebra, such as the theory of groups, lattices, fields, etc. Each of these disciplines can be developed as a purely deductive system on the basis of a suitable set of postulates. If P be the conjunction of the postulates for a given theory, then the proof of a proposition T of that theory consists in deducing T from P by means of the principles of formal logic. What is established by the proof is therefore not the truth of T, but rather the fact that T is true provided that the postulates are. But since both P and T contain certain primitive terms of the theory, to which no specific meaning is assigned, it is not strictly possible to speak of the truth of either P or T; it is therefore more adequate to state the point as follows: If a proposition T is logically deduced from P, then every specific interpretation of the primitives which turns all the postulates of P into true statements, will also render T a true statement.—Up to this point, the analysis is exactly analogous to that of arithmetic as based on Peano's set of postulates. In the case of arithmetic, however, it proved possible to go a step further, namely to define the customary meanings of the primitives in terms of purely logical concepts and to show that the postulates—and therefore also the theorems—of arithmetic are unconditionally true by virtue of these definitions. An analogous procedure is not applicable to those disciplines which are not outgrowths of arithmetic: The primitives of the various branches of abstract algebra have no specific "customary meaning"; and if geometry in its customary interpretation is thought of as a theory of the structure of physical space, then its primitives have to be construed as referring to certain types of physical entities, and the question of the truth of a geometrical theory in this interpretation turns into an *empirical* problem.[14] For the purpose of applying any one of these nonarithmetical disciplines to some specific field of mathematics or empirical science, it is therefore necessary first to assign to the primitives some specific meaning and then to ascertain whether in this interpretation the postulates turn into true statements. If this is the case, then we can be sure that all the theorems are true statements too, because they are logically derived from the postulates and thus simply explicate the content of the latter in the given interpretation.—In their application to empirical subject matter, therefore, these mathematical theories no less than those which grow out of arithmetic and ultimately out of pure logic, have the function of an analytic tool, which brings to light the implications of a given set of assumptions but adds nothing to their content.

But while mathematics in no case contributes anything to the content of our knowledge of empirical matters, it is entirely indispensable as an instrument for the validation and even for the linguistic expression of such knowledge: The majority of the more far-reaching theories in empirical science—including those which lend themselves most eminently to prediction or to practical application—are stated with the help of mathematical concepts; the formulation of these theories makes use, in particular, of the number system, and of functional relationships among different metrical variables. Furthermore, the scientific test of these theories, the establishment of predictions by means of them, and finally their practical application, all require the deduction, from the general theory, of certain specific consequences; and such deduction would be entirely impossible without the techniques

---

[14] For a more detailed discussion of this point, cf. the article mentioned in footnote 1.

of mathematics which reveal what the given general theory implicitly asserts about a certain special case.

Thus, the analysis outlined on these pages exhibits the system of mathematics as a vast and ingenious conceptual structure without empirical content and yet an indispensable and powerful theoretical instrument for the scientific understanding and mastery of the world of our experience.

W. V. O. QUINE

Two Dogmas of Empiricism

Modern empiricism has been conditioned in large part by two dogmas. One is a belief in some fundamental cleavage between truths which are *analytic,* or grounded in meanings independently of matters of fact, and truths which are *synthetic,* or grounded in fact. The other dogma is *reductionism:* the belief that each meaningful statement is equivalent to some logical construct upon terms which refer to immediate experience. Both dogmas, I shall argue, are ill-founded. One effect of abandoning them is, as we shall see, a blurring of the supposed boundary between speculative metaphysics and natural science. Another effect is a shift toward pragmatism.

1. BACKGROUND FOR ANALYTICITY

Kant's cleavage between analytic and synthetic truths was foreshadowed in Hume's distinction between relations of ideas and matters of fact, and in Leibniz's distinction between truths of reason and truths of fact. Leibniz spoke of the truths of reason as true in all possible worlds. Picturesqueness aside, this is to say that the truths of reason are those which could not possibly be false. In the some vein we hear analytic statements defined as statements whose denials are self-contradictory. But this definition has small explanatory value; for the notion of self-contradictoriness, in the quite broad sense needed for this definition of analyticity, stands in exactly the same need of clarifica-

* Reprinted by permission of the publishers from Willard Van Orman Quine, *From a Logical Point of View.* Cambridge, Mass.: Harvard University Press, Copyright, 1953, 1961, by the President and Fellows of Harvard College.

tion as does the notion of analyticity itself. The two notions are the two sides of a single dubious coin.

Kant conceived of an analytic statement as one that attributes to its subject no more than is already conceptually contained in the subject. This formulation has two shortcomings: it limits itself to statements of subject-predicate form, and it appeals to a notion of containment which is left at a metaphorical level. But Kant's intent, evident more from the use he makes of the notion of analyticity than from his definition of it, can be restated thus: a statement is analytic when it is true by virtue of meanings and independently of fact. Pursuing this line, let us examine the concept of *meaning* which is presupposed.

Meaning, let us remember, is not to be identified with naming. Frege's example of 'Evening Star' and 'Morning Star', and Russell's of 'Scott' and 'the author of *Waverly*', illustrate that terms can name the same thing but differ in meaning. The distinction between meaning and naming is no less important at the level of abstract terms. The terms '9' and 'the number of the planets' name one and the same abstract entity but presumably must be regarded as unlike in meaning; for astronomical observation was needed, and not mere reflection on meanings, to determine the sameness of the entity in question.

The above examples consist of singular terms, concrete and abstract. With general terms, or predicates, the situation is somewhat different but parallel. Whereas a singular term purports to name an entity, abstract or concrete, a general term does not; but a general term is *true* of an entity, or of each of many, or of none. The class of all entities of which a general term is true is called the *extension* of the term. Now paralleling the contrast between the meaning of a singular term and the entity named, we must distinguish equally between the meaning of a general term and its extension. The general terms 'creature with a heart' and 'creature with kidneys,' for example, are perhaps alike in extension but unlike in meaning.

Confusion of meaning with extension, in the case of general terms, is less common than confusion of meaning with naming in the case of singular terms. It is indeed a commonplace in philosophy to oppose intension (or meaning) to extension, or, in a variant vocabulary, connotation to denotation.

The Aristotelian notion of essence was the forerunner, no doubt, of the modern notion of intension or meaning. For Aristotle it was essential in men to be rational, accidental to be two-legged. But there is an important difference between this attitude and the doctrine of meaning. From the latter point of view it may indeed be conceded (if only for the sake of argument) that rationality is involved in the meaning of the word 'man' while two-leggedness is not; but two-leggedness may at the same time be viewed as involved in the meaning of 'biped' while rationality is not. Thus from the point of view of the doctrine of meaning it makes no sense to say of the actual individual, who is at once a man and a biped, that his rationality is essential and his two-leggedness accidental or vice versa. Things had essences, for Aristotle, but only linguistic forms have meanings. Meaning is what essence becomes when it is divorced from the object of reference and wedded to the word.

For the theory of meaning a conspicuous question is the nature of its objects: what sort of things are meanings? A felt need for meant entities may derive from an earlier failure to appreciate that meaning and reference are distinct. Once the theory of meaning is sharply separated from the theory of reference, it is a short step to recognizing as the primary business of the theory of meaning simply the synonymy of linguistic forms and the analyticity of statements; meanings themselves, as obscure intermediary entities, may well be abandoned.

The problem of analyticity then confronts us anew. Statements which are analytic by general philosophical acclaim are not, indeed, far to seek. They fall into two classes. Those of the first class, which may be called *logically true,* are typified by:

(1) No unmarried man is married.

The relevant feature of this example is that it not merely is true as it stands, but remains true under any and all reinterpretations of 'man' and 'married.' If we suppose a prior inventory of *logical* particles, comprising 'no,' 'un-,' 'not,' 'if,' 'then,' 'and,' and so forth, then in general a logical truth is a statement which is true and remains true under all reinterpretations of its components other than the logical particles.

But there is also a second class of analytic statements, typified by:

(2) No bachelor is married.

The characteristic of such a statement is that it can be turned into a logical truth by putting synonyms for synonyms; thus (2) can be turned into (1) by putting 'unmarried man' for its synonym 'bachelor.' We still lack a proper characterization of this second class of analytic statements, and therewith of analyticity generally, inasmuch as we have had in the above description to lean on a notion of "synonymy" which is no less in need of clarification than analyticity itself.

In recent years Carnap has tended to explain analyticity by appeal to what he calls state-descriptions. A state-description is any exhaustive assignment of truth values to the atomic, or noncompound, statements of the language. All other statements of the language are, Carnap assumes, built up of their component clauses by means of the familiar logical devices, in such a way that the truth value of any complex statement is fixed for each state-description by specifiable logical laws. A statement is then explained as analytic when it comes out true under every state-description. This account is an adaptation of Leibniz's "true in all possible worlds." But note that this version of analyticity serves its purpose only if the atomic statements of the language are, unlike 'John is a bachelor' and 'John is married,' mutually independent. Otherwise there would be a state-description which assigned truth to 'John is a bachelor' and to 'John is married,' and consequently 'No bachelors are married' would turn out synthetic rather than analytic under the proposed criterion. Thus the criterion of analyticity in terms of state-descriptions serves only for languages devoid of extralogical synonym-pairs, such as 'bachelor' and 'unmarried man'—synonym-pairs of the type which give rise to the "second class" of analytic statements. The criterion in terms of state-descriptions is a reconstruction at best of logical truth, not of analyticity.

I do not mean to suggest that Carnap is under any illusions on this point. His simplified model language with its state-descriptions is aimed primarily not at the general problem of analyticity but at another purpose, the clarification of probability and induction. Our problem, however, is analyticity; and here the major difficulty lies not in the first class of analytic statements, the logical truths, but rather in the second class, which depends on the notion of synonymy.

2. DEFINITION

There are those who find it soothing to say that the analytic statements of the second class reduce to those of the first class, the logical truths, by *definition*; 'bachelor', for example, is *defined* as 'unmarried man.' But how do we find that 'bachelor' is defined as 'unmarried man'? Who defined it thus, and when? Are we to appeal to the nearest dictionary, and accept the lexicographer's formulation as law? Clearly this would be to put the cart before the horse. The lexicographer is an empirical scientist, whose business is the recording of antecedent facts; and if he glosses 'bachelor' as 'unmarried man' it is because of his belief that there is a relation of synonymy between those forms, implicit in general or preferred usage prior to his own work. The notion of synonymy presupposed here has still to be clarified, presumably in terms relating to linguistic behavior. Certainly the "definition" which is the lexicographer's report of an observed synonymy cannot be taken as the ground of the synonymy.

Definition is not, indeed, an activity exclusively of philologists. Philosophers and scientists frequently have occasion to "define" a recondite term by paraphrasing it into terms of a more familiar vocabulary. But ordinarily such a definition, like the philologist's, is pure lexicography, affirming a relation of synonymy antecedent to the exposition in hand.

Just what it means to affirm synonymy, just what the interconnections may be which are necessary and sufficient in order that two linguistic forms be properly describable as synonymous, is far from clear; but, whatever these interconnections may be, ordinarily they are grounded in usage. Definitions reporting selected instances of synonymy come then as reports upon usage.

There is also, however, a variant type of definitional activity which does not limit itself to the reporting of preëxisting synonymies. I have in mind what Carnap calls *explication*—an activity to which philosophers are given, and scientists also in their more philosophical moments. In explication the purpose is not merely to paraphrase the definiendum into an outright synonym, but actually to improve upon the definiendum by refining or supplementing its meaning. But even explication, though not merely reporting a preëxisting synonymy between definiendum and definiens, does rest nevertheless on *other* preëxisting synonymies. The matter may be viewed as follows. Any word worth explicating has some contexts which, as wholes, are clear and precise enough to be useful; and the purpose of explication is to preserve the usage of these favored contexts while sharpening the usage of other contexts. In order that a given definition be suitable for purposes of explication, therefore, what is required is not that the definiendum in its antecedent usage be synonymous with the definiens, but just that each of these favored contexts of the definiendum, taken as a whole in its antecedent usage, be synonymous with the corresponding context of the definiens.

Two alternative definientia may be equally appropriate for the purposes of a given task of explication and yet not be synonymous with each other; for they may serve interchangeably within the favored contexts but diverge elsewhere. By cleaving to one of these definientia rather than the other, a definition of explicative kind generates, by fiat, a relation of synonymy between definiendum and definiens which did not hold before. But such a definition still owes its explicative function, as seen, to preëxisting synonymies.

There does, however, remain still an extreme sort of definition which does not hark back to prior synonymies at all: namely, the explicitly conventional introduction of novel notations for purposes of sheer abbreviation. Here the definiendum becomes synonymous with the definiens simply because it has been created expressly for the purpose of being synonymous with the definiens. Here we have a really transparent case of synonymy created by definition; would that all species of synonymy were as intelligible. For the rest, definition rests on synonymy rather than explaining it.

The word "definition" has come to have a dangerously reassuring sound, owing no doubt to its frequent occurrence in logical and mathematical writings. We shall do well to digress now into a brief appraisal of the role of definition in formal work.

In logical and mathematical systems either of two mutually antagonistic types of economy may be striven for, and each has its peculiar practical utility. On the one hand we may seek economy of practical expression—ease and brevity in the statement of multifarious relations. This sort of economy calls usually for distinctive concise notations for a wealth of concepts. Second, however, and oppositely, we may seek economy in grammar and vocabulary; we may try to find a minimum of basic concepts such that, once a distinctive notation has been appropriated to each of them, it becomes possible to express any desired further concept by mere combination and iteration of our basic notations. This second sort of economy is impractical in one way, since a poverty in basic idioms tends to a necessary lengthening of discourse. But it is practical in another way: it greatly simplifies theoretical discourse *about* the language, through minimizing the terms and the forms of construction wherein the language consists.

Both sorts of economy, though *prima facie* incompatible, are valuable in their separate ways. The custom has consequently arisen of combining both sorts of economy by forging in effect two languages, the one a part of the other. The inclusive language, though redundant in grammar and vocabulary, is economical in message lengths, while the part, called primitive notation, is economical in grammar and vocabulary. Whole and part are correlated by rules of translation whereby each idiom not in primitive notation is equated to some complex built up of primitive notation. These rules of translation are the so-called *definitions* which appear in formalized systems. They are best viewed not as adjuncts to one language but as correlations between two languages, the one a part of the other.

But these correlations are not arbitrary. They are supposed to show how the primitive notations can accomplish all purposes, save brevity and convenience, of the redundant language. Hence the definiendum and its definiens may be expected, in each case, to be related in one or another of the three ways lately noted. The definiens may be a faithful paraphrase of the definiendum into the narrower notation, preserving a direct synonymy as of antecedent usage; or the definiens may, in the spirit of explication, improve upon the antecedent usage of the definiendum; or finally, the definiendum may be a newly created notation, newly endowed with meaning here and now.

In formal and informal work alike, thus, we find that definition—

except in the extreme case of the explicitly conventional introduction
of new notations—hinges on prior relations of synonymy. Recognizing
then that the notion of definition does not hold the key to synonymy
and analyticity, let us look further into synonymy and say no more
of definition.

3. INTERCHANGEABILITY

A natural suggestion, deserving close examination, is that the synonymy of two linguistic forms consists simply in their interchangeability in all contexts without change of truth value—interchangeability,
in Leibniz's phrase, *salva veritate*. Note that synonyms so conceived
need not even be free from vagueness, as long as the vaguenesses match.

But it is not quite true that the synonyms 'bachelor' and 'unmarried man' are everywhere interchangeable *salva veritate*. Truths
which become false under substitution of 'unmarried man' for 'bachelor' are easily constructed with the help of 'bachelor of arts' or 'bachelor's buttons'; also with the help of quotation, thus:

'Bachelor' has less than ten letters.

Such counterinstances can, however, perhaps be set aside by treating
the phrases 'bachelor of arts' and 'bachelor's buttons' and the quotation ' 'bachelor' ' each as a single indivisible word and then stipulat-
ing that the interchangeability *salva veritate* which is to be the touch-
stone of synonymy is not supposed to apply to fragmentary occurrences
inside of a word. This account of synonymy, supposing it acceptable
on other counts, has indeed the drawback of appealing to a prior con-
conception of "word" which can be counted on to present difficulties
of formulation in its turn. Nevertheless some progress might be
claimed in having reduced the problem of synonymy to a problem of
wordhood. Let us pursue this line a bit, taking "word" for granted.

The question remains whether interchangeability *salva veritate*
(apart from occurrences within words) is a strong enough condition
for synonymy, or whether, on the contrary, some heteronymous expressions might be thus interchangeable. Now let us be clear that we
are not concerned here with synonymy in the sense of complete identity
in psychological associations or poetic quality; indeed no two expressions are synonymous in such a sense. We are concerned only with
what may be called *cognitive* synonymy. Just what this is cannot be
said without successfully finishing the present study; but we know
something about it from the need which arose for it in connection with
analyticity in §1. The sort of synonymy needed there was merely such
that any analytic statement could be turned into a logical truth by

putting synonyms for synonyms. Turning the tables and assuming analyticity, indeed, we could explain cognitive synonymy of terms as follows (keeping to the familiar example): to say that 'bachelor' and 'unmarried man' are cognitively synonymous is to say nò more nor less than that the statement:

(3) All and only bachelors are unmarried men

is analytic.

What we need is an account of cognitive synonymy not presupposing analyticity—if we are to explain analyticity conversely with help of cognitive synonymy as undertaken in §1. And indeed such an independent account of cognitive synonymy is at present up for consideration, namely, interchangeability *salva veritate* everywhere except within words. The question before us, to resume the thread at last, is whether such interchangeability is a sufficient condition for cognitive synonymy. We can quickly assure ourselves that it is, by examples of the following sort. The statement:

(4) Necessarily all and only bachelors are bachelors

is evidently true, even supposing 'necessarily' so narrowly construed as to be truly applicable only to analytic statements. Then, if 'bachelor' and 'unmarried man' are interchangeable *salva veritate,* the result:

(5) Necessarily all and only bachelors are unmarried men

of putting 'unmarried man' for an occurrence of 'bachelor' in (4) must, like (4), be true. But to say that (5) is true is to say that (3) is analytic, and hence that 'bachelor' and 'unmarried man' are cognitively synonymous.

Let us see what there is about the above argument that gives it its air of hocus-pocus. The condition of interchangeability *salva veritate* varies in its force with variations in the richness of the language at hand. The above argument supposes we are working with a language rich enough to contain the adverb 'necessarily', this adverb being so construed as to yield truth when and only when applied to an analytic statement. But can we condone a language which contains such an adverb? Does the adverb really make sense? To suppose that it does is to suppose that we have already made satisfactory sense of 'analytic'. Then what are we so hard at work on right now?

Our argument is not flatly circular, but something like it. It has the form, figuratively speaking, of a closed curve in space.

Interchangeability *salva veritate* is meaningless until relativized to a language whose extent is specified in relevant respects. Suppose now we consider a language containing just the following materials.

There is an indefinitely large stock of one-place predicates (for example, 'F' where 'Fx' means that x is a man) and many-place predicates (for example, 'G' where 'Gxy' means that x loves y), mostly having to do with extralogical subject matter. The rest of the language is logical. The atomic sentences consist each of a predicate followed by one or more variables 'x', 'y', and so forth; and the complex sentences are built up of the atomic ones by truth functions ('not', 'and', 'or', *etc.*) and quantification. In effect such a language enjoys the benefits also of descriptions and indeed singular terms generally, these being contextually definable in known ways. Even abstract singular terms naming classes, classes of classes, and so forth, are contextually definable in case the assumed stock of predicates includes the two-place predicate of class membership. Such a language can be adequate to classical mathematics and indeed to scientific discourse generally, except in so far as the latter involves debatable devices such as contrary-to-fact conditionals or modal adverbs like 'necessarily'. Now a language of this type is extensional, in this sense: any two predicates which agree extensionally (that is, are true of the same objects) are interchangeable *salva veritate*.

In an extensional language, therefore, interchangeability *salva veritate* is no assurance of cognitive synonymy of the desired type. That 'bachelor' and 'unmarried man' are interchangeable *salva veritate* in an extensional language assures us of no more than that (3) is true. There is no assurance here that the extensional agreement of 'bachelor' and 'unmarried man' rests on meaning rather than merely on accidental matters of fact, as does the extensional agreement of 'creature with a heart' and 'creature with kidneys.'

For most purposes extensional agreement is the nearest approximation to synonymy we need care about. But the fact remains that extensional agreement falls far short of cognitive synonymy of the type required for explaining analyticity in the manner of §1. The type of cognitive synonymy required there is such as to equate the synonymy of 'bachelor' and 'unmarried man' with the analyticity of (3), not merely with the truth of (3).

So we must recognize that interchangeability *salva veritate,* if construed in relation to an extensional language, is not a sufficient condition of cognitive synonymy in the sense needed for deriving analyticity in the manner of §1. If a language contains an intensional adverb 'necessarily' in the sense lately noted, or other particles to the same effect, then interchangeability *salva veritate* in such a language does afford a sufficient condition of cognitive synonymy; but such a language is intelligible only in so far as the notion of analyticity is already understood in advance.

The effort to explain cognitive synonymy first, for the sake of deriving analyticity from it afterward as in §1, is perhaps the wrong approach. Instead we might try explaining analyticity somehow without appeal to cognitive synonymy. Afterward we could doubtless derive cognitive synonymy from analyticity satisfactorily enough if desired. We have seen that cognitive synonymy of 'bachelor' and 'unmarried man' can be explained as analyticity of (3). The same explanation works for any pair of one-place predicates, of course, and it can be extended in obvious fashion to many-place predicates. Other syntactical categories can also be accommodated in fairly parallel fashion. Singular terms may be said to be cognitively synonymous when the statement of identity formed by putting '=' between them is analytic. Statements may be said simply to be cognitively synonymous when their biconditional (the result of joining them by 'if and only if') is analytic. If we care to lump all categories into a single formulation, at the expense of assuming again the notion of "word" which was appealed to early in this section, we can describe any two linguistic forms as cognitively synonymous when the two forms are interchangeable (apart from occurrences within "words") *salva* (no longer *veritate* but) *analyticitate*. Certain technical questions arise, indeed, over cases of ambiguity or homonymy; let us not pause for them, however, for we are already digressing. Let us rather turn our backs on the problem of synonymy and address ourselves anew to that of analyticity.

4. SEMANTICAL RULES

Analyticity at first seemed most naturally definable by appeal to a realm of meanings. On refinement, the appeal to meanings gave way to an appeal to synonymy or definition. But definition turned out to be a will-o'-the-wisp, and synonymy turned out to be best understood only by dint of a prior appeal to analyticity itself. So we are back at the problem of analyticity.

I do not know whether the statement 'Everything green is extended' is analytic. Now does my indecision over this example really betray an incomplete understanding, an incomplete grasp of the "meanings", of 'green' and 'extended'? I think not. The trouble is not with 'green' or 'extended', but with 'analytic'.

It is often hinted that the difficulty in separating analytic statements from synthetic ones in ordinary language is due to the vagueness of ordinary language and that the distinction is clear when we have a precise artificial language with explicit "semantical rules." This, however, as I shall now attempt to show, is a confusion.

The notion of analyticity about which we are worrying is a purported relation between statements and languages: a statement S is said to be *analytic for* a language *L*, and the problem is to make sense of this relation generally, that is, for variable '*S*' and '*L*'. The gravity of this problem is not perceptibly less for artificial languages than for natural ones. The problem of making sense of the idiom '*S* is analytic for *L*', with variable '*S*' and '*L*', retains its stubbornness even if we limit the range of the variable '*L*' to artificial languages. Let me now try to make this point evident.

For artificial languages and semantical rules we look naturally to the writings of Carnap. His semantical rules take various forms, and to make any point I shall have to distinguish certain of the forms. Let us suppose, to begin with, an artificial language L_0 whose semantical rules have the form explicitly of a specification, by recursion or otherwise, of all the analytic statements of L_0. The rules tell us that such and such statements, and only those, are the analytic statements of L_0. Now here the difficulty is simply that the rules contain the word 'analytic', which we do not understand! We understand what expressions the rules attribute analyticity to, but we do not understand what the rules attribute to those expressions. In short, before we can understand a rule which begins 'A statement *S* is analytic for language L_0 if and only if . . . ', we must understand the general relative term 'analytic for', we must understand '*S* is analytic for *L*' where '*S*' and '*L*' are variables.

Alternatively we may, indeed, view the so-called rule as a conventional definition of a new simple symbol 'analytic-for-L_0', which might better be written untendentiously as '*K*' so as not to seem to throw light on the interesting word 'analytic'. Obviously any number of classes *K*, *M*, *N*, and so forth of statements of L_0 can be specified for various purposes or for no purposes; what does it mean to say that *K*, as against *M*, *N*, and so forth, is the class of the "analytic" statements of L_0?

By saying what statements are analytic for L_0 we explain 'analytic-for-L_0' but not 'analytic', not 'analytic for'. We do not begin to explain the idiom '*S* is analytic for *L*' with variable '*S*' and '*L*', even if we are content to limit the range of '*L*' to the realm of artificial languages.

Actually we do know enough about the intended significance of 'analytic' to know that analytic statements are supposed to be true. Let us then turn to a second form of semantical rule, which says not that such and such statements are analytic but simply that such and such statements are included among the truths. Such a rule is not subject to the criticism of containing the un-understood word 'analytic', and we may grant for the sake of argument that there is no difficulty over the broader term 'true'. A semantical rule of this second type, a rule of truth, is not supposed to specify all the truths of the language; it merely stipulates, recursively or otherwise, a certain multitude of statements which, along with others unspecified, are to count as true. Such a rule may be conceded to be quite clear. Derivatively, afterward, analyticity can be demarcated thus: a statement is analytic if it is (not merely true but) true according to the semantical rule.

Still there is really no progress. Instead of appealing to an unexplained word 'analytic', we are now appealing to an unexplained phrase 'semantical rule'. Not every true statement which says that the statements of some class are true can count as a semantical rule—otherwise *all* truths would be "analytic" in the sense of being true according to semantical rules. Semantical rules are distinguishable, apparently, only by the fact of appearing on a page under the heading 'Semantical Rules'; and this heading is itself then meaningless.

We can say indeed that a statement is *analytic-for-L_0* if and only if it is true according to such and such specifically appended "semantical rules," but then we find ourselves back at essentially the same case which was originally discussed: 'S is analytic-for-L_0 if and only if . . .' Once we seek to explain 'S is analytic for L' generally for variable 'L' (even allowing limitation of 'L' to artificial languages), the explanation 'true according to the semantical rules of L' is unavailing; for the relative term 'semantical rule of' is as much in need of clarification, at least, as 'analytic for'.

It may be instructive to compare the notion of semantical rule with that of postulate. Relative to a given set of postulates, it is easy to say what a postulate is: it is a member of the set. Relative to a given set of semantical rules, it is equally easy to say what a semantical rule is. But given simply a notation, mathematical or otherwise, and indeed as thoroughly understood a notation as you please in point of the translations or truth conditions of its statements, who can say which of its true statements rank as postulates? Obviously the question is meaningless—as meaningless as asking which points in Ohio are starting points. Any finite (or effectively specifiable infinite) selection of statements (preferably true ones, perhaps) is as much *a* set of postulates as any other. The word 'postulate' is significant only relative to an act of inquiry; we apply the word to a set of statements just in so far as we happen, for the year or the moment, to be thinking of those statements in relation to the statements which can be reached from them by some set of transformations to which we have seen fit to direct our attention. Now the notion of semantical rule is as sensible and meaningful as that of postulate, if conceived in a similarly relative spirit—relative, this time, to one or another particular enterprise of schooling unconversant persons in sufficient conditions for truth of statements of some natural or artificial language L. But from this point of view no one signalization of a subclass of the truths of L is intrinsically more a semantical rule than another; and, if 'analytic' means 'true by semantical rules', no one truth of *L* is analytic to the exclusion of another.

It might conceivably be protested that an artificial language *L* (unlike a natural one) is a language in the ordinary sense *plus* a set of explicit semantical rules—the whole constituting, let us say, an ordered pair; and that the semantical rules of *L* then are specifiable simply as the second component of the pair *L*. But, by the same token and more simply, we might construe an artificial language *L* outright as an ordered pair whose second component is the class of its analytic statements; and then the analytic statements of *L* become specifiable simply as the statements in the second component of *L*. Or better still, we might just stop tugging at our bootstraps altogether.

Not all the explanations of analyticity known to Carnap and his readers have been covered explicitly in the above considerations, but the extension to other forms is not hard to see. Just one additional factor should be mentioned which sometimes enters: sometimes the semantical rules are in effect rules of translation into ordinary language, in which case the analytic statements of the artificial language are in effect recognized as such from the analyticity of their specified translations in ordinary language. Here certainly there can be no thought of an illumination of the problem of analyticity from the side of the artificial language.

From the point of view of the problem of analyticity the notion of an artificial language with semantical rules is a *feu follet par excellence*. Semantical rules determining the analytic statements of an artificial language are of interest only in so far as we already understand the notion of analyticity; they are of no help in gaining this understanding.

Appeal to hypothetical languages of an artificially simple kind could conceivably be useful in clarifying analyticity, if the mental or behavioral or cultural factors relevant to analyticity—whatever they may be—were somehow sketched into the simplified model. But a model which takes analyticity merely as an irreducible character is unlikely to throw light on the problem of explicating analyticity.

It is obvious that truth in general depends on both language and extralinguistic fact. The statement 'Brutus killed Caesar' would be false if the world had been different in certain ways, but it would also be false if the word 'killed' happened rather to have the sense of 'begat'. Thus one is tempted to suppose in general that the truth of a statement is somehow analyzable into a linguistic component and a factual component. Given this supposition, it next seems reasonable that in some statements the factual component should be null; and these are the analytic statements. But, for all its *a priori* reasonableness, a boundary between analytic and synthetic statements simply has not been drawn. That there is such a distinction to be drawn at all is an unempirical dogma of empiricists, a metaphysical article of faith.

5. THE VERIFICATION THEORY AND REDUCTIONISM

In the course of these somber reflections we have taken a dim view first of the notion of meaning, then of the notion of cognitive synonymy, and finally of the notion of analyticity. But what, it may be asked, of the verification theory of meaning? This phrase has established itself so firmly as a catchword of empiricism that we should be very unscientific indeed not to look beneath it for a possible key to the problem of meaning and the associated problems.

The verification theory of meaning, which has been conspicuous in the literature from Peirce onward, is that the meaning of a statement is the method of empirically confirming or infirming it. An analytic statement is that limiting case which is confirmed no matter what.

As urged in §1, we can as well pass over the question of meanings as entities and move straight to sameness of meaning, or synonymy. Then what the verification theory says is that statements are synonymous if and only if they are alike in point of method of empirical confirmation or infirmation.

This is an account of cognitive synonymy not of linguistic forms generally, but of statements. However, from the concept of synonymy of statements we could derive the concept of synonymy for other linguistic forms, by considerations somewhat similar to those at the end of §3. Assuming the notion of "word," indeed, we could explain any two forms as synonymous when the putting of the one form for an occurrence of the other in any statement (apart from occurrences within "words") yields a synonymous statement. Finally, given the concept of synonymy thus for linguistic forms generally, we could define analyticity in terms of synonymy and logical truth as in §1. For that matter, we could define analyticity more simply in terms of just synonymy of statements together with logical truth; it is not necessary to appeal to synonymy of linguistic forms other than statements. For a statement may be described as analytic simply when it is synonymous with a logically true statement.

So, if the verification theory can be accepted as an adequate account of statement synonymy, the notion of analyticity is saved after all. However, let us reflect. Statement synonymy is said to be likeness of method of empirical confirmation or infirmation. Just what are these methods which are to be compared for likeness? What, in other words, is the nature of the relation between a statement and the experiences which contribute to or detract from its confirmation?

The most naïve view of the relation is that it is one of direct report. This is *radical reductionism*. Every meaningful statement is held to be translatable into a statement (true or false) about immediate experience. Radical reductionism, in one form or another, well antedates the verification theory of meaning explicitly so called. Thus Locke and Hume held that every idea must either originate directly in sense experience or else be compounded of ideas thus originating; and taking a hint from Tooke we might rephrase this doctrine in semantical jargon by saying that a term, to be significant at all, must be either a name of a sense datum or a compound of such names or an abbreviation of such a compound. So stated, the doctrine remains ambiguous as between sense data as sensory events and sense data as sensory qualities; and it remains vague as to the admissible ways of compounding. Moreover, the doctrine is unnecessarily and intolerably restrictive in the term-by-term critique which it imposes. More reasonably, and without yet exceeding the limits of what I have called radical reductionism, we may take full statements as our significant units— thus demanding that our statements as wholes be translatable into sense-datum language, but not that they be translatable term by term.

This emendation would unquestionably have been welcome to Locke and Hume and Tooke, but historically it had to await an important reorientation in semantics—the reorientation whereby the primary vehicle of meaning came to be seen no longer in the term but in the statement. This reorientation, explicit in Frege,[1] underlies Russell's concept of incomplete symbols defined in use, also it is implicit in the verification theory of meaning, since the objects of verification are statements.

Radical reductionism, conceived now with statements as units, set itself the task of specifying a sense-datum language and showing how to translate the rest of significant discourse, statement by statement, into it. Carnap embarked on this project in the *Aufbau*.

The language which Carnap adopted as his starting point was not a sense-datum language in the narrowest conceivable sense, for it included also the notations of logic, up through higher set theory. In effect it included the whole language of pure mathematics. The ontology implicit in it (that is, the range of values of its variables) embraced not only sensory events but classes, classes of classes, and so on. Empiricists there are who would boggle at such prodigality. Carnap's

[1] G. Frege, *Foundations of Arithmetic* (New York: Philosophical Library, Inc., 1950).

starting point is very parsimonious, however, in its extralogical or sensory part. In a series of constructions in which he exploits the resources of modern logic with much ingenuity, Carnap succeeds in defining a wide array of important additional sensory concepts which, but for his constructions, one would not have dreamed were definable on so slender a basis. He was the first empiricist who, not content with asserting the reducibility of science to terms of immediate experience, took serious steps toward carrying out the reduction.

If Carnap's starting point is satisfactory, still his constructions were, as he himself stressed, only a fragment of the full program. The construction of even the simplest statements about the physical world was left in a sketchy state. Carnap's suggestions on this subject were, despite their sketchiness, very suggestive. He explained spatio-temporal point-instants as quadruples of real numbers and envisaged assignment of sense qualities to point-instants according to certain canons. Roughly summarized, the plan was that qualities should be assigned to point-instants in such a way as to achieve the laziest world compatible with our experience. The principle of least action was to be our guide in constructing a world from experience.

Carnap did not seem to recognize, however, that his treatment of physical objects fell short of reduction not merely through sketchiness, but in principle. Statements of the form 'Quality q is at point-instant $x;y;z;t$' were, according to his canons, to be apportioned truth values in such a way as to maximize and minimize certain over-all features, and with growth of experience the truth values were to be progressively revised in the same spirit. I think this is a good schematization (deliberately oversimplified, to be sure) of what science really does; but it provides no indication, not even the sketchiest, of how a statement of the form 'Quality q is at $x;y;z;t$' could ever be translated into Carnap's initial language of sense data and logic. The connective 'is at' remains an added undefined connective; the canons counsel us in its use but not in its elimination.

Carnap seems to have appreciated this point afterward; for in his later writings he abandoned all notion of the translatability of statements about the physical world into statements about immediate experience. Reductionism in its radical form has long since ceased to figure in Carnap's philosophy.

But the dogma of reductionism has, in a subtler and more tenuous form, continued to influence the thought of empiricists. The notion lingers that to each statement, or each synthetic statement, there is associated a unique range of possible sensory events such that the occurrence of any of them would add to the likelihood of truth of the statement, and that there is associated also another unique range of possible sensory events whose occurrence would detract from that like-lihood. This notion is of course implicit in the verification theory of meaning.

The dogma of reductionism survives in the supposition that each statement, taken in isolation from its fellows, can admit of confirmation or infirmation at all. My countersuggestion, issuing essentially from Carnap's doctrine of the physical world in the *Aufbau,* is that our statements about the external world face the tribunal of sense experience not individually but only as a corporate body.

The dogma of reductionism, even in its attenuated form, is intimately connected with the other dogma—that there is a cleavage between the analytic and the synthetic. We have found ourselves led, indeed, from the latter problem to the former through the verification theory of meaning. More directly, the one dogma clearly supports the other in this way: as long as it is taken to be significant in general to speak of the confirmation and infirmation of a statement, it seems significant to speak also of a limiting kind of statement which is vacuously confirmed, *ipso facto,* come what may; and such a statement is analytic.

The two dogmas are, indeed, at root identical. We lately reflected that in general the truth of statements does obviously depend both upon language and upon extralinguistic fact; and we noted that this obvious circumstance carries in its train, not logically but all too naturally, a feeling that the truth of a statement is somehow analyz-able into a linguistic component and a factual component. The factual component must, if we are empiricists, boil down to a range of confirmatory experiences. In the extreme case where the linguistic component is all that matters, a true statement is analytic. But I hope we are now impressed with how stubbornly the distinction between analytic and synthetic has resisted any straightforward drawing. I am impressed also, apart from prefabricated examples of black and white balls in an urn, with how baffling the problem has always been of arriving at any explicit theory of the empirical confirmation of a synthetic statement. My present suggestion is that it is nonsense, and the root of much nonsense, to speak of a linguistic component and a factual component in the truth of any individual statement. Taken collectively, science has its double dependence upon language and experience; but this duality is not significantly traceable into the statements of science taken one by one.

The idea of defining a symbol in use was, as remarked, an advance over the impossible term-by-term empiricism of Locke and Hume. The statement, rather than the term, came with Frege to be recognized as the unit accountable to an empiricist critique. But what I am now urging is that even in taking the statement as unit we have drawn our grid too finely. The unit of empirical significance is the whole of science.

6. EMPIRICISM WITHOUT THE DOGMAS

The totality of our so-called knowledge or beliefs, from the most casual matters of geography and history to the profoundest laws of atomic physics or even of pure mathematics and logic, is a man-made fabric which impinges on experience only along the edges. Or, to change the figure, total science is like a field of force whose boundary conditions are experience. A conflict with experience at the periphery occasions readjustments in the interior of the field. Truth values have to be redistributed over some of our statements. Reëvaluation of some statements entails reëvaluation of others, because of their logical inter-connections—the logical laws being in turn simply certain further statements of the system, certain further elements of the field. Having reëvaluated one statement we must reëvaluate some others, which may be statements logically connected with the first or may be the state-ments of logical connections themselves. But the total field is so un-derdetermined by its boundary conditions, experience, that there is much latitude of choice as to what statements to reëvaluate in the light of any single contrary experience. No particular experiences are linked with any particular statements in the interior of the field, except in-directly through considerations of equilibrium affecting the field as a whole.

If this view is right, it is misleading to speak of the empirical content of an individual statement—especially if it is a statement at all remote from the experiential periphery of the field. Furthermore it becomes folly to seek a boundary between synthetic statements, which hold contingently on experience, and analytic statements, which hold come what may. Any statement can be held true come what may, if we make drastic enough adjustments elsewhere in the system. Even a statement very close to the periphery can be held true in the face of recalcitrant experience by pleading hallucination or by amending certain state-ments of the kind called logical laws. Conversely, by the same token, no statement is immune to revision. Revision even of the logical law of the excluded middle has been proposed as a means of simplifying quantum mechanics; and what difference is there in principle be-tween such a shift and the shift whereby Kepler superseded Ptolemy, or Einstein Newton, or Darwin Aristotle?

For vividness I have been speaking in terms of varying distances from a sensory periphery. Let me try now to clarify this notion without metaphor. Certain statements, though *about* physical objects and not sense experience, seem peculiarly germane to sense experience—and in a selective way: some statements to some experiences, others to others. Such statements, especially germane to particular experiences, I picture as near the periphery. But in this relation of "germaneness" I envisage nothing more than a loose association reflecting the relative likelihood, in practice, of our choosing one statement rather than another for revision in the event of recalcitrant experience. For example, we can imagine recalcitrant experiences to which we would surely be inclined to accommodate our system by reëvaluating just the statement that there are brick houses on Elm Street, together with related statements on the same topic. We can imagine other recalcitrant experiences to which we would be inclined to accommodate our system by reëvaluating just the statement that there are no centaurs, along with kindred statements. A recalcitrant experience can, I have urged, be accommodated by any of various alternative reëvaluations in various alternative quarters of the total system; but, in the cases which we are now imagining, our natural tendency to disturb the total system as little as possible would lead us to focus our revisions upon these specific statements concerning brick houses or centaurs. These statements are felt, therefore, to have a sharper empirical reference than highly theoretical statements of physics or logic or ontology. The latter statements may be thought of as relatively centrally located within the total network, meaning merely that little preferential connection with any particular sense data obtrudes itself.

As an empiricist I continue to think of the conceptual scheme of science as a tool, ultimately, for predicting future experience in the light of past experience. Physical objects are conceptually imported into the situation as convenient intermediaries—not by definition in terms of experience, but simply as irreducible posits comparable, epistemologically, to the gods of Homer. For my part I do, qua lay physicist, believe in physical objects and not in Homer's gods; and I consider it a scientific error to believe otherwise. But in point of epistemological footing the physical objects and the gods differ only in degree and not in kind. Both sorts of entities enter our conception only as cultural posits. The myth of physical objects is epistemologically superior to most in that it has proved more efficacious than other myths as a device for working a manageable structure into the flux of experience.

Positing does not stop with macroscopic physical objects. Objects at the atomic level are posited to make the laws of macroscopic objects, and ultimately the laws of experience, simpler and more manageable; and we need not expect or demand full definition of atomic and subatomic entities in terms of macroscopic ones, any more than definition of macroscopic things in terms of sense data. Science is a continuation of common sense, and it continues the common-sense expedient of swelling ontology to simplify theory.

Physical objects, small and large, are not the only posits. Forces are another example; and indeed we are told nowadays that the boundary between energy and matter is obsolete. Moreover, the abstract entities which are the substance of mathematics—ultimately classes and classes of classes and so on up—are another posit in the same spirit. Epistemologically these are myths on the same footing with physical objects and gods, neither better nor worse except for differences in the degree to which they expedite our dealings with sense experiences.

The over-all algebra of rational and irrational numbers is underdetermined by the algebra of rational numbers, but is smoother and more convenient; and it includes the algebra of rational numbers as a jagged or gerrymandered part. Total science, mathematical and natural and human, is similarly but more extremely underdetermined by experience. The edge of the system must be kept squared with experience; the rest, with all its elaborate myths or fictions, has as its objective the simplicity of laws.

Ontological questions, under this view, are on a par with questions of natural science. Consider the question whether to countenance classes as entities. This, as I have argued elsewhere, is the question whether to quantify with respect to variables which take classes as values. Now Carnap[2] has maintained that this is a question not of matters of fact but of choosing a convenient language form, a convenient conceptual scheme or framework for science. With this I agree, but only on the proviso that the same be conceded regarding scientific hypotheses generally. Carnap[3] has recognized that he is able to preserve a double standard for ontological questions and scientific hypotheses only by assuming an absolute distinction between the analytic and the synthetic; and I need not say again that this is a distinction which I reject.

The issue over there being classes seems more a question of convenient conceptual scheme; the issue over there being centaurs, or brick houses on Elm Street, seems more a question of fact. But I have been urging that this difference is only one of degree, and that it turns upon our vaguely pragmatic inclination to adjust one strand of the fabric of science rather than another in accommodating some particular recalcitrant experience. Conservatism figures in such choices, and so does the quest for simplicity.

---

[2] R. Carnap, "Empiricism, Semantics, and Ontology," *Revue Internationale de Philosophie* (1950).

[3] *Ibid.*, p. 32n.

Carnap, Lewis, and others take a pragmatic stand on the question of choosing between language forms, scientific frameworks; but their pragmatism leaves off at the imagined boundary between the analytic and the synthetic. In repudiating such a boundary I espouse a more thorough pragmatism. Each man is given a scientific heritage plus a continuing barrage of sensory stimulation; and the considerations which guide him in warping his scientific heritage to fit his continuing sensory promptings are, where rational, pragmatic.

H. P. GRICE / P. F. STRAWSON

In Defense of a Dogma

In his article "Two Dogmas of Empiricism," [1] Professor Quine advances a number of criticisms of the supposed distinction between analytic and synthetic statements, and of other associated notions. It is, he says, a distinction which he rejects.[2] We wish to show that his criticisms of the distinction do not justify his rejection of it.

There are many ways in which a distinction can be criticized, and more than one in which it can be rejected. It can be criticized for not being a sharp distinction (for admitting of cases which do not fall clearly on either side of it); or on the ground that the terms in which it is customarily drawn are ambiguous (have more than one meaning); or on the ground that it is confused (the different meanings being habitually conflated). Such criticisms alone would scarcely amount to a rejection of the distinction. They would, rather, be a prelude to clarification. It is not this sort of criticism which Quine makes.

Again, a distinction can be criticized on the ground that it is not useful. It can be said to be useless for certain purposes, or useless altogether, and, perhaps, pedantic. One who criticizes in this way may indeed be said to reject a distinction, but in a sense which also requires him to acknowledge its existence. He simply declares he can get on without it. But Quine's rejection of the analytic-synthetic distinction appears to be more radical than this. He would certainly say he could

---

* Reprinted from *The Philosophical Review*, vol. LXV, no. 2 (April, 1956). Used by permission of the editor and the authors.

[1] W. V. O. Quine, *From a Logical Point of View* (Cambridge, Mass., 1953), pp. 20–46. All references are to page numbers in this book. [Quine's essay is reprinted in this volume. Page references are also given for this—ed.]

[2] Page 46. [See this volume, p. 71—ed.]

get on without the distinction, but not in a sense which would commit him to acknowledging its existence.

Or again, one could criticize the way or ways in which a distinction is customarily expounded or explained on the ground that these explanations did not make it really clear. And Quine certainly makes such criticisms in the case of the analytic-synthetic distinction.

But he does, or seems to do, a great deal more. He declares, or seems to declare, not merely that the distinction is useless or inadequately clarified, but also that it is altogether illusory, that the belief in its existence is a philosophical mistake. "That there is such a distinction to be drawn at all," he says, "is an unempirical dogma of empiricists, a metaphysical article of faith." [3] It is the existence of the distinction that he here calls in question; so his rejection of it would seem to amount to a denial of its existence.

Evidently such a position of extreme skepticism about a distinction is not in general justified merely by criticisms, however just in themselves, of philosophical attempts to clarify it. There are doubtless plenty of distinctions, drawn in philosophy and outside it, which still await adequate philosophical elucidation, but which few would want on this account to declare illusory. Quine's article, however, does not consist wholly, though it does consist largely, in criticizing attempts at elucidation. He does try also to diagnose the causes of the belief in the distinction, and he offers some positive doctrine, acceptance of which he represents as incompatible with this belief. If there is any general prior presumption in favor of the existence of the distinction, it seems that Quine's radical rejection of it must rest quite heavily on this part of his article, since the force of any such presumption is not even impaired by philosophical failures to clarify a distinction so supported.

Is there such a presumption in favor of the distinction's existence? Prima facie, it must be admitted that there is. An appeal to philosophical tradition is perhaps unimpressive and is certainly unnecessary. But it is worth pointing out that Quine's objection is not simply to the words "analytic" and "synthetic," but to a distinction which they are supposed to express, and which at different times philosophers have supposed themselves to be expressing by means of such pairs of words or phrases as "necessary" and "contingent," "a priori" and "empirical," "truth of reason" and "truth of fact"; so Quine is certainly at odds with a philosophical tradition which is long and not wholly disreputable. But there is no need to appeal only to tradition; for there is also present practice. We can appeal, that is, to the fact that those who use the terms "analytic" and "synthetic" do to a very considerable extent agree in the applications they make of them. They apply the term "analytic" to more or less the same cases, withhold it from more or less the same cases, and hesitate over more or less the same cases. This agreement extends not only to cases which they have been *taught* so to characterize, but to new cases. In short, "analytic" and "synthetic" have a more or less established philosophical *use;* and this seems to suggest that it is absurd, even senseless, to say that there is no such distinction. For, in general, if a pair of contrasting expressions are habitually and generally used in application to the same cases, *where these cases do not form a closed list,* this is a sufficient condition for saying that there are *kinds* of cases to which the expressions apply; and nothing more is needed for them to mark a distinction.

In view of the possibility of this kind of argument, one may begin to doubt whether Quine really holds the extreme thesis which his words encourage one to attribute to him. It is for this reason that we made the attribution tentative. For on at least one natural interpretation of this extreme thesis, when we say of something true that it is analytic and of another true thing that it is synthetic, it simply never is the case that we thereby mark a distinction between them. And this view seems terribly difficult to reconcile with the fact of an established philosophical usage (*i.e.,* of general agreement in application in an open class). For this reason, Quine's thesis might be better represented not as the thesis that there is *no difference at all* marked by the use of these expressions, but as the thesis that the nature of, and reasons for, the difference or differences are totally misunderstood by those who use the expressions, that the stories they tell themselves *about* the difference are full of illusion.

We think Quine might be prepared to accept this amendment. If so, it could, in the following way, be made the basis of something like an answer to the argument which prompted it. Philosophers are notoriously subject to illusion, and to mistaken theories. Suppose there were a particular mistaken theory about language or knowledge, such that, seen in the light of this theory, some statements (or propositions or sentences) appeared to have a characteristic which no statements really have, or even, perhaps, which it does not make sense to suppose that any statement has, and which no one who was not consciously or subconsciously influenced by this theory would ascribe to any statement. And suppose that there were other statements which, seen in this light, did not appear to have this characteristic, and others again which presented an uncertain appearance. Then philosophers who were under the influence of this theory would tend to mark the supposed presence or absence of this characteristic by a pair of contrasting expressions, say "analytic" and "synthetic." Now in these circumstances it still could not be said that there was no distinction at all being

marked by the use of these expressions, for there would be at least
the distinction we have just described (the distinction, namely, between those statements which appeared to have and those which appeared to lack a certain characteristic), and there might well be other
assignable differences too, which would account for the difference in
appearance; but it certainly could be said that *the* difference these
philosophers supposed themselves to be marking by the use of the
expressions simply did not exist, and perhaps also (supposing the
characteristic in question to be one which it was absurd to ascribe to
any statement) that these expressions, as so used, were senseless or
without meaning. We should only have to suppose that such a mistaken theory was very plausible and attractive, in order to reconcile
the fact of an established philosophical usage for a pair of contrasting
terms with the claim that *the* distinction which the terms purported
to mark did not exist at all, though not with the claim that there
simply did not exist a difference of any kind between the classes of
statements so characterized. We think that the former claim would
probably be sufficient for Quine's purposes. But to establish such a
claim on the sort of grounds we have indicated evidently requires a
great deal more argument than is involved in showing that certain explanations of a term do not measure up to certain requirements of
adequacy in philosophical clarification—and not only more argument,
but argument of a very different kind. For it would surely be too harsh
to maintain that the *general* presumption is that philosophical distinctions embody the kind of illusion we have described. On the
whole, it seems that philosophers are prone to make too few distinctions rather than too many. It is their assimilations, rather than their
distinctions, which tend to be spurious.

So far we have argued as if the prior presumption in favor of the
existence of the distinction which Quine questions rested solely on the
fact of an agreed *philosophical* usage for the terms "analytic" and "synthetic." A presumption with only this basis could no doubt be coun-
tered by a strategy such as we have just outlined. But, in fact, if we are
to accept Quine's account of the matter, the presumption in question
is not only so based. For among the notions which belong to the ana-
lyticity-group is one which Quine calls "cognitive synonymy," and in
terms of which he allows that the notion of analyticity could at any
rate be formally explained. Unfortunately, he adds, the notion of
cognitive synonymy is just as unclarified as that of analyticity. To
say that two expressions x and y are cognitively synonymous seems to
correspond, at any rate roughly, to what we should ordinarily express
by saying that x and y have the same meaning or that x means the
same as y. If Quine is to be consistent in his adherence to the extreme
thesis, then it appears that he must maintain not only that the distinc-

tion we suppose ourselves to be marking by the use of the terms "analytic" and "synthetic" does not exist, but also that the distinction we suppose ourselves to be marking by the use of the expressions "means the same as," "does not mean the same as" does not exist either. At least, he must maintain this insofar as the notion of *meaning the same as,* in its application to predicate-expressions, is supposed to differ from and go beyond the notion of *being true of just the same objects as.* (This latter notion—which we might call that of "coextensionality"—he is prepared to allow to be intelligible, though, as he rightly says, it is not sufficient for the explanation of analyticity.) Now since he cannot claim this time that the pair of expressions in question (*viz.,* "means the same," "does not mean the same") is the special property of philosophers, the strategy outlined above of countering the presumption in favor of their marking a genuine distinction is not available here (or is at least enormously less plausible). Yet the denial that the distinction (taken as different from the distinction between the coextensional and the non-coextensional) really exists, is extremely paradoxical. It involves saying, for example, that anyone who seriously remarks that "bachelor" means the same as "unmarried man" but that "creature with kidneys" does not mean the same as "creature with a heart"—supposing the last two expressions to be coextensional —*either* is not in fact drawing attention to any distinction at all between the relations between the members of each pair of expressions *or* is making a philosophical mistake about the nature of the distinction between them. In either case, what he says, taken as he intends it to be taken, is senseless or absurd. More generally, it involves saying that it is always senseless or absurd to make a statement of the form "Predicates x and y in fact apply to the same objects, but do not have the same meaning." But the paradox is more violent than this. For we frequently talk of the presence or absence of relations of synonymy between kinds of expressions—for example, conjunctions, particles of many kinds, whole sentences—where there does not appear to be any obvious substitute for the ordinary notion of synonymy, in the way in which coextensionality is said to be a substitute for synonymy of predicates. Is all such talk meaningless? Is all talk of correct or incorrect or incorrect *translation* of sentences of one language into sentences of another meaningless? It is hard to believe that it is. But if we do successfully make the effort to believe it, we have still harder renunciations before us. If talk of sentence-synonymy is meaningless, then it seems that talk of sentences having a meaning at all must be meaningless too. For if it made sense to talk of a sentence have a meaning, or meaning something, then presumably it would make sense to ask "What does it mean?" And if it made sense to ask "What does it mean?" of a sentence, then sentence-synonymy could be roughly defined as follows: Two sentences are synonymous if and only if any true answer to the question "What does it mean?" asked of one of them, is a true answer to the same question, asked of the other. We do not, of course, claim any clarifying power for this definition. We want only to point out that if we are to give up the notion of sentence-synonymy as senseless, we must give up the notion of sentence-significance (of a sentence having meaning) as senseless too. But then perhaps we might as well give up the notion of sense.—It seems clear that we have here a typical example of a philosopher's paradox. Instead of examining the actual use that we make of the notion of *meaning the same*, the philosopher measures it by some perhaps inappropriate standard (in this case some standard of clarifiability), and because it falls short of this standard, or seems to do so, denies its reality, declares it illusory.

We have argued so far that there is a strong presumption in favor of the existence of the distinction, or distinctions, which Quine challenges—a presumption resting both on philosophical and on ordinary usage—and that this presumption is not in the least shaken by the fact, if it is a fact, that the distinctions in question have not been, in some sense, adequately clarified. It is perhaps time to look at what Quine's notion of adequate clarification is.

The main theme of his article can be roughly summarized as follows. There is a certain circle or family of expressions, of which "analytic" is one, such that if any one member of the circle could be taken to be satisfactorily understood or explained, then other members of the circle could be verbally, and hence satisfactorily, explained in terms of it. Other members of the family are: "self-contradictory" (in a broad sense), "necessary," "synonymous," "semantical rule," and perhaps (but again in a broad sense) "definition." The list could be added to. Unfortunately each member of the family is in as great need of explanation as any other. We give some sample quotations: "The notion of self-contradictoriness (in the required broad sense of inconsistency) stands in exactly the same need of clarification as does the notion of analyticity itself." [4] Again, Quine speaks of "a notion of synonymy which is no less in need of clarification than analyticity itself." [5] Again, of the adverb "necessarily," as a candidate for use in the explanation of synonymy, he says, "Does the adverb *really make sense?* To suppose that it does is to suppose that we have already *made satisfactory sense* of 'analytic.' " [6] To make "satisfactory sense" of one of these expressions would seem to involve two things.

[4] Page 20. [See this volume, pp. 52–53—ed.]

[5] Page 23. [See this volume, p. 54—ed.]

[6] Page 30, our italics. [See this volume, p. 59—ed.]

(1) It would seem to involve providing an explanation which does not incorporate any expression belonging to the family-circle. (2) It would seem that the explanation provided must be of the same general character as those rejected explanations which do incorporate members of the family-circle (*i.e.*, it must specify some feature common and peculiar to all cases to which, for example, the word "analytic" is to be applied; it must have the same general form as an explanation beginning, "a statement is analytic if and only if . . ."). It is true that Quine does not explicitly state the second requirement; but since he does not even consider the question whether any other kind of explanation would be relevant, it seems reasonable to attribute it to him. If we take these two conditions together, and generalize the result, it would seem that Quine requires of a satisfactory explanation of an expression that it should take the form of a pretty strict definition but should not make use of any member of a group of interdefinable terms to which the expression belongs. We may well begin to feel that a satisfactory explanation is hard to come by. The other element in Quine's position is one we have already commented on in general, before enquiring what (according to him) is to count as a satisfactory explanation. It is the step from "We have not made satisfactory sense (provided a satisfactory explanation) of *x*" to "*x* does not make sense."

It would seem fairly clearly unreasonable to insist *in general* that the availability of a satisfactory explanation in the sense sketched above is a necessary condition of an expression's making sense. It is perhaps dubious whether *any* such explanations can *ever* be given. (The hope that they can be is, or was, the hope of reductive analysis in general.) Even if such explanations can be given in some cases, it would be pretty generally agreed that there are other cases in which they cannot. One might think, for example, of the group of expressions which includes "morally wrong," "blameworthy," "breach of moral rules," and so forth; or of the group which includes the propositional connectives and the words "true" and "false," "statement," "fact," "denial," "assertion." Few people would want to say that the expressions belonging to either of these groups were senseless on the ground that they have not been formally defined (or even on the ground that it was impossible formally to define them) except in terms of members of the same group. It might, however, be said that while the unavailability of a satisfactory explanation in the special sense described was not a *generally* sufficient reason for declaring that a given expression was senseless, it was a sufficient reason in the case of the expressions of the analyticity group. But anyone who said this would have to advance a reason for discriminating in this way against the expressions of this group. The only plausible reason for being harder on these expressions than on others is a refinement on a consideration which we have already had before us. It starts from the point that "analytic" and "synthetic" themselves are technical philosophical expressions. To the rejoinder that other expressions of the family concerned, such as "means the same as" or "is inconsistent with," or "self-contradictory," are not at all technical expressions, but are common property, the reply would doubtless be that, to qualify for inclusion in the family circle, these expressions have to be used in specially adjusted and precise senses (or pseudo-senses) which they do not ordinarily possess. It is the fact, then, that all the terms belonging to the circle are *either* technical terms *or* ordinary terms used in specially adjusted senses, that might be held to justify us in being particularly suspicious of the claims of members of the circle to have any sense at all, and hence to justify us in requiring them to pass a test for significance which would admittedly be too stringent if generally applied. This point has some force, though we doubt if the special adjustments spoken of are in every case as considerable as it suggests. (This seems particularly doubtful in the case of the word "inconsistent"—a perfectly good member of the nontechnician's meta-logical vocabulary.) But though the point has some force, it does not have whatever force would be required to justify us in insisting that the expressions concerned should pass exactly that test for significance which is in question. The fact, if it is a fact, that the expressions cannot be explained in precisely the way which Quine seems to require, does not mean that they cannot be explained at all. There is no need to try to pass them off as expressing innate ideas. They can be and are explained, though in other and less formal ways than that which Quine considers. (And the fact that they are so explained fits with the facts, first, that there is a generally agreed philosophical use for them, and second, that this use is technical or specially adjusted.) To illustrate the point briefly for one member of the analyticity family. Let us suppose we are trying to explain to someone the notion of *logical impossibility* (a member of the family which Quine presumably regards as no clearer than any of the others) and we decide to do it by bringing out the contrast between logical and natural (or causal) impossibility. We might take as our examples the logical impossibility of a child of three's being an adult, and the natural impossibility of a child of three's understanding Russell's Theory of Types. We might instruct our pupil to imagine two conversations one of which begins by someone (X) making the claim:

(1) "My neighbor's three-year-old child understands Russell's Theory of Types,"

and the other of which begins by someone (Y) making the claim:

(1′) "My neighbor's three-year-old child is an adult."

It would not be inappropriate to reply to X, taking the remark as a hyperbole:

(2) "You mean the child is a particularly bright lad."

If X were to say:

(3) "No, I mean what I say—he really does understand it,"

one might be inclined to reply:

(4) "I don't believe you—the thing's impossible."

But if the child were then produced, and did (as one knows he would not) expound the theory correctly, answer questions on it, criticize it, and so on, one would in the end be forced to acknowledge that the claim was literally true and that the child was a prodigy. Now consider one's reaction to Y's claim. To begin with, it might be somewhat similar to the previous case. One might say:

(2′) "You mean he's uncommonly sensible or very advanced for his age."

If Y replies:

(3′) "No, I mean what I say,"

we might reply:

(4′) "Perhaps you mean that he won't grow any more, or that he's a sort of freak, that he's already fully developed."

Y replies:

(5′) "No, he's not a freak, he's just an adult."

At this stage—or possibly if we are patient, a little later—we shall be inclined to say that we just don't understand what Y is saying, and to suspect that he just does not know the meaning of some of the words he is using. For unless he is prepared to admit that he is using words in a figurative or unusual sense, we shall say, not that we don't believe him, but that his words have *no* sense. And whatever kind of creature is ultimately produced for our inspection, it will not lead us to say that what Y said was literally true, but at most to say that we now see what he meant. As a summary of the difference between the two imaginary conversations, we might say that in both cases we would tend to begin by supposing that the other speaker was using words in a figurative or unusual or restricted way; but in the face of his repeated claim to be speaking literally, it would be appropriate in the first case to say that we did not believe him and in the second case to say that we did not understand him. If, like Pascal, we thought it prudent to prepare against very long chances, we should in the first case know what to prepare for; in the second, we should have no idea. We give this as an example of just one type of informal explanation which we might have recourse to in the case of one notion of the analyticity group. (We do not wish to suggest it is the only type.) Further examples, with different though connected types of treatment, might be necessary to teach our pupil the use of the notion of logical impossibility in its application to more complicated cases—if indeed he did not pick it up from the one case. Now of course this type of explanation does not yield a formal statement of necessary and sufficient conditions for the application of the notion concerned. So it does not fulfill one of the conditions which Quine seems to require of a satisfactory explanation. On the other hand, it does appear to fulfill the other. It breaks out of the family circle. The distinction in which we ultimately come to rest is that between not believing something and not understanding something; or between incredulity yielding to conviction, and incomprehension yielding to comprehension. It would be rash to maintain that *this* distinction does not need clarification; but it would be absurd to maintain that it does not exist. In the face of the availability of this informal type of explanation for the notions of the analyticity group, the fact that they have not received another type of explanation (which it is dubious whether *any* expressions *ever* receive) seems a wholly inadequate ground for the conclusion that the notions are pseudo-notions, that the expressions which purport to express them have no sense. To say this is not to deny that it would be philosophically desirable, and a proper object of philosophical endeavor, to find a more illuminating general characterization of the notions of this group than any that has been so far given. But the question of how, if at all, this can be done is quite irrelevant to the question of whether or not the expressions which belong to the circle have an intelligible use and mark genuine distinctions.

So far we have tried to show that sections 1 to 4 of Quine's article—the burden of which is that the notions of the analyticity group have not been satisfactorily explained—do not establish the extreme thesis for which he appears to be arguing. It remains to be seen whether sections 5 and 6, in which diagnosis and positive theory are offered, are any more successful. But before we turn to them, there are two further points worth making which arise out of the first two sections.

1. One concerns what Quine says about *definition* and *synonymy*. He remarks that definition does not, as some have supposed, "hold the key to synonymy and analyticity," since "definition—except in the

extreme case of the explicitly conventional introduction of new notations—hinges on prior relations of synonymy." [7] But now consider
what he says of these extreme cases. He says: "Here the definiendum
becomes synonymous with the definiens simply because it has been expressly created for the purpose of being synonymous with the definiens.
Here we have a really transparent case of synonymy created by definition; would that all species of synonymy were as intelligible." Now if
we are to take these words of Quine seriously, then his position *as a
whole* is incoherent. It is like the position of a man to whom we are
trying to explain, say, the idea of one thing fitting into another thing,
or two things fitting together, and who says: "I can understand what
it means to say that one thing fits into another, or that two things fit
together, in the case where one was specially made to fit the other; but
I cannot understand what it means to say this in any other case." Perhaps we should not take Quine's words here too seriously. But if not,
then we have the right to ask him exactly what state of affairs he
thinks *is* brought about by explicit definition, what relation between
expressions *is* established by this procedure, and why he thinks it unintelligible to suggest that the same (or a closely analogous) state of
affairs, or relation, should exist in the absence of this procedure. For
our part, we should be inclined to take Quine's words (or some of
them) seriously, and reverse his conclusions; and maintain that the
notion of synonymy by explicit convention would be unintelligible if
the notion of synonymy by usage were not presupposed. There cannot be law where there is no custom, or rules where there are not
practices (though perhaps we can understand better what a practice is
by looking at a rule).

2. The second point arises out of a paragraph on page 32 of Quine's
book.* We quote:

> I do not know whether the statement "Everything green is extended" is
> analytic. Now does my indecision over this example really betray an incom-
> plete understanding, an incomplete grasp of the "meanings" of "green"
> and "extended"? I think not. The trouble is not with "green" or "ex-
> tended," but with "analytic."

If, as Quine says, the trouble is with "analytic," then the trouble
should doubtless disappear when "analytic" is removed. So let us remove it, and replace it with a word which Quine himself has con-
trasted favorably with "analytic" in respect of perspicuity—the word
"true." Does the indecision at once disappear? We think not. The

indecision over "analytic" (and equally, in this case, the indecision over "true") arises, of course, from a further indecision: namely, that which we feel when confronted with such questions as "Should we count a *point* of green light as *extended* or not?" As is frequent enough in such cases, the hesitation arises from the fact that the boundaries of application of words are not determined by usage in all possible directions. But the example Quine has chosen is particularly unfortunate for his thesis, in that it is only too evident that our hesitations are not *here* attributable to obscurities in "analytic." It would be possible to choose other examples in which we should hesitate between "analytic" and "synthetic" and have few qualms about "true." But no more in these cases than in the sample case does the hesitation necessarily imply any obscurity in the notion of analyticity; since the hesitation would be sufficiently accounted for by the same or a similar kind of indeterminacy in the relations between the words occurring within the statement about which the question, whether it is analytic or synthetic, is raised.

Let us now consider briefly Quine's positive theory of the relations between the statements we accept as true or reject as false on the one hand and the "experiences" in the light of which we do this accepting and rejecting on the other. This theory is boldly sketched rather than precisely stated.[8] We shall merely extract from it two assertions, one of which Quine clearly takes to be incompatible with acceptance of the distinction between analytic and synthetic statements, and the other of which he regards as barring one way to an explanation of that distinction. We shall seek to show that the first assertion is not incompatible with acceptance of the distinction, but is, on the contrary, most intelligibly interpreted in a way quite consistent with it, and that the second assertion leaves the way open to just the kind of explanation which Quine thinks it precludes. The two assertions are the following:

1. It is an illusion to suppose that there is any class of accepted statements the members of which are in principle "immune from revision" in the light of experience, that is, any that we accept as true and must continue to accept as true whatever happens.

2. It is an illusion to suppose that an individual statement, taken in isolation from its fellows, can admit of confirmation or disconfirmation at all. There is no particular statement such that a particular experience or set of experiences decides once for all whether that statement is true or false, independently of our attitudes to all other statements.

The apparent connection between these two doctrines may be summed up as follows. Whatever our experience may be, it is in prin-

---

[8] Cf. pages 37–46. [See this volume, pp. 65–72—ed.]

ciple possible to hold on to, or reject, any particular statement we like, so long as we are prepared to make extensive enough revisions elsewhere in our system of beliefs. In practice our choices are governed largely by considerations of convenience: we wish our system to be as simple as possible, but we also wish disturbances to it, as it exists, to be as small as possible.

The apparent relevance of these doctrines to the analytic-synthetic distinction is obvious in the first case, less so in the second.

1. Since it is an illusion to suppose that the characteristic of immunity in principle from revision, come what may, belongs, or could belong, to any statement, it is an illusion to suppose that there is a distinction to be drawn between statements which possess this characteristic and statements which lack it. Yet, Quine suggests, this is precisely the distinction which those who use the terms "analytic" and "synthetic" suppose themselves to be drawing. Quine's view would perhaps also be (though he does not explicitly say this in the article under consideration) that those who believe in the distinction are inclined at least sometimes to mistake the characteristic of strongly resisting revision (which belongs to beliefs very centrally situated in the system) for the mythical characteristic of total immunity from revision.

2. The connection between the second doctrine and the analytic-synthetic distinction runs, according to Quine, through the verification theory of meaning. He says: "If the verification theory can be accepted as an adequate account of statement synonymy, the notion of analyticity is saved after all." [9] For, in the first place, two statements might be said to be synonymous if and only if any experiences which contribute to, or detract from, the confirmation of one contribute to, or detract from, the confirmation of the other, to the same degree; and, in the second place, synonymy could be used to explain analyticity. But, Quine seems to argue, acceptance of any such account of synonymy can only rest on the mistaken belief that individual statements, taken in isolation from their fellows, can admit of confirmation or disconfirmation at all. As soon as we give up the idea of a set of experiential truth-conditions for each statement taken separately, we must give up the idea of explaining synonymy in terms of identity of such sets.

Now to show that the relations between these doctrines and the analytic-synthetic distinction are not as Quine supposes. Let us take the second doctrine first. It is easy to see that acceptance of the second doctrine would not compel one to abandon, but only to revise, the suggested explanation of synonymy. Quine does not deny that individual statements are regarded as confirmed or disconfirmed, are in fact rejected or accepted, in the light of experience. He denies only that these relations between single statements and experience hold independently of our attitudes to *other* statements. He means that experience can confirm or disconfirm an individual statement, only given certain assumptions about the truth or falsity of other statements. When we are faced with a "recalcitrant experience," he says, we always have a choice of what statements to amend. What we have to renounce is determined by what we are anxious to keep. This view, however, requires only a slight modification of the definition of statement-synonymy in terms of confirmation and disconfirmation. All we have to say now is that two statements are synonymous if and only if any experiences which, *on certain assumptions about the truth-values of other statements,* confirm or disconfirm one of the pair, also, *on the same assumptions,* confirm or disconfirm the other to the same degree. More generally, Quine wishes to substitute for what he conceives to be an oversimple picture of the confirmation-relations between particular statements and particular experiences, the idea of a looser relation which he calls "germaneness" (p. 43).* But however loosely "germaneness" is to be understood, it would apparently continue to make sense to speak of two statements as standing in the same germaneness-relation to the same particular experiences. So Quine's views are not only consistent with, but even suggest, an amended account of statement-synonymy along these lines. We are not, of course, concerned to defend such an account, or even to state it with any precision. We are only concerned to show that acceptance of Quine's doctrine of empirical confirmation does not, as he says it does, entail giving up the attempt to define statement-synonymy in terms of confirmation.

Now for the doctrine that there is no statement which is in principle immune from revision, no statement which might not be given up in the face of experience. Acceptance of this doctrine is quite consistent with adherence to the distinction between analytic and synthetic statements. Only, the adherent of *this* distinction must also insist on another; on the distinction between that kind of giving up which consists in merely admitting falsity, and that kind of giving up which involves changing or dropping a concept or set of concepts. Any form of words at one time held to express something true may, no doubt, at another time, come to be held to express something false. But it is not only philosophers who would distinguish between the case where this happens as the result of a change of opinion solely as to matters of fact, and the case where this happens at least partly as a result of a shift in the sense of the words. Where such a shift in the sense of the words is a necessary condition of the change in truth-value, then the adherent of the distinction will say that the form of words in question

---

* [See this volume, p. 70—ed.]

changes from expressing an analytic statement to expressing a synthetic statement. We are not now concerned, or called upon, to elaborate an adequate theory of conceptual revision, any more than we were called upon, just now, to elaborate an adequate theory of synonymy. If we can make sense of the idea that the same form of words, taken in one way (or bearing one sense), may express something true, and taken in another way (or bearing another sense), may express something false, then we can make sense of the idea of conceptual revision. And if we can make sense of this idea, then we can perfectly well preserve the distinction between the analytic and the synthetic, while conceding to Quine the revisability-in-principle of everything we say. As for the idea that the same form of words, taken in different ways, may bear different senses and perhaps be used to say things with different truth-values, the onus of showing that this is somehow a mistaken or confused idea rests squarely on Quine. The point of substance (or one of them) that Quine is making, by this emphasis on revisability, is that there is no absolute necessity about the adoption or use of any conceptual scheme whatever, or, more narrowly and in terms that he would reject, that there is no analytic proposition such that we *must* have linguistic forms bearing just the sense required to express that proposition. But it is one thing to admit this, and quite another thing to say that there are no necessities within any conceptual scheme we adopt or use, or, more narrowly again, that there are no linguistic forms which do express analytic propositions.

The adherent of the analytic-synthetic distinction may go further and admit that there may be cases (particularly perhaps in the field of science) where it would be pointless to press the question whether a change in the attributed truth-value of a statement represented a conceptual revision or not, and correspondingly pointless to press the analytic-synthetic distinction. We cannot quote such cases, but this inability may well be the result of ignorance of the sciences. In any case, the existence, if they do exist, of statements about which it is pointless to press the question whether they are analytic or synthetic, does not entail the nonexistence of statements which are clearly classifiable in one or other of these ways and of statements our hesitation over which has different sources, such as the possibility of alternative interpretations of the linguistic forms in which they are expressed.

This concludes our examination of Quine's article. It will be evident that our purpose has been wholly negative. We have aimed to show merely that Quine's case against the existence of the analytic-synthetic distinction is not made out. His article has two parts. In one of them, the notions of the analyticity group are criticized on the ground that they have not been adequately explained. In the other, a positive theory of truth is outlined, purporting to be incompatible with views to which believers in the analytic-synthetic distinction either must be, or are likely to be, committed. In fact, we have contended, no single point is established which those who accept the notions of the analyticity group would feel any strain in accommodating in their own system of beliefs. This is not to deny that many of the points raised are of the first importance in connection with the problem of giving a satisfactory general account of analyticity and related concepts. We are here only criticizing the contention that these points justify the rejection, as illusory, of the analytic-synthetic distinction and the notions which belong to the same family.

ANTHONY QUINTON

The a Priori and the Analytic

I

There is something unsatisfactory about the way in which the doctrine that all *a priori* statements are analytic—I shall call it the analytic thesis for convenience—is ordinarily defended. In its great days,
thirty years ago, its opponents would ask: what is the status of the
thesis itself? It is not empirical, but it does not appear to be analytic
either. Therefore it is a refutation of itself. Those of its defenders who
did not take refuge behind the insecure defense of the theory of types,
admitting that it was *a priori*, insisted that it was, despite appearances,
analytic. But they did not treat it as if it were. Instead of attempting
to prove it they put it forward more as an hypothesis, supporting it
with representative pieces of favourable evidence and attempting to
dispose of apparent counter-examples. In practice controversy settled,
or bogged, down around a handful of particular cases: for example,
'nothing can be red and green all over' and the transitivity of 'earlier
than'.

If the thesis is analytic this kind of inductive argument is misplaced.
Examples may suggest an analytic generalization in the first place and
be used to illustrate and clarify it, to make the theoretical arguments
for it more concrete and intelligible, but they cannot establish it.
It was a bad habit of Moore's to base conceptual truths on particular
instances. In his attack on naturalism he inferred that 'good' was
different in meaning from any natural or descriptive term whatever

* Reprinted from *Proceedings of the Aristotelian Society*, Vol. 64 (1963–4), pp.
31–54. Reprinted by courtesy of the Editor of The Aristotelian Society. Copyright
1963–64 The Aristotelian Society.

from the application of a dubious technique of conceptual intuition to a few selected instances of naturalistic definition. No proof or explanation of the general differences between the ethical and the non-ethical was offered. In the same way he concluded that 'exists' was not a predicate from some particular differences of logical behaviour between it and some ordinary predicates.

How should *a priori* truths be established? Something like the traditional view that *a priori* knowledge rests on intuition or demonstration must be correct. *A priori* truths must be established either directly or by deduction from those that have been. They must be seen or shown to be true. If any are to be demonstrated some must be intuited as self-evident in order to halt the regress of demonstration by providing ultimate premisses and to supply the rules of inference that are applied to them. The discovery that a body of *a priori* truths can be deduced equally well from distinct sets of axioms has brought this notion of logical intuition into disfavour. But it does not follow from the fact that there is no unique set of formally sufficient axioms, complete, consistent and independent, that there is no question of material adequacy. It is one thing for the theorems of a system to follow from its axioms, another for either of them to be acceptable as true. Axioms only confer truth on theorems if they are true themselves. A formally sufficient axiom will be materially adequate only if it is intuitive. According to the analytic thesis, an *a priori* truth is intuitive if its acceptance as true is a condition of understanding the terms it contains.

It is fairly clear that the analytic thesis is not intuitive. The fact of controversy about the thesis is not quite conclusive since it is abstractly possible that the defenders of the thesis attach a different sense to the term 'analytic' from the sense or senses ascribed by its opponents, one in which 'analytic' and '*a priori*' are bare synonyms. If this were the case it could not go undetected for it would be the only way in which defenders of the thesis, taking it to be intuitive, could account for the obvious fact of hostility to it. The fact that there are familiar explicit definitions of the crucial terms involved, in none of which is either term straightforwardly defined by reference to the other, shows that this general misunderstanding does not obtain in practice. '*A priori*' means either, widely, 'non-empirical' or, narrowly, following Kant, 'necessary'. To assimilate these is to make the questionable assumption that all non-empirical truths are necessary which I shall discuss later. 'Analytic', I would suggest, has had four main interpretations. (i) In the first and widest, an analytic statement is one true in virtue of the meaning of the terms it contains. (ii) As understood by Leibniz and Kant, an analytic statement is a tautology that repeats itself, asserts no more than it assumes, is an instance of the law of identity whose denial is an explicit contradiction. (iii) As understood by those who take Hobbes's view of necessary truth, an analytic statement is one that is true in virtue of the conventions of language. (iv) Finally, as understood by Frege and most modern logicians, an analytic statement is a truth of logic or reducible to one with the help of definitions. The identity of these four definitions of 'analytic' with the two definitions of 'a priori' is not intuitively obvious, nor is their identity with each other. In this paper I propose to argue, first, that all *necessary a priori* truths are analytic in the first and widest sense and then, building on this conclusion, which is not itself contentious, that such truths are also analytic in the other three senses. And for each of the four identifications involved I shall offer a general argument.

II

I shall begin with a proof of the analytic thesis in the widest interpretation of the two crucial terms involved: that all non-empirical statements are true (or false) in virtue of their meaning. I hasten to admit that it will seem disappointingly trivial. I shall also consider an objection which, by casting doubt on one side of the thesis in this form without, however, touching the essentials of the thesis, provides a good reason for interpreting it in accordance with the narrower, Kantian sense of 'a priori' as: all necessary statements are true (or false) in virtue of their meaning. For convenience of exposition I shall speak only of true statements hereafter but the adjustments required to include false statements are obvious.

The proof starts from the commonplace distinction between necessary and contingent statements. A necessary truth is one that is true in itself, true, in Lewis's phrase, 'no matter what', must be true and cannot be false. A contingent truth, as etymology suggests, is one that is true dependently on or because of something else, something outside itself. As depending on this something else it does not have to be true. The necessary and the contingent make an exclusive and exhaustive division of the realm of truths. I shall argue that the correlated distinctions of the analytic from the synthetic and of the *a priori* from the empirical coincide with the distinction of the necessary from the contingent since they both arise from elucidations of one of the none too sharply defined elements of that distinction.

To start with the distinction of analytic and synthetic. Here 'analytic' is the positive element. It is a development or elucidation of the idea of the necessary. If a truth is necessary it is true in itself and independently of everything outside it. The statement itself consists of a form of words with a meaning attached. But it is not the form of words that determines the truth of the statement. If 'lie' is defined as 'false statement made with intent to deceive' the words 'every lie is a falsehood' express a necessary truth but if 'lie' is defined as 'statement believed false made with intent to deceive' then they express a contingent falsehood. Since there is nothing more to the statement than the words it is composed of and the meaning they are given and since the words do not determine its truth, if it is true in itself it must be true in virtue of its meaning.

In the *a priori*-empirical distinction the positive element is 'empirical'. The term '*a priori*' just sweeps up the residue of non-empirical truths. The idea of the empirical is a development or elucidation of the idea of the contingent. It aims to explain how a statement can owe its truth to something else, what conditions the something else must satisfy if it is to confer truth on a statement. To require it to be experience is to say that unless it is something of whose existence we can in principle become aware then the form of words involved has not made out its claim to be a statement. No limit is set here to the possible forms of experience or awareness, in particular no equation of experience and sense-experience is implied. For a form of words to be understood as a statement we must know what its truth-conditions are and to know this is to be able to recognize them when they occur, to know what it would be like to experience them.

If these arguments are correct all and only necessary truths are analytic and all and only contingent truths are empirical. Since necessary and contingent truths are exclusive no truth is *both* analytic *and* empirical, since they are exhaustive every truth is *either* analytic *or* empirical. Since 'synthetic' means 'non-analytic' and '*a priori*' means 'non-empirical' every truth is synthetic or *a priori* and no truth is both.

This excessively tidy-looking argument explains why there should be many defenders of synthetic *a priori* truths but none for analytic empirical truths. 'Analytic' and 'empirical' are both positively defined. If a statement is analytic it is true in virtue of its meaning, if empirical in virtue of experience. But if it is true in virtue of its meaning there is no room left for experience to have any effect on it and if it is true in virtue of experience then its meaning cannot have been sufficient to determine its truth. The synthetic and the *a priori*, on the other hand, are defined negatively, by exclusion. If a statement is synthetic it does not owe its truth to its meaning, if *a priori* not to experience. But might it not owe its truth to some third consideration beyond both of them? If, as I have argued, the analytic and the empirical are simply elucidations of the exhaustive concepts of the necessary and the contingent there is no third possibility. Meaning and experience must be as exhaustive as the two concepts they are used to explain.

One part of the analytic thesis in the interpretation we are considering, its claim that all contingent statements are empirical, has recently been challenged in a way that does not touch the main point at issue and enables it to be more sharply defined. Watkins, following Popper, has argued that statements which are both universally and existentially quantified, like 'every event has a cause' and 'every metal has a solvent', are neither analytic nor empirical. He points out that an important class of metaphysical propositions are of this form and are, therefore, synthetic *a priori*. They are not empirical, he maintains, because, like all unrestricted existential statements, they cannot be conclusively falsified. So far we have taken an empirical statement to be one that is true (or false) in virtue of experience. But this is not clear. We can interpret 'empirical' strongly, as 'conclusively verifiable or falsifiable by experience', or weakly, as 'confirmable or disconfirmable by experience'. Popper chooses a definition falling between these extremes for two main reasons. First, science consists mainly of universal statements which are essential for explanation and prediction. The only existential statements it contains are restricted or circumscribed, asserting that something of a certain sort exists, not at some unspecified place and time, but in a circumscribed spatio-temporal region, and such statements can be falsified. Secondly, an empirical statement is one that can be empirically tested and to test something is to see how much it can stand, to see whether it can be destroyed. So the empirical test of a statement is its exposure to the possibility of refutation, of conclusive falsification. That which cannot in principle be refuted cannot be seriously tested.

If we accept conclusive falsifiability by experience as a criterion of the empirical it follows that all unrestricted existential statements are non-empirical. But such statements are ordinarily synthetic so they are synthetic *a priori* in the wide sense of the latter term. But it is important to notice that they are also contingent. They are not *a priori* in the strong, Kantian sense that implies necessity. It is only because of the hold of Kant's identification of the *a priori* with the necessary that this defence of the synthetic *a priori* seems at first sight to conflict with the analytic thesis. What emerges is that the essential content of the thesis is that all *necessary* truths are analytic.

Now if this is taken to mean, in accordance with the first and widest definition of 'analytic', that all necessary truths are true in virtue of the meaning of the terms they contain it will be objected, not that it is false, but that it lacks substance. Certainly most of the leading defenders of the synthetic *a priori* agree that necessary truths owe their truth to their meaning. In *The Problems Of Philosophy*, Russell says, "all *a priori* knowledge deals exclusively with the relations of universals" (p. 103). Since universals are at any rate the meanings of general terms this amounts to an acceptance of the present form of the thesis. Broad says that an *a priori* proposition is either one that can be seen to be true "by merely inspecting it and reflecting on its terms and their mode of combination" or else the logical consequence of such a proposition (Proceedings of the Aristotelian Society *Supp. Vol.* 15 (1936), p. 102). Ewing says that the truth of an *a priori* proposition "depends wholly on the meaning of the terms used" (Proceedings of the Aristotelian Society 1939–40, p. 231). Kneale, finally, says that "anything we come to know *a priori* . . . is learnt by reflection on the meanings of words or other symbols" (*The Development of Logic,* p. 636). Pap sums the matter up in a criticism of C. I. Lewis. "The term 'analytic' is sometimes used in the strict sense of demonstrability on the basis of definitions and principles of logic, sometimes in a broader sense which is often expressed as 'certifiable as true by reflection upon meanings alone' . . . The broader sense of 'analytic' is not distinguishable at all from the sense of '*a priori*', so that by this interpretation the empiricist thesis is true but trivial" (*Semantics And Necessary Truth,* p. 89).

This cloud of witnesses shows that no philosopher who has seriously considered the question is prepared to dispute the view that necessary truth is determined by meaning. But this is not the same thing as triviality. Since I hold that 'necessary' and 'analytic' are demonstrably the same in meaning I am, of course, committed to the position that these concepts are, in the end, indistinguishable. But this is not to say that they are trivially indistinguishable. The definitions of the two terms are not verbally identical and a simple argument is needed to make the step from one to the other. 'Analytic' as 'true in virtue of meaning' gives a little more clarity of outline to the relatively amorphous notion of the necessary as that which is true in itself, no matter what. My witnesses are content to assert that necessary truth depends on meaning without giving reasons for doing so.

The main result of the glimpses into the obvious we have taken so far is that the issue between the defenders and the opponents of the analytic thesis is now more precisely identified. Its defenders believe that necessary truths are also analytic in some or all of the other three senses enumerated at the end of the first section and these further interpretations of the thesis are rejected by its opponents. I shall argue not merely that the three principles embodied in these interpretations, that necessary truths are identities, are true by convention and are reducible to truths of logic, are in fact correct, but that they follow from the first and widest version of the analytic thesis we have so far been dealing with. The three principles are not obviously equivalent for there is no obvious absurdity in accepting some and rejecting the others. I accept all three of them, though the third only with certain qualifications. In each case I shall argue that the principle is a con-

The a Priori and the Analytic / 95

sequence of the original, most inclusive and generally accepted form of the thesis.

III

The principle that necessary truth depends on identity or repetition is a natural development of the thesis that necessity depends on meaning. The claim that we discover the necessary truth of a statement by reflecting on the meaning of its terms, though helpful in a preliminary way, is more suggestive than explanatory. What are we supposed to look for in this process of reflection? How can meanings be so related or connected in a statement that its falsity is ruled out and its truth, therefore, certified?

The answer proposed by the Leibnizian principle rests on a general account of the nature of statements as containing two sorts of factor —I shall call them the assumption and the assertion—which generalizes the familar idea that every statement contains a subject or referring element and a predicate or describing element. This duality has two different forms. The first is categorical. In a categorical statement 'S is P' to utter the subject-expression 'S' is to assume the existence of what it refers to. The statement then goes on to assert the predicate 'P' of the S that has been assumed to exist. The second form of the duality is hypothetical. In an hypothetical statement 'if p then q', the antecedent makes the hypothetical supposition that the fact obtains which 'p' by itself could be used to state categorically. A categorical necessary truth, then, according to this principle, is of the form 'the F is F' and an hypothetical necessary statement is of the form 'if p then p'. In either case denial involves contradiction: 'the F is not F' and 'p and not-p'.

The question was: how can the meaning of a statement be such as to rule out the possibility of its falsehood and thus make it necessarily true? The reply is that if a statement makes some assumption, categorical or hypothetical, as to how things are and then does no more than assert all or part of what has been thus assumed it runs no risk of falsification. The only way to guarantee that what a statement asserts is correct is to assume that it is. Unless the occurrence of something incompatible with what is asserted is ruled out by the assumption of the statement the assertion may turn out to be false. Necessary truth, then, depends on repetition.

There will be no objection to the claim that if a statement asserts no more than it assumes it is necessarily true. It is the converse claim that is controversial. Unfortunately those who reject it give no clear account of the relation between meanings other than identity they have in mind. The obscurity of their position is compounded by the fact that they are not explicit about how identity succeeds in rendering necessary the statements whose elements' meanings it relates, though they usually agree that it does. Blanshard, for example, says that "elements really different may be intelligibly connected" (*The Nature Of Thought*, Vol. II, p. 408). Certainly elements that are verbally different may be identical in meaning. And elements that differ in meaning may be intelligibly connected in the sense that a reason can be given for the fact that one applies to everything to which the other applies. But these admissions are consistent with the Leibnizian principle. In the first, necessity remains grounded in identity of meaning; in the second, the 'intelligible connexion' is not an identity of meaning but it is not a necessary connexion either.

Underlying these protests on behalf of a non-identical connexion of meanings there seems to be a vivid but unacceptable picture of the Platonic realm of meanings or essences in which they are conceived as being related in as many different ways as are particulars in space and time. To oppose this picture is not to call in question the propriety of conceiving meanings as objects existing in a realm of their own. It is only to insist that if this conception, or way of speaking, is adopted its use should be guided by the actual nature of the things so conceived and not irrelevantly proliferated by unfounded analogies with a more familiar order of things. Meanings, conceived as objects, are not in time or space. It is only through their relations to the devices men have used to express them that they come to have any relations other than identity, total or partial, and distinctness.

We can examine the question at a less breathlessly abstract level by considering a distinction drawn by Ewing between two senses in which the conclusion of a valid deductive inference can be contained in its premisses. It may be contained as a part, the position of the Leibnizian principle, or as merely being entailed by them. As an example of this substantial variety of entailment that does not rest on identity he offers the entailment of q by the conjunction of p and if p then q. Certainly the categorical assertion of q is not explicitly present in the premisses. Nor is the joint assertion of the premisses together with the negation of the conclusion explicitly self-contradictory. But we can easily turn it into an explicit self-contradiction by substituting 'not (p and not-q)' for 'if p then q' in the formula '(if p then q) and p and not-q'. The same operation can be applied to more complicated laws, for example, the truth-functional law of the transitivity of implication.

The ultimate reason for saying that identity is the relation between meanings that gives rise to necessary truth is that identity and its opposite are the only relations that meanings, considered in themselves, can have. The principle that necessity rests on identity of meaning does not strictly entail the position that all necessary truth is categorical or hypothetical. But since I do not see how identity of meaning could make statements necessarily true in any other way I must take serious account of the objection that there are necessary truths which are not of these logical forms.

Two possible examples are easy to deal with. Mathematical equations can be represented as biconditionals about classes or sets: thus '5 + 7 = 12' means the same as 'all and only sets with 5 + 7 members have 12 members'. Negative existential statements like 'there are no round squares' can be understood as hypothetical statements with a negative consequent: 'if anything is round it is not square'. Affirmative existential statements are more troublesome. I would suggest that 'there is a prime number between 5 and 11' can only be established as a consequence of the more specific statement '7 is prime and between 5 and 11' whose three constituents, '7 is prime', '7 is greater than 5' and '7 is less than 11' can be dealt with along the lines suggested for '5 + 7 = 12'.

IV

The argument to show that necessary truth is a matter of convention is very simple. A statement is a necessary truth because of the meaning of the words of which it is composed. The meaning that words have is assigned to them by convention. Therefore it is linguistic convention that makes a form of words express a necessary truth. This Hobbesian view makes necessity unmysterious by treating it, not as something objectively discoverable in the nature of things, but as a matter of human decision. The impossibility of falsification that is characteristic of necessary truths is not a brute ontological fact; it is brought about by our refusal from the start to let any falsification occur.

But this simplicity is not to all tastes. Many who know the difficulty of mathematical work from direct experience resent what they take as an insult to mathematicians. We do not decide that

$$x = \frac{-b \pm \sqrt{b^2 - 4ac}}{2a} \quad \text{if} \quad ax^2 + bx + c = o;$$

we find it out, if we have the skill, after heavy labour. The theorems of mathematics are discoveries not arbitrary whims. The view that mathematical propositions are tautologies with its apparent implication that they are obvious evokes a similar emotion. Kneale observes, with barely concealed indignation, that Leibniz knew too much about mathematics to regard it as conventional (*op. cit.*, p. 312).* But he did not, it seems, know enough about it to realize that its propositions were not identities.

In fact neither of these offensive implications follows from the principles in question. The two equations in the last paragraph are identical in meaning as can readily be shown by substituting the value given for x in the first for the occurrences of x in the second. This is mildly laborious but not difficult. What is hard is to discover the identity in the first place. But an identity is none the less an identity for being deeply hidden. Similarly, the view that necessary truth is conventional does not trivialize it. Kneale's argument about mathematics could just as well be applied to chess to show that its rules are not conventional. To say that it is a game is not to assimilate it to the activity of a child idly kicking a stone along a road.

It follows from the principle that necessity is conventional that the conventions actually in force could have been different from what they are. The fact that the meanings of many non-logical words have changed in the course of time enforces a general agreement that the rules governing them are alterable. But, it is claimed, there is a limit to this alterability. Some hold that no logical law can be replaced by some other rule for the use of logical words. Others, more cautiously, regard the law of contradiction, at least, as indispensable.

The existence of alternative logics with no law of excluded middle is a difficulty for the wider view about the limits of convention. The defence that such systems are only called logics by courtesy, because of their formal analogies to classical logic, is too like obscurantist resistances to non-Euclidean geometry to be very convincing. But there is a sense in which the law of contradiction is unalterable. For no system that rejected it could be used as a logic, a system of the general rules of inference of a language, since no practice of utterance that failed to abide by the law would be a language. If an utterance has a meaning there must, in general, be occasions on which it is correct and occasions on which it is incorrect to make it. This selective feature of its utterance constitutes the existence of a rule for its use. To impart such rules to others we must be able to correct their errors and for our own use to be critical we must be able to cancel our own mistakes. Language requires rule-governed utterance, and the existence of conventions of affirmation and negation is an indispensable minimum of rules. The difference between a language and a practice of making arbitrary noises is that the former embodies a concept of negation. And the law of contradiction is an essential part of all definitions of negation, even if the law of excluded middle is not. But this primacy

* [The Development of Logic.]

does not show the law of contradiction to be non-conventional. To choose to speak rather than babble is, amongst other things, to accept the law of contradiction. But to speak is still a choice and the law of contradiction still a convention even though its abandonment would put us in a position where we should no longer be able to say, or even see, what we had done.

Most arguments against the view that necessity is conventional start by misstating it. Broad said that if necessary truths report the existence of linguistic conventions they must be synthetic and empirical. No doubt they would be but what the thesis says is that they are made necessary by convention not that they describe the conventions that prevail. To move your knight in accordance with the relevant rule of chess is not to say that that rule obtains. It is argued again that if to assert a necessary truth is to adopt a convention it would be a matter of free choice. But, according to the thesis, although the necessity of a statement *reflects* the existence of a convention its assertion is not ordinarily a way of *instituting* it. When you move your knight in accordance with the rules of chess you are not reinventing the game and when you move it in a currently forbidden way you are not setting up a new game of your own. Once in a while new conventions are set up in this comparatively inarticulate way. There is the case of William Webb Ellis who first picked up the ball and ran with it, thus inventing rugby football. The performance of a counter-conventional act may be striking enough to recommend a new convention by a concrete display of its possibilities. Poets are the chief William Webb Ellises of language.

A more serious objection, raised by Lewis in his *Analysis of Knowledge and Valuation,* is that the conventionality principle fails to distinguish sentences from the propositions they express. Since the meaning of a sentence is due to convention the fact that a sentence expresses a necessary proposition is conventional. But it does not follow, and is not the case, that the necessity of the proposition expressed is conventional. The relation of meanings in which it consists is an objective and timeless necessity which obtains whether anybody is aware of it, or has conventionally instituted any terms to express it, or not.

Some of the force of this argument is removed by the consideration that if it applies to any necessary truth it applies to all of them. Defenders of the synthetic *a priori* have usually wanted to distinguish between trifling, verbal, analytic necessities, such as 'all bald men are bald', and serious substantial, synthetic ones, such as 'nothing can be red and green all over' or 'there is no largest prime number'. But if 'nothing can be red and green all over' owes its necessity to a non-conventional relation of meanings which it is used by convention to express then so does 'all bald men are bald'. If the convention governing the use of 'all' were exchanged for that now governing 'not all' the sentence 'all bald men are bald' would come to express a contradiction but the proposition it originally expressed would remain necessarily true. Supporters of the argument must then agree that no necessary propositions whatever are true by convention but that all sentences expressing necessary propositions are.

But even if Lewis's argument fails to distinguish two kinds of necessity it is still an objection to the thesis. I shall argue that the distinction it draws between the conventionally introduced relations between words in virtue of the meanings they have been given and the supposedly non-conventional relations between the meanings themselves cannot be drawn.

It will be simplest to consider it in application to verbal definitions, as a way of showing that they are not conventional. Both sides agree that the identity of meaning of two synonymous expressions is established by convention. But the anti-conventionalist maintains that there is a non-conventional identity of concepts, lying behind the conventional synonymy of terms, which would still exist even if no means of expressing the concepts had ever been devised. The actual use of the expressions 'bachelor' and 'unmarried man' is something that has been conventionally set up in the course of human history. But it is only because there is a non-conventional identity between the timeless and objective concepts that these terms have been chosen to express that the terms are synonymous.

There is a suggestive incoherence in the formulation of this principle about conceptual identity. On the one hand it says that there are two concepts involved, one corresponding to each of the synonymous expressions; on the other that there is only a single concept which is the meaning common to both. What has happened is that the anti-conventionalist has seen two senses in statements of identity of meaning where in fact there is only one. He wants to say that it is a matter of convention that the meaning of '*bachelor*' is the same as the meaning of '*unmarried man*' but that it is an objective fact that *this* concept (the one conventionally expressed by the word 'bachelor' as it happens) is identical with *this* one (the one conventionally expressed by the phrase 'unmarried man' as it happens). But identity-statements do not correlate objects considered in themselves, they can correlate objects only under a certain description. The only way in which concepts can be identifyingly described is by reference to the words that express them. Of course every concept, like everything else, is what it is. But we can only say what it is by correlating one description of it with another.

What suggests that there is an objective relation of self-identity, over and above the identity asserted of the concept under two descriptions, is the fact that I can know what the meaning of 'X' is and know what the meaning of 'Y' is without realizing that 'X' and 'Y' have the same meaning. But this is because I can know what the meaning of 'X' is without knowing everything about the meaning of 'X'. To know the meaning of a non-logical term, at any rate, is to be able to decide about any particular thing, actual or possible, whether or not the term applies to it. To decide whether two terms are the same in meaning I have to exercise this capacity by considering whether there is any particular thing, actual or possible, to which I would apply one term but not the other. The meaning is not some kind of wholly transparent object present to consciousness in all its details. Consider the identification of ordinary concrete objects. I can know which hook my coat is hanging on, the unpainted one let us say, and which hook your coat is hanging on, let us say the one nearest the light switch. But I may not realize that our coats are hanging on the same hook. I can be in a position to identify our respective hooks without realizing that they are one and the same. What I fail to realize is not the self-identity of an object considered in itself but that two descriptions, 'the unpainted hook' and 'the hook nearest the light switch' refer to the same thing.

The object referred to in a true identity-statement does not have, in itself, the duality which makes identification possible. Duality only comes in with the ways in which the object is described and conceived. One identity-statement can be grounded in another as the example about the hooks shows. But such a process of support will only replace some descriptions by others. It will never terminate in a statement in which the object, innocent of all description, will be identified with itself.

V

The third and final principle I have undertaken to derive from the thesis that necessary truth depends on meaning corresponds to Frege's definition of an analytic statement as one for whose proof nothing is required beyond logical laws and definitions of extra-logical terms. To accept the definition is not to endorse the view that all necessity is logical: Frege himself thought geometry was necessary but, in this sense, synthetic.

The outlines of an argument to prove that if necessity depends on meaning it depends on logic and definitions are to be found in Wittgenstein's *Tractatus*. How are the expressions given the meanings from which the necessity of statements arises? Either indirectly, by definition in terms of other expressions already understood, or in a direct way. The direct definition of non-logical terms is carried out by ostension, their correlation with observable features of the world. Logical terms are implicitly defined by means of logical laws. These logical laws, implicitly definitive of the basic logical terms, provide an initial stock of necessary truths. Others are generated by substitution in them in accordance with explicit definitions. Two non-logical terms with the same ostensive definition can be explicitly defined in terms of each other. Two such terms with different ostensive definitions are distinct in meaning and thus not related in the way that gives rise to necessity. Therefore the only conventions of meaning that can render statements containing the terms they relate to necessary are (i) logical laws implicitly defining logical terms, (ii) explicit definitions and (iii) identical ostensive definitions of non-logical terms which could be replaced by explicit definitions of either in terms of the other.

An objection of principle to this argument is that it assumes that the expressions of our language can be exclusively separated into the logical and the non-logical. Though this may look a reasonable assumption at first glance in fact the argument does not represent logical and non-logical terms in a necessarily exclusive way. For it takes a logical term to be one whose meaning is *wholly* determined, in the end and after explicit definitions have been applied, by logical laws and a non-logical term to be one whose meaning is *wholly* determined, in the end, by ostension. It leaves out the possibility of mixed terms whose meaning is partly fixed by ostension and partly by the kind of implicit definition given for the basic logical terms. Simple descriptive predicates like 'red' suggest that this possibility is realized. It is not sufficient for an understanding of 'red' to have been shown enough red things to be able to tell whether further things are red or not. The use of the term must also be circumscribed by the realization that if a thing is red it cannot also be of another colour as well. Must we then admit that some necessities depend on non-logical laws, implicitly definitive of non-logical terms, as well as logical laws and explicit definitions? To decide this question we need a criterion for distinguishing between logical and non-logical laws and terms.

Before considering this obscurity in the principle that all necessity is logical and in the Fregean definition of 'analytic' to which it corresponds three preliminary points should be mentioned. First, Frege's definition draws some of its attraction from the idea that it improves on the Leibnizian definition in terms of identity and contradiction in that it does not accord a mistakenly elevated place to the traditional laws of thought. Russell and others thought this elevation to be a mistake because the ancient laws did not figure in any of the recognized sets of axioms sufficiently powerful for the derivation of ordinary logic. It may be that this dethronement was premature. We have already seen one reason for giving a special place to the law of contradiction; no system without it is a logic. Furthermore it plays a fundamental part in two non-axiomatic methods of demonstration. It is the final court of appeal in demonstration by reductio ad absurdum (cf. K. R. Popper, 'Logic Without Assumptions', Proceedings of the Aristotelian Society, 1946–7) and it is presupposed by the mechanical method of truth-tables in the rule that a sentence-element cannot have more than one truth-value (cf. G. H. von Wright, *Logical Studies*, p. 8). Secondly, the contracted version of Frege's definition now in general currency as one true in virtue of logical laws alone or as one reducible with the help of definitions to a truth of logic has led some philosophers to conclude that the laws of logic are not themselves analytic (cf. W. T. Stace, *Theory of Knowledge and Existence*, p. 361; W. H. Walsh, *Reason and Experience*, p. 50). This is, of course, a misunderstanding. What is reducible to a law of logic is identical in meaning to it and must have the same logical status as it has. But it does point to a weakness of the Fregean definition which is that it wholly trivializes the statement that logical truths are analytic. It would certainly be an achievement to show that all necessity was logical but, in the first place, this does not throw any light on the nature of logical truths themselves and, secondly, it can only be done after it has first been shown that all necessary truths are analytic in the wider sense that they depend for their truth on their meaning.

The most serious deficiency of the Fregean definition, which must infect the corresponding principle, remains to be discussed: the fact that the concept of a logical law or truth on which it turns is thoroughly indeterminate. At one end the concept is firmly fixed by highly abstract elementary principles which would be universally accepted as laws of logic. But how far down into the body of truths as a whole does the class of logical truths extend?

One familiar and reasonable criterion for a statement's being a logical truth is that logical terms alone should occur essentially in it. When Russell made this suggestion, he was conscious of its limitations: it provides a necessary, but not a sufficient, condition of being a logical truth (*Introduction to Mathematical Philosophy*, p. 202). In the plainly contingent statements that something exists $((\exists x)x = x)$, that at least two things exist $((\exists x)(\exists y)x \neq y)$ . . . logical terms alone occur essentially. The further necessary condition required to exclude such cases is that logical truths are necessary. If logical truth is thus defined as a necessary truth in which only logical terms occur essentially the principle corresponding to Frege's sense of 'analytic' takes the form: every necessary truth in which non-logical terms occur essentially can be reduced with the help of definitions to one in which they do not.

The crucial need at this point is for an account of logical terms to

104 / DE DICTO

be given which is precise enough for the principle to be discussed. It would, of course, be circular to define a logical term as one that occurs essentially in a logical truth. Essential occurrence in necessary truths is not much better. In the first place it would make any term logical since every term occurs essentially in some necessary truth: 'bachelor' in 'all bachelors are unmarried', 'red' in 'nothing can be red and green all over'. Secondly, this proposal would trivialize the principle under discussion in equating logical and necessary truth by fiat.

Logicians in recent times, following Tarski, have been sceptical about arriving at any general criterion for logical terms. Quine simply enumerates a set of logical primitives, regarding these and anything wholly definable in terms of them as logical. He adheres to a roughly conformist principle of selection in assembling his primitives: it is the smallest set capable of yielding the vocabulary of what has traditionally passed as logic.

Can anything be done that it is less passive and more explanatory? It is an agreed and obvious feature of admitted logical terms that they are neutral as between topics and capable of figuring in discourse about any sort of subject-matter. I suggest that the essential character of logical terms can be made clearer if we reflect on the reasons for this fact. For it is a consequence of the particular way in which logical terms are endowed with meaning. Whereas topical, non-logical, terms are introduced, directly or indirectly, by some kind of ostension, which correlates them with particular regions or features of the extra-linguistic world, the topic-neutral terms of logic are introduced by implicit definition. For example, the ordinary concept of negation is introduced by the laws of contradiction and excluded middle, which are general formulae whose variable elements can take statements about any subject-matter whatever as their values. Logical terms are purely syntactical. Their function is to arrange or organize discourse, not to refer to anything in the extra-linguistic world. We can thus define a logical term as one whose meaning is wholly specified by implicit definitions.

In his justly celebrated essay *Truth By Convention* Quine makes an objection to this proposal, which has been very influential and is, I believe, mistaken. Comparing various ways in which mathematics might be reduced to logic he comes finally to the view that they might be identified as containing only terms whose meaning is wholly introducible by conventional assignment of truth to implicit definitions. His objection is that this criterion is wholly undiscriminating. Certainly sense can be given to 'not', 'if' and 'every' by implicit definition but so can it to every other term. The example he considers in detail is 'later than'. Its meaning can be fixed, he claims, by the conventional assignment of truth to all statements in which only 'later than' and the admitted logical primitives occur essentially. From this he infers that the technique can be extended to any term whatever.

Now the statements in which only 'later than' and the logical primitives occur essentially can indeed be regarded as logical truths. But they do not suffice to fix the sense of 'later than' and a part of this term, the element 'late', does not occur in them essentially. The relevant statements are that if x is later than y, y is not later than x and that if x is later than y and y than z then x is later than z. These two statements are instances of general principles of asymmetry and transitivity for the radically topic-neutral term 'more than' or 'more ϕ than': $(x)\ (y)\ (\phi)\ (x > \phi y) \rightarrow \sim (y > \phi x)$ and $(x)\ (y)\ (z)\ (\phi)\ ((x > \phi y).$ $(y > \phi z)) \rightarrow (x > \phi z)$. These wholly topic-neutral necessary truths give only part of the meaning of 'later than'. It must also be correlated with particular pairs of temporally distinct events. Statements reporting these indispensable correlative facts will not serve as implicit definitions. First, though this is not a reason that would weigh with Quine, because they are contingent. Secondly, because they must contain terms other than 'later than' and the logical primitive which occur essentially in them. These terms will identify the temporally distinct events involved, as in 'the accession of Richard I is later than the accession of Henry I'.

The account I have given of logical terms contains the defensible part of the theory of innate ideas. Logical concepts are not acquired by ostension. The attempts of Russell and others to find empirical correlates for the logical terms in the feelings of their users have been much criticized. Geach has pointed out (*Mental Acts*, p. 23) that a feeling of hesitation does not universally accompany the use of 'or', a threatening feeling is quite as appropriate. Also it is hard to see what feeling is to go with 'and', 'if' and 'all'. But the crucial point is that the feelings that accompany a logical term are not criteria for their correct use. An extreme of hesitation on my part does not make a statement of the form 'p or q' true. Logical concepts are innate in the harmless sense of being not empirical but syntactical.

The necessary transitivity of 'later than' is not, then a refutation of the principle that all necessity is logical. It is an instance of a logical truth in which only 'and', 'if', the universal quantifier and the topic-neutral term 'more ϕ than' occur essentially, while the element 'late', with its topical reference to time, occurs vacuously. There is, however, a difficulty here which was pointed out to me by Mr. P. F. Strawson. The principles of asymmetry and transitivity do not wholly fix the sense of 'more ϕ than' since they remain necessarily true if 'less ϕ than' is substituted and 'more' and 'less' do not mean the same. But however this objection is to be dealt with it does not show 'more ϕ

than' to be a non-logical term. For the difference between 'more' and 'less' must be as topic-neutral as they are.

Can we deal with 'nothing can be red and green all over', which is equally resistant to reduction to ordinary logical laws, in the same way? The only definition of 'red' that would make 'this is red and green' reducible to an explicit contradiction defines 'red' as 'not green and not blue and . . .' It is objectionable, first, because it is open-ended and, secondly, because it can only be applied to one colour term if circularity is to be avoided and in that case 'nothing can be blue and white all over' and the rest still resist reduction.

It could be said that 'nothing can be red and green all over' is an instance of the highly abstract law: 'nothing can be a member of two species of a genus'. Like the transitivity of 'more ϕ than' it fixes only part of the sense of the terms involved but it is as topic-neutral as could be wished. This is too informal a step to settle the question of whether all necessity is logical. But it does formulate the question in a way that allows it to be settled by decision. If the principle is interpreted narrowly, as saying that all necessary truths can be reduced with the help of definitions to necessary truths in which only terms whose meaning is *wholly* given by implicit definitions occur essentially, then 'nothing can be red and green all over' is a falsifying exception to it. If, on the other hand, it is interpreted broadly, as saying that all necessary truths implicitly define their terms or are reducible to those that do, the principle is correct.

VI

So far I have taken it for granted that there is a distinction between the necessary and the contingent, and my aim has been to show that it coincides with four other distinctions all of which have been taken to distinguish the analytic from the synthetic: (i) statements true in virtue of meaning and of experience, (ii) statements which assert no more and more than they assume, (iii) statements true by convention and on non-conventional grounds and (iv) statements logically and non-logically true. Quine's critique of analyticity questions the assumption I have made that there is a distinction to discuss. Against theological dualism which sees a fundamental difference of kind between necessary and contingent he sees only continuity.

There is an interesting peculiarity about the tactics of his argument. The concept of synonymy whose intelligibility he questions is not really central to the Fregean definition of 'analytic statement' as either a truth of logic or else reducible to one by the replacement of synonyms on which he concentrates. Even if his objections to synonymy were well-founded his argument would not show that there are no analytic statements. It would show, rather, that explicit truths of logic were the only unequivocally analytic statements. His argument has more damaging implications but they are rhetorically suggested rather than argued for. If all and only logical truths are analytic the term 'analytic' explains nothing about logical truth and is not worth introducing. Furthermore his defeatist account of logical truth in terms of a pretty arbitrarily enumerated set of logical primitives, the consequence of his mistaken belief that any term whatever can have its whole sense given by implicit definition, implies that there is important difference of kind between logical and non-logical truths. Finally if there is no clear concept of synonymy the Leibnizian principle which grounds necessity on the fact that what some statements assert is partly or wholly identical in meaning with what they assume falls to the ground. But the direct force of his argument is restricted by the limitations of the Fregean concept of the analytic on which it turns.

But how well-founded are his doubts about synonymy? Grice and Strawson have shown that the supposed circle of intensional terms—synonymous, analytic, contradictory, and so forth—which cannot be defined except in terms of one another can be broken (*Philosophical Review*, 1956). 'Synonymous' means the same as 'means the same as' and the latter is no philosopher's technicality but a perfectly familiar expression. An idea does not become technical simply by being dressed up in an ungainly polysyllable. I shall develop this argument by showing that Quine cannot consistently raise the doubt he does about the concept of synonymy unless he already understands it.

How, he asks, are relations of synonymy to be discovered? By the observation of linguistic behaviour. He confines this observation to the application of terms by those who understand them. But all that application can show is identity of extension which according to defenders of analyticity is not the same as, even if it follows from, identity of meaning. Synonymy, he infers, is empirically undiscoverable.

But why should observation of linguistic behaviour be only of the application of terms and not of the learning that preceded it? We learn to use words both ostensively, by noticing and imitating the applications made by the fully-fledged language-users around us, and lexically, by becoming aware of the conventionally established identity of meaning between new words and words whose meaning we already understand. These processes are more closely interwoven, no doubt, than the theory of simple and complex ideas allows but there are pure cases: 'horses' ostensive and 'bachelor' lexical.

Now Quine deprives himself, as linguistic observer, of reliance on the fact of lexical learning which was part of his training as a linguis-

tic agent. This cannot be reasonable unless language is wholly ostensive and there is no such thing as lexical learning. If that were the
case there would be no word-word correlations to observe but only
word-thing correlations. We should have to learn the use of 'featherless
biped' as we now learn the use of 'man'. But in that case the two terms
would have the same meaning. In a purely ostensive language there
would be no difference between coextensiveness and synonymy. If exactly the same ostensible specimens will serve equally well for the
introduction of either term each will be associated with the same
recognitional capacity. It would be idle to envisage deviant applications of the two terms. It would be a conjecture, with no more evidence in its favour than that there are the two different terms, about
the possibility of deviating application in the future by more expert
language-users than oneself.

We can envisage a featherless biped that is not a man because
'featherless biped' is a lexically learnt term. It is learnt through the
rather undramatic lexical formula: 'x is a featherless biped' $=$ 'x is
featherless and x is a biped'. Idioms like 'French polisher' show that
this formula cannot be generalized without qualification: not all
French polishers are French. The two elements in the defining part of
the formula are learnt ostensively and the extension of the defined
term is fixed indirectly as the logical product of the extensions of its
constituents. There are plenty of non-men in these constituent extensions: snakes and chickens, for example. Terms can only be coextensive
without identity of meaning if there are antecedent relations of synonymy that fix indirectly the extensions of at least one of the terms
involved. In Quine's ostensive language, all true biconditionals like
'all and only men are featherless bipeds' would be analytic. Observation of linguistic behaviour restricted to application alone could only
discover coextensiveness that did not entail identity of meaning in a
language that contained lexically learnt terms and thus allowed for a
less restricted kind of observation. In both types of language 'this is a
featherless biped' would be synthetic and so the analytic-synthetic distinction would persist in a purely ostensive language. The synthetic
biconditional which, according to Quine, are all that linguistic observation can discover, could only exist in a language where the conventional assertion of analytic biconditionals was part of the learning
process.

It is not *inconceivable* that ostensively learnt terms with the same
extension should differ in meaning. Mr. D. F. Pears has pointed out
to me that a learner might connect two such coextensive terms with
different recurrent aspects or features of the common stock of situa-
tions with which they were correlated. But this would be gratuitous
in the circumstances. Ostension correlates a term with a class of spatio-

temporal regions. Though several distinct common properties or resemblances may characterize such a class it will be natural for learners to fasten on the most obvious of them (cf. my 'Properties and Classes', *Proceedings of the Aristotelian Society*, 1958–9). What makes such differing interpretations seem likely is that we can conceive, for example, that all and only things of a certain shape, say seashells, might be of a certain colour, say pink. We should retain distinct concepts of seashell and pink provided there was no general coincidence of particular shapes with particular colours. In the absence of such a coincidence we could form the generic concepts of shape and colour and use them to guide or focus the learning of 'sea-shell' and 'pink' ('this *thing* is a seashell', 'this is pink in *colour*'). But then they would not be purely ostensive terms.

RODERICK CHISHOLM

The Truths of Reason

A TRADITIONAL VIEW

"There are also two kinds of truths: those of reasoning and those of fact. The truths of reasoning are necessary, and their opposite is impossible. Those of fact, however, are contingent, and their opposite is possible. When a truth is necessary, we can find the reason by analysis, resolving the truth into simpler ideas and simpler truths until we reach those that are primary." [Leibniz, *Monadology*, 33]

"Reason," as we have noted, is sometimes said to function along with "experience" as a "source" of knowledge. One traditional view of the subject matter of the knowledge thus attributed to reason seems to be based upon the assumptions that there is a valid distinction to be drawn between properties and concrete individual things, or substances; that there is an analogous distinction to be drawn between states of affairs and concrete events; that properties may be related to each other by entailment, or inclusion, and by exclusion; that states of affairs may be similarly related; and that such relations hold necessarily. All of these assumptions are properly said to be metaphysical.

This view also involves the epistemological assumption that in certain instances, we can know that these relations hold, and that they hold necessarily, and what is more, that we can know these truths of reason *a priori*.

And finally, it involves the assumption that some of these truths of reason are what constitute the subject matter of logic.

As in the other spheres of knowledge we have just considered, there

* Roderick M. Chisholm, *Theory of Knowledge* © 1966. Reprinted by permission of Prentice-Hall, Inc., Englewood Cliffs, New Jersey. Revised by the author.

is also the possibility of scepticism—in the present case, scepticism with respect to the "truths of reason." The apparent impasses that arise between sceptic and nonsceptic, once again, are difficult, if not impossible, to remove. Some of those who are sceptical with respect to metaphysics attempt to "reduce" the truths of reason to other, less objectionable truths; but these attempts at reduction seem to be no more plausible than those considered earlier.

Let us begin by attempting to sketch the metaphysical interpretation of these truths.

INCLUSION AND EXCLUSION

Some properties (for example, that of being a horse, or being equine) are exemplified in several different individual things (for there are many different horses); other properties (for example, that of being perfectly round) are not exemplified in any individual thing; still other properties (for example, that of being the fastest runner) are exemplified in only one individual thing.

The relation of *entailment* or *inclusion* among properties is exemplified by these facts: The property of being square includes that of being rectangular, and that of being red includes that of being colored. The relation of *exclusion* is exemplified by these facts: The property of being square excludes that of being circular, and that of being red excludes that of being blue. To say that one property excludes another, therefore, is to say more than that the one fails to include the other. Being red fails to include being heavy, but it does not exclude being heavy; if it excluded being heavy, as it excludes being blue, then nothing could be both red and heavy.[1]

There are also compound properties—for example, that of being either red or blue, that of being both red and warm, that of being nonred, and that of being red-if-colored. Relations of inclusion and exclusion involving such properties may be illustrated in obvious ways: Being both red and square includes being red and excludes being circular; being both red and warm-if-red includes being warm; being both nonwarm and warm-if-red excludes being red.

Relations, on this view, may be thought of as being a kind of property. Among the properties of Socrates is that of being older than Plato, and hence, also that of being older than someone, as well as that of being older than anything that Plato is older than. Relations, like

---

[1] "Being red excludes being blue" should not be taken to rule out the possibility of a thing being red in one part and blue in another; it tells us only that being red in one part at one time excludes being blue in exactly that same part at exactly that same time.

other properties, may be thought of as being themselves related by inclusion and exclusion. For example, bearing warmer-than to any particular thing x includes, and is included by, being borne cooler-than to by x; it also includes bearing warmer-than to whatever x bears warmer-than to, and it excludes being borne warmer-than to by x.

There are also certain more general truths about the relations of inclusion and exclusion. For example, every property F and every property G is such that F's excluding G includes G's excluding F; F's excluding G includes F's including not-G; F excludes non-F, and includes F-or-G.

States of affairs (or to use a different terminology, possible states of affairs) are analogous to properties. Where a property may be exemplified in several different things, a state of affairs (for example, Socrates being in Athens) is exemplified in several different concrete events; other states of affairs (for example, Socrates being in Rome) are not exemplified in any concrete event. Still other states of affairs (for example, Socrates dying in 399 B.C.) are exemplified in only one concrete event.[2]

States of affairs, like properties, are related by inclusion and exclusion; for example, some men being Greeks includes, and is included by, some Greeks being men, and excludes no Greeks being men. States of affairs, like properties, may be compound; for example, some men being Greek and Plato being Roman; Socrates receiving inspiration being a sufficient condition for Socrates becoming a philosopher. Examples of relations of inclusion and exclusion involving compound states of affairs are: the conjunctive state of affairs, composed of (1) Socrates receiving inspiration and (2) Socrates receiving inspiration being a sufficient condition for Socrates becoming a philosopher, includes (3) Socrates becoming a philosopher; and the conjunctive state of affairs, composed of (1) Socrates not becoming a philosopher and (2) Socrates receiving inspiration being a sufficient condition for Socrates becoming a philosopher, excludes (3) Socrates receiving inspiration. These two examples are instances of more general truths: For every state of affairs, p and q, the conjunctive state of affairs, composed of p and of p being a sufficient condition of q, includes q;

---

[2] There is no accepted uniform terminology for expressing this distinction. Where I have said "(possible) state of affairs" and "concrete events," others have said: "eternal object" and "occasion" (Whitehead); "states of affairs" and "space-time slabs of reality" (Lewis); and "generic propositions" and "individual propositions" (von Wright). Cf. A. N. Whitehead, *Science and the Modern World* (New York: The Macmillan Company, 1930), pp. 32–39; C. I. Lewis, *An Analysis of Knowledge and Valuation* (La Salle, Ill.: Open Court Publishing Co., 1946), pp. 52–55; and G. H. von Wright, *Norm and Action* (London: Routledge & Kegan Paul, Ltd., 1963), pp. 23–25. And where I said "properties," others have said "attributes," "essences," "meanings," "universals," or "intensions."

and the conjunctive state of affairs, composed of not-q and of p being a sufficient condition of q, excludes p. These latter "truths of reason" are thus said to be the kind of truth with which the logic of propositions is concerned.

And more generally, according to the present doctrine, when one sentence can be said necessarily to imply another, then the state of affairs intended by the one sentence includes the state of affairs intended by the other.

KNOWLEDGE OF NECESSITY IS NOT A POSTERIORI

When it is said that these truths of reason are known (or are capable of being known) *a priori*, part of what is meant is that if they are known they are not known *a posteriori*. A single example may suggest what is intended when it is said that these truths are not known *a posteriori*.

Corresponding to "Necessarily, being red excludes being blue," which is a truth about properties, the following general statement is a truth about individual things: "Necessarily, every individual thing, past, present, or future, is such that if it is red then it is not blue." If the latter truth were known *a posteriori*, then it would be justified by some induction or inductions; our evidence presumably would consist in the fact that a great variety of red things and a great variety of non-blue things have been observed in the past, and that up to now, no red things have been blue. We might thus inductively confirm "Every individual thing, past, present, or future, is such that if it is red then it is not blue"; we might then proceed to the further conclusion, "Necessarily, being red excludes being blue," and finally, to "Necessarily, every individual thing, past, present, or future, is such that if it is red then it is not blue."

Thus, there might be said to be three steps involved in an inductive justification of "Necessarily, being red excludes being blue": (1) the accumulation of instances—"This red thing is not blue," "That blue thing is not red," and so on—along with the summary statement "No red thing observed up to now has been blue"; (2) the inductive inference from these data to "Every individual thing, past, present, and future, is such that if it is red then it is not blue"; (3) the step from this inductive conclusion to "Necessarily, being red excludes being blue," and then to "Necessarily, every individual thing, past, present, or future, is such that if it is red then it is not blue."

Why *not* say that such "truths of reason" are thus known *a posteriori?*

For one thing, some of these truths pertain to properties that have never been exemplified. If we take "square," "rectangular," and "circular" in the precise way in which these words are usually interpreted in geometry, we must say that nothing is square, rectangular, or circular; things in nature, as Plato said, "fall short" of having such properties.[3] Hence, to justify "Necessarily, being square includes being rectangular and excludes being circular," we cannot even take the first of the three steps illustrated above; there being no squares, we cannot collect instances of squares that are rectangles and squares that are not circles.

For another thing, application of induction would seem to presuppose a knowledge of the "truths of reason." In setting out to confirm an inductive hypothesis, we must be able to recognize what its consequences would be. Ordinarily, to recognize these we must apply deduction; we take the hypothesis along with other things that we know and we see what is then implied. All of this, it would seem, involves apprehension of truths of reason—such truths as may be suggested by "For every state of affairs, p and q, the conjunctive state of affairs, composed of p and of either not-p or q, includes q," and "All A's being B excludes some A's not being B." Hence, even if we are able to justify some of the "truths of reason" by inductive procedures, any such justification will presuppose others, and we will be left with some "truths of reason" which we have not justified by means of induction.[4]

And finally, the last of the three steps described above—the step from the inductive generalization "Every individual thing, past, present, and future, is such that if it is red then it is not blue" to "Necessarily, being red excludes being blue"—is not itself a matter of induction. This is best seen if we note that there are other inductive generalizations which obviously do not warrant a comparable step. Perhaps we are justified in saying, for example, "Every individual thing, past, present, and future, is such that if it is human then it does not live to be 200 years old" and "Every individual thing, past, present, and future, is such that if it is a quintuplet named 'Dionne' then it is not male.' But these facts do not warrant the further conclusions "Necessarily, being human excludes being 200 years old" and "necessarily, being a quintuplet named 'Dionne' excludes being male." Hence, the fact that we have justified the inductive generalization involved in the second of our three steps is not in itself sufficient to justify the necessary truth involved in the third.[5]

---

[3] *Phaedo*, 75a.

[4] Cf. Gottlob Frege, *The Foundations of Arithmetic* (Oxford: Basil Blackwell, 1950), pp. 16–17; first published in 1884.

[5] "Experience cannot offer the smallest ground for the necessity of a proposition. She can observe and record what has happened; but she cannot find, in any case, or in any accumulation of cases, any reason for what *must* happen. She may see

Thus, Kant said that *necessity* is a mark, or criterion, of the *a priori*.[6] If what we know is a necessary truth—if we may formulate it in a sentence prefixed by the modal operator "necessarily," or "it is necessary that"—then our knowledge is not *a posteriori*.

A PRIORI KNOWLEDGE

Here, as elsewhere, the "sceptic" and the "intuitionist" may appeal to the same fact. Affirming that ordinary empirical procedures yield no knowledge of necessary truths, the "sceptic" will conclude that there is no such knowledge and the "intuitionist," that such knowledge is intuitive. The "intuitionist's" case, for whatever it may be worth, is somewhat better here than it is in some of the other controversial areas of knowledge to which we have referred. For in some of those other areas, the "intuition" to which he wants to appeal seems simply not to be found. But in the present area, the experience to which he refers is a familiar one—whether or not that experience yields the knowledge that he thinks it does. In support of this contention only—that the experience to which the intuitionist refers is a familiar one—let us try to locate and identify the experience that he calls "intuitive." The best way to do this, I believe, is to follow the traditional account.

"Contemplation of essences," a phrase that is frequently used in this connection, is misleading, for it suggests Plato's doctrine that in order to acquire a knowledge of necessity, we should turn away from "the twilight of becoming and perishing" and contemplate the world of "the absolute and eternal and immutable."[7] According to Aristotle, however, and to subsequent philosophers in the tradition with which we are here concerned, one way of obtaining the requisite intuition is to consider the particular, perishable things of this world.

---

objects side by side, but she cannot see a reason why they must ever be side by side. She finds certain events to occur in succession; but the succession supplies, in its occurrence, no reasons for its recurrence; she contemplates external objects; but she cannot detect any internal bond, which indissolubly connects the future with the past, the possible with the real. To learn a proposition by experience, and to see it to be necessarily true, are two altogether different processes of thought. . . . If anyone does not clearly comprehend this distinction of necessary and contingent truths, he will not be able to go along with us in our researches into the foundations of human knowledge; nor indeed, to pursue with success any speculation on the subject." William Whewell, *Philosophy of the Inductive Sciences Founded upon Their History*, I (London: J. W. Parker & Son, 1840), 59–61.

[6] *Critique of Pure Reason*, B4; cf. *Immanuel Kant's Critique of Pure Reason*, ed. Norman Kemp Smith (London: Macmillan & Co., Ltd., 1933), p. 44. [See this volume, p. 26—ed.]

[7] *The Republic*, 479–508.

As a result of perceiving a particular blue thing, or a number of particular blue things, we may come to know what it is for a thing to be blue, and thus, we may be said to know what the property of being blue is. And as a result of perceiving a particular red thing, or a number of particular red things, we may come to know what it is for a thing to be red, and thus, to know what the property of being red is. Then, having this knowledge of what it is to be red and of what it is to be blue, we are able to see that being red excludes being blue, and that this is necessarily so.

Thus, Aristotle tells us that as a result of perceiving Callias and a number of other particular men, we come to see what it is for a thing to have the property of being human. And then, by considering the property of being human, we come to see that being human includes being animal, and that this is necessarily so.[8]

The following stages seem to be present in both of these examples: (1) the perception of the individual things—in the one case, the perception of the particular red things and blue things, and in the other, the perception of Callias and the other particular men; (2) a process of abstraction—we come to see what it is for a thing to be red and for a thing to be blue, and we come to see what it is for a thing to be a man; (3) the intuitive apprehension of certain relations holding between properties—in the one case, apprehension of the fact that being red excludes being blue, and in the other, apprehension of the fact that being rational and animal includes being animal; and (4) this intuitive knowledge justifies a universal generalization about particular things—"Necessarily, everything is such that if it is red then it is not blue" and "Necessarily, everything is such that if it is human then it is animal."

Aristotle called this process "induction." But since it differs in essential respects from what subsequently came to be known as "induction," some other term, say, "intuitive induction," may be less misleading.[9]

If we have performed an "intuitive induction" in the manner described, then we may say that the proposition concerning the relation between properties ("Necessarily, being red excludes being blue") justifies the universal generalization about particular things ("Necessarily, everything is such that if it is red then it is not blue"). And we can say, therefore, that the universal generalization, as well as the proposition about properties, is known *a priori*. The order of justifica-

---

[8] *Posterior Analytics*, 100a–100b.

[9] This term was proposed by W. E. Johnson, *Logic* (London: Cambridge University Press, 1921), Part II, pp. 191ff. Aristotle uses the term "induction" in the passages cited in the *Posterior Analytics*; cf. *The Nicomachean Ethics*, Book VI, Chap. 3, 1139b.

tion thus differs from that of the enumerative induction considered earlier, where one attempts to justify the statement about properties by reference to a generalization about particular things.

There is a superficial resemblance between "intuitive induction" and "induction by simple enumeration," since in each case, we start with particular instances and then proceed beyond them. Thus, when we make an induction by enumeration, we may proceed from "This *A* is *B*," "That *A* is *B*," and so on, to "In all probability, all *A*'s are *B*'s," or to "In all probability, the next *A* is *B*." But in an induction by enumeration, the function of the particular instances is to *justify* the conclusion. If we find subsequently that our perceptions of the particular instances were unveridical, say, that the things we took to be *A*'s were not *A*'s at all, then the inductive argument would lose whatever force it may have had. In an "intuitive induction," however, the particular perceptions are only incidental to the conclusion. This may be seen in the following way.

Let us suppose that the knowledge expressed by the two sentences "necessarily, being red excludes being blue" and "Necessarily, being human includes being animal" is arrived at by intuitive induction; and let us suppose further that in each case, the process began with the perception of certain particular things. Neither conclusion depends for its *justification* upon the particular perceptions which led to the knowledge concerned. As Duns Scotus put it, the perception of the particular things is only the "occasion" of acquiring the knowledge. If we happen to find our perception was unveridical, this finding will have no bearing upon the result. "If the senses from which these terms were received were all false, or what is more deceptive, if some were false and others true, I still maintain that the intellect would not be deceived about such principles. . . ." [10] If what we take to be Callias is not a man at all, but only a clever imitation of a man, then, if the imitation is clever enough, our deceptive experience will still be an occasion for contemplating the property of being human—the property of being both rational and animal—and thus, for coming to know that being human includes being animal.

It may be, indeed, that to perform an intuitive induction—that is, to "abstract" a certain property, contemplate it, and then see what it in-

[10] *Philosophical Writings*, ed. and trans. Allan Wolter (New York: Thomas Nelson & Sons, 1962), p. 109 (the Nelson philosophical text); cf. p. 103. Cf. Leibniz: "It is also well to observe that if I should discover any demonstrative truth, mathematical or other, while dreaming (as might in fact be), it would be just as certain as if I had been awake. This shows us how intelligible truth is independent of the truth or of the existence outside of us of sensible and material things." *The Philosophical Works of Leibniz*, ed. G. M. Duncan (New Haven: The Tittle, Morehouse & Taylor Co., 1908), p. 161.

cludes and excludes—we need only to *think* of some individual thing as having that property. By thinking about a blue thing and a red thing, for example, we may come to see that being blue excludes being red. Thus, Ernst Mach spoke of "experiments in the imagination." [11] And E. Husserl, whose language may have been needlessly Platonic, said, "The Eidos, the *pure essence,* can be exemplified intuitively in the data of experience, data of perception, memory, and so forth, but just as readily *also in the mere data of fancy. . . .*" [12]

One could go on to say that "intuitive induction" enables us to know those truths about *states of affairs* which, according to the view we are trying to set forth, comprise the subject matter of logic. As a result of our perception, possibly unveridical, of some actual event, we come to consider a certain state of affairs which this event (we believe) happens to exemplify; by contemplating this state of affairs (say, the sun being in the sky and people standing in the road) we come to see that it excludes a certain other state of affairs (that disjunctive state of affairs which is either the sun not being in the sky or there being no people in the road). By contemplating this general state of affairs, we arrive at the intuitive knowledge of an even more general truth—the one that the logician might put by saying, "For any propositions *p* and *q,* the conjunction of *p* and *q* is true if, and only if, the disjunction of not-*p* and not-*q* is false."

But some of the truths of reason are said to be known "by demonstration" and not "by intuition." Thus, Locke tells us that we acquire "demonstrative knowledge" in the following situation: We have intuitive knowledge that a certain state of affairs *A* obtains; we also have intuitive knowledge that *A* includes a state of affairs *B*; and further, we have intuitive knowledge that *B* includes a state of affairs *C*; in which case (Locke says), whether or not we have intuitive knowledge that *C* obtains, we have all that is necessary in order to "demonstrate" to ourselves that *C* obtains. Locke reminds us, however, that proofs involving a number of steps take time, with the result that the "evident lustre" of the early steps may be lost by the time we reach the conclusion: "In long deductions, and the use of many proofs, the memory does not always so readily retain." Therefore, he said demonstrative knowledge "is more imperfect than intuitive knowledge." [13]

[11] *Erkenntnis und Irrtum* (Leipzig: Felix Meiner, 1905), p. 180ff.

[12] *Ideas: General Introduction to Phenomenology* (New York: The Macmillan Company, 1931), p. 57.

[13] *Essay Concerning Human Understanding,* Book IV, Chap. 2, Sec. 7. Descartes also notes that memory is essential to demonstrative knowledge. He remarks in *Rules for the Direction of the Mind* that if we can *remember* having deduced a certain conclusion step by step from a set of premises that are "known by intuition," then, even though we may not now recall each of the particular steps, we are jus-

The various truths of reason, whether they are themselves the objects of intuitive knowledge or of demonstrative knowledge, are thus said to be at the basis of all demonstrative knowledge. We might say in more general terms: if a man knows that a certain state of affairs A necessarily obtains, and if he has intuitive or demonstrative knowledge that A includes a state of affairs B, then (provided he concludes that B obtains) he has demonstrative knowledge that B obtains.

SCEPTICISM AND "PSYCHOLOGISM"

One alternative to this metaphysical account of our knowledge of the truths of reason is scepticism: one may deny that we have such knowledge.

As we have seen, the general reply to a scepticism that addresses itself to an entire area of knowledge can only be this: we do have the knowledge in question, and therefore, any philosophical theory implying that we do not is false. This way of looking at the matter may seem especially plausible in the present instance. It is tempting to say of scepticism, with respect to the truths of reason, what Leonard Nelson said of it, with respect to the truths of mathematics. The advocate of such a sceptism, Nelson said, has invited us to "sacrifice the clearest and most lucid knowledge that we possess—indeed, the *only* knowledge that is clear and lucid *per se*. I prefer to strike the opposite course. If a philosophy, no matter how attractive or plausible or ingenious it may be, brings me into conflict with mathematics, I conclude that not mathematics but my philosophy is on the wrong track." [14] There is certainly no *better* ground for scepticism with respect to our knowledge of the truths of reason than there is for scepticism with respect to our knowledge of physical things.[15] But we

---

tified in saying that the conclusion is "known by deduction." See *The Philosophical Works of Descartes*, ed. E. S. Haldane and G. R. T. Ross, I (London: Cambridge University Press, 1934), 8. Some version of Descartes' principle should be added to the principles about memory set forth in Chap. 3. Cf. Norman Malcolm's suggestion: "If a man previously had grounds for being sure that *p*, and now remembers that *p*, but does not remember what his grounds were," then he "*has* the same grounds he previously had." *Knowledge and Certainty* (Englewood Cliffs: Prentice-Hall, Inc., 1963), p. 230.

[14] Leonard Nelson, *Socratic Method and Critical Philosophy* (New Haven: Yale University Press, 1949), p. 184.

[15] "The preference of (say) seeing over understanding as a method of observation seems to me capricious. For just as an opaque body may be seen, so a concept may be understood or grasped." Alonzo Church, "Abstract Entities in Semantic Analysis," *Proceedings of the American Academy of Arts and Sciences*, Vol. 80 (1951), 100–112; the quotation is on p. 104.

should remind ourselves, at this point, of the general difficulties we encountered in trying to deal with the problem of the criterion.

The "dialectic" will proceed as before: We look for a "reductive" alternative to scepticism and intuitionism, one that will translate sentences expressing the truths in question into sentences referring to a less objectionable subject matter. Of the attempts at such reduction, the only ones worthy of consideration are, first, the view that came to be known in the nineteenth century as "psychologism," and secondly, its contemporary counterpart, which we might call "linguisticism." Much of what can be said in criticism of the one can also be said, mutatis mutandis, in criticism of the other.

Theodore Lipps wrote, in 1880, that "logic is either the physics of thought or nothing at all" and he tried to show that the truths of logic are, in fact, truths about the ways in which people think.[16] This is the view that was called "psychologism" and it was applied generally to the subject matter of the truths of reason.

A psychologistic interpretation of "Necessarily, being red excludes being blue" might be: "Everyone is so constituted psychologically that if he thinks of a thing as being red then he cannot help but think of it as not being blue." And a psychologistic interpretation of the logical truth "For any propositions p and q, if p is true and p implies q, then q is true" might be: "Everyone is so constituted psychologically that if he believes that p is true, and if he believes that p implies q, then he cannot help but believe that q is true."

But obviously, these psychological sentences do not at all convey what is intended by the sentences they are supposed to translate. The psychological sentences are empirical generalizations about the ways in which people think, and as such, they can be supported only by extensive psychological investigation. Thus, Gottlob Frege said, in connection with the psychologistic interpretation of mathematics: "It would be strange if the most exact of all the sciences had to seek support from psychology, which is still feeling its way none too surely." [17] And

---

[16] "Die Aufgabe der Erkenntnistheorie," *Philosophische Monatshefte*, Vol. XVI, (1880); quoted by Husserl, in *Logische Untersuchungen*, Vol. I (Halle: Max Niemeyer, 1928). In his *Philosophie der Arithmetik* (Leipzig: C. E. M. Pfeffer, 1891), Husserl defended a version of "psychologism," but he criticizes that view in the *Logische Untersuchungen*.

[17] *The Foundations of Arithmetic* (Oxford: Basil Blackwell, 1950), p. 38; Frege's work was first published in 1884. Cf. Philip E. B. Jourdain, *The Philosophy of Mr. B*rtr*nd R*ss*ll* (London: George Allen & Unwin, 1918), p. 88: "The psychological founding of logic appears to be not without analogy with the surprising method of advocates of evolutionary ethics, who expect to discover what *is* good by inquiring what cannibals have *thought* good. I sometimes feel inclined to apply the historical method to the multiplication table. I should make a statistical inquiry among school-children, before their pristine wisdom has been biased by teachers. I should put down their answers as to what 6 times 9 amounts to, I should work

being empirical generalizations, the psychological sentences are probable at best and are at the mercy of contrary instances. The existence somewhere of one unreasonable individual—one man who believed that some things are both red and blue, or one man who believed that a certain proposition p is true and also that p implies q, and who yet refused to believe that q is true—would be sufficient to insure that the psychological sentence is false. And we know, all too well, that there are such men. Their existence, however, has no bearing upon the truths expressed by "Necessarily, being red excludes being blue" and "Necessarily, for any propositions p and q, if p is true and if p implies q, then q is true."

In the face of such difficulties, the proponent of psychologism is likely to modify his view. He will say of sentences expressing the laws of logic and the other truths of reason, that they really express *rules of thought,* and that they are not descriptive sentences telling us how people actually do think. But to see the hopelessness of this approach we have only to consider the possible ways of interpreting the sentence "The laws of logic are rules of thought."

(1) One interpretation would be: "The laws of logic are ethical truths pertaining to our duties and obligations with respect to thinking." In this case, the problem of our knowledge of the laws of logic is transferred to the (more difficult) problem of our knowledge of the truths (if any) of ethics.

(2) "The laws of logic are imperatives commanding us to think in certain ways—and imperatives are neither true nor false." This way of looking at the matter leaves us with the problem of distinguishing between valid and invalid imperatives. For there is a distinction between "Do not believe, with respect to any particular thing, both that it is red and that it is blue" and "Do not believe, with respect to any particular thing, that that thing is either red or not red." The former imperative, surely, is correct or valid, and the latter, incorrect or invalid. If we are not to fall back into scepticism, we must also say that the former is known to be valid and the latter is known to be invalid. Moreover, it is not possible to construe all of the statements of logic as imperatives. For the logician can also tell us nonimperatively such things as: If you believe that p, and if you believe that p implies q, and if you conform to the imperative, modus ponens, then you will also believe that q. This statement is a necessary truth. (A manual of chess, similarly, may give us certain rules in the form of imperatives: "Move the king only one square at a time." And possibly these im-

out the average of their answers to six places of decimals, and should then decide that, at the present stage of human development, this average is of the value of 6 times 9."

peratives are neither valid nor invalid. But whether or not they are valid, the chess manual will also contain true indicative sentences— sentences which are not themselves imperatives but which tell us what will happen when, in accordance with the imperatives that the manual lays down, we move the pieces into various positions. "It is impossible, if white is in such and such a position, for black to win in less than seven moves." And these statements are also necessary truths.)

(3) "The laws of logic tell us which ways of believing will lead to truth and which will lead to falsehood." According to this interpretation, our two examples might be thought of as telling us respectively: "A necessary condition of avoiding false beliefs is to refrain from believing, with respect to any particular thing, both that that thing is red and also that it is blue" and "A necessary condition of avoiding false beliefs is to refrain from believing, at one and the same time, with respect to any propositions p and q, that p is true, that p implies q, and that q is false." To see that this way of formulating psychologism leaves us with our problem, let us compare it with a similar psychologistic interpretation of some other subject matter, say, astronomy. We may say, if we like, that what the statement "There are nine planets" really tells us is that if we wish to avoid error with respect to the number of planets, it is essential to refrain from believing that there are not nine planets; it also tells us that if we wish to arrive at the truth about the number of planets, it is essential to believe that there *are* nine planets. It is not likely that in so spinning out what is conveyed by "There are nine planets," we can throw any light upon what the astronomer thinks he knows. In any case, our problem reappears when we compare our new versions of the statements of logic with those of the statements of astronomy. The former, but not the latter, can be prefixed by "It is necessary that," and unless we give in to scepticism (which it was the point of psychologism to avoid) we must say that the result of such a prefixing is also a statement we can know to be true.[18]

"LINGUISTICISM"

A popular conception of the truths of reason at the present time is the linguistic analogue of psychologism. Versions of "linguisticism" may be obtained merely by altering our exposition of psychologism. We may replace the references to ways in which people *think* by refer-

---

[18] Cf. the criticism of psychologism in Husserl's *Logische Untersuchungen*, I, 154ff., and Rudolf Carnap, *The Logical Foundations of Probability* (Chicago: University of Chicago Press, 1950), pp. 37–42.

ences to ways in which they *use language,* replace the references to what people *believe* by references to what they *write* or *say,* replace "avoiding false belief" by "avoiding absurdity," and replace "rules of thought" by "rules of language." The result could then be criticized substantially, mutatis mutandis, as before.

Some of the versions of linguisticism, however, are less straightforward. It is often said, for example, that the sentences formulating the truths of logic are "true in virtue of the rules of language" and hence, that they are "true in virtue of the way in which we use words." What could this possibly mean?

The two English sentences, "Being red excludes being blue" and "Being rational and animal includes being animal," could plausibly be said to "owe their truth," in part, to the way in which we use words. If we used "being blue" to refer to the property of being heavy, and not to that of being blue, then the first sentence (provided the other words in it had their present use) would be false instead of true. And if we used the word "and" to express the relation of disjunction instead of conjunction, then the second sentence (again, provided that the other words in it had their present use) would also be false instead of true. But as W. V. Quine has reminded us, "even so factual a sentence as 'Brutus killed Caesar' owes its truth not only to the killing but equally to our using the component words as we do." [19] Had "killed," for example, been given the use that "was survived by" happens to have, then, other things being the same, "Brutus killed Caesar" would be false instead of true.

It might be suggested, therefore, that the truths of logic and other truths of reason stand in this peculiar relationship to language: they are true "solely in virtue of the rules of our language," or "solely in virtue of the ways in which we use words." But if we take the phrase "solely in virtue of" in the way in which it would naturally be taken, then the suggestion is obviously false.

To say of a sentence that it is true *solely* in virtue of the ways in which we use words, or that it is true *solely* in virtue of the rules of our language, would be to say that the only condition that needs to obtain in order for the sentence to be true is that we use words in certain ways or that there be certain rules pertaining to the way in which words are to be used. But let us consider what conditions must obtain if the English sentence "Being red excludes being blue" is to be true. One such condition is indicated by the following sentence which we may call "*T*":

[19] W. V. Quine, "Carnap and Logical Truth," *The Philosophy of Rudolf Carnap,* ed. P. A. Schilpp (La Salle, Ill.: Open Court Publishing Co., 1963), p. 386.

The English sentence "Being blue excludes being red" is true if, and only if, being blue excludes being red.

Clearly, the final part of T, the part following the second "if," formulates a necessary condition for the truth of the English sentence "Being red excludes being blue"; but it refers to a relationship among properties and not to rules of language or ways in which we use words (To suppose otherwise would be to make the mistake, once again, of confusing use and mention of language). Hence, we cannot say that the only conditions that need to obtain in order for "Being red excludes being blue" to be true is that we use words in certain ways or that there be certain rules pertaining to the ways in which words are to be used; and therefore, the sentence cannot be said to be true solely in virtue of the ways in which we use words.

LOGICAL TRUTH AND THE ANALYTIC

Another epistemological problem involving the truths of reason concerns the status of "the synthetic *a priori*." To understand this problem, we must first explicate the terms involved.

Let us consider, once again, the epistemological terms *a priori* and *a posteriori*. What they are intended to refer to may be conveyed in this way: We have said that those necessary truths that are known by "intuitive induction" or "by demonstration," in the manner set forth above, are truths that are known *a priori*. Let us also say that those universal generalizations that are justified reference to such truths are known *a priori;* hence, both "Being red excludes being blue" and "Every individual thing is such that if it is red then it is not blue" will be statements expressing what we know *a priori*. And let us say that what is known, but not known *a priori*, is known *a posteriori*. Thus, we can say, with Kant, that *necessity* is a mark or criterion of the *a priori*.

The terms "analytic" and "synthetic" were introduced by Kant in order to contrast two types of categorical judgment. They are used in much of contemporary philosophy to refer instead to the types of *sentence* that express the types of judgment to which Kant referred. An analytic *judgment*, according to Kant, is a judgment in which "the predicate adds nothing to the concept of the subject." If I judge that all squares are rectangles, then, in Kant's terminology, the concept of the subject of my judgment is the property of being square, and the concept of the predicate is the property of being rectangular. Kant uses the term "analytic," since, he says, the concept of the predicate helps to "break up the concept of the subject into those constituent concepts that have all along been thought in it." [20] Since being square is the conjunctive property of being equilateral and rectangular, the predicate of the judgment expressed by "All squares are rectangular" may be said to "analyze out" what is contained in the subject. An analytic judgment, then, may be expressed in the form of an explicit redundancy: for example, "Everything is such that if it is both equilateral and rectangular then it is rectangular." To deny such an explicit redundancy would be to affirm a *contradictio in adjecto*, for it would be to judge that there are things which both have and do not have a certain property—in the present instance, that there is something that both is and is not rectangular. Hence, Kant said that "the common principle of all analytic judgments is the law of contradiction." [21]

If we wish to apply Kant's distinction to *sentences*, as distinguished from *judgments*, and if we are to be otherwise faithful to what it was that he had in mind, we might proceed in the following way.

Consider a sentence that can be expressed in the form "All things that are *S* are *P*"; or more exactly, consider a sentence such that what it expresses can also be expressed in an English sentence of the form "All things that are *S* are *P*." One example of such a sentence is, "All things that are square are rectangular"; another is, "No bachelors are married," for what this sentence expresses may also be expressed obversely by, "All things that are bachelors are nonmarried." Let us say of such a sentence that it is *analytic* provided that the predicate term *P* (i.e., the term occupying the place of "*P*") can be "analyzed out" of the subject term *S*. And let us say that the predicate term *P* can be *analyzed out* of the subject term *S* provided that any one of the following three conditions holds.

1. The terms *S* and *P* are synonymous (are used with the same meaning).
2. There is a term *Q* such that *S* is synonymous with the conjunction of *Q* and *P*, and *Q* is not synonymous either with *S* or with the disjunction of *S* and the negation of *P*.
3. *P* is synonymous with a disjunctive term, P^1 or P^2, which is such that P^1 can be analyzed out of *S*, and P^2 cannot be analyzed out of *S*.

Thus, if we use "equilateral and rectangular" as a synonym for "square," we may say that in virtue of (1), the sentence "All things that are equilateral and rectangular are square," as well as "All things that are square are square," and "All things that are equilateral and

[20] *Critique of Pure Reason*, A7; trans. Norman Kemp Smith.

[21] *Prolegomena to Any Future Metaphysics*, Sec. 2.

rectangular are equilateral and rectangular," is analytic. We may say that in virtue of (2), the sentence "All things that are equilateral and rectangular are rectangular" is analytic. And if we use "parents" as a synonym for "fathers or mothers," then we may say that in virtue of (3), the sentence "All fathers are parents" is analytic.

Completing this Kant-like account, we could now say that a catgorical sentence—a sentence expressible in the form "All things that are S are P," "No things that are S are P," "Some things that are S are P," and "Some things that are S are not P"—is *synthetic* provided that neither it nor its negation is analytic. (Kant did not himself provide a term for the negations of analytic judgments—those judgments expressible in such sentences as "Some squares are not rectangles" and "Some bachelors are married." We could say, however, that the sentences expressing such judgments are "analytically false"—in which case we would have a motive for replacing Kant's "analytic" by "analytically true.")

If we thus restrict "analytic" and "synthetic" to categorical sentences, then we should distinguish the concept of the *analytic* from the wider, but closely related, concept of *logical truth*. It is sometimes said that a sentence is logically true if it is true "in virtue of its form alone." It would be very difficult to define this phrase precisely, but what it intends may be suggested by the following procedure, set forth by W. V. Quine.

Quine enumerates a list of expressions that he calls "logical expressions"; the list includes "and," "or," "not," "all," "every," "some," "if," "then," "it is true that," and "it is false that." He then proposes that a sentence may be called logically true provided it is one in which only the logical expressions *occur essentially*. In "If no Greeks are Romans then it is false that some Romans are Greeks," the logical expressions "no," "it is false that," "some," "if," and "then" occur essentially, but the nonlogical expressions, "are," "Greeks," and "Romans," do not. One might say that the truth of the sentence is independent of the nonlogical expressions that occur in it. Or more exactly, the sentence is one such that, if we alter it only by replacing some of its nonlogical expressions by other "grammatically admissible" expression (making sure that all occurrences of the old word are replaced by occurrences of the same new word), the result will be true. Thus, if we replace "Greeks" by "Algerians," and "Romans" by "Alaskans," the result will be true; this would also hold true for any other plural nouns we might select. But if we replace some of the logical expressions by other logical expressions (*e.g.*, "no" by "some") we may get a falsehood. A logical truth, according to this interpretation, is a sentence "which is true and remains true under all reinterpretations of its components other than logical particles." [22] Or we could say, somewhat more broadly, that a logical truth is any sentence which is such that what is expressed can also be expressed in a sentence of the sort that Quine describes.

The class of logical truths, then, is not restricted to sentences that are categorical; hence, it is wider than the class of sentences we have described as being "analytic." But all analytic sentences may be said to be logically true. Thus, again, if we use "square" as a synonym for "equilateral and rectangular," we may express "All things that are square are rectangular" as "All things that are equilateral and rectangular are rectangular"; the latter sentence could be said to be logically true, or "true in virtue of its form," since replacement of "equilateral" by any other adjective, and of each occurrence of "rectangular" by any other adjective (the same adjective each time), will result in a sentence that is also true.

We may thus divide meaningful indicative sentences into three groups: (1) those sentences that are *logically true*—analytic sentences comprise a subclass of sentences that are logically true; (2) the negations or contradictories of sentences that are logically true—these, we may say, are *logically false;* (3) and finally, all other meaningful indicative sentences—these, some of which are true and some of which are false, may be said to be *synthetic,* in a broad sense of the term "synthetic." (Using "synthetic" in this broad sense, we depart somewhat from the Kantian tradition.)

But many philosophers now believe that the distinction between the analytic and the synthetic has been shown to be untenable; we should consider what reasons there might be for such a belief. Ordinarily, it is defended by reference to the following facts. (1) In drawing a distinction between analytic and synthetic sentences, one must use such a term as "synonym"; we have said, for example, that "both equilateral and rectangular" may be used as a synonym for "square." (2) The traditional account of synonymy refers to abstract entities; one term is said to be used synonymously with another term if the two terms are used to connote the same properties. (3) There is no reliable way of telling, merely by observing a man's behavior, what properties, if any, he is using any given word to connote. And (4) it is not possible to define "synonym" merely by reference to linguistic behavior. [23]

[22] Cf. W. V. Quine, *From a Logical Point of View* (Cambridge: Harvard University Press, 1953), pp. 22–23. [See this volume, p. 54—ed.]

[23] Cf. W. V. Quine, "Two Dogmas of Empiricism," in *From a Logical Point of View,* esp. pp. 20–37. [See this volume, pp. 52–65—ed.], and Morton White, "The Analytic and the Synthetic: An Untenable Dualism," in Leonard Linsky, ed. *Seman-*

But these four propositions, even if they are true, are not sufficient to yield the conclusion (5) that the distinction between the analytic and the synthetic is untenable. If we attempt to formulate the additional premise that would be needed to make the argument valid, we will see that it must involve a philosophical generalization—a generalization concerning what conditions must obtain if the distinction between the analytic and the synthetic is to be tenable. And how would the generalization be defended? This question should be considered in the light of what we have said about scepticism and the problem of the criterion. Of the philosophical generalizations that would make the above argument valid, none of them, so far as I know, has ever been defended. It is not accurate, therefore, to say that the distinction between the analytic and the synthetic has been *shown* to be untenable.

THE SYNTHETIC A PRIORI

Some of the things that we know *a priori* are expressible in sentences that are logically true. Presumably, all of the logical truths cited up to now are necessary truths that are shown to be true *a priori*. Some of the things that we know *a posteriori* are expressible in sentences that are synthetic, for example, "There are kangaroos in New Zealand." We leave open the question whether we have *a posteriori* knowledge of any necessary truths. (What if a man accepts a certain logical principle merely on the ground that all reputable logicians affirm that it is necessary? If we decide that such a man may know *a posteriori* that the principle is necessary, then we must qualify Kant's *dictum* according to which knowledge of necessity is a mark of the *a priori*.) The question of the synthetic *a priori* now becomes: Of the things that we know *a priori* to be true, are any of them expressible in sentences that are synthetic? Or more briefly: Is there a synthetic *a priori*?

Obviously, it would be very difficult indeed to *prove* either that there is a synthetic *a priori* or that there is not. But there are sentences which seem to express what is known *a priori*, and which, up to now, have not been shown to be logically true. This fact may be *some* presumption in favor of the view that there is a synthetic *a priori*. And if there is a synthetic *a priori*, then this fact, in turn, might be taken to have important bearing upon the nature of the human mind (it would imply, for example, that our *a priori* knowledge is not restricted to knowledge of "formal" truths).

Let us consider, then, certain possible examples of the synthetic *a priori*.

(1) One important candidate for the synthetic *a priori* is the knowledge that might be expressed either by saying "Being red includes being colored" or "Necessarily, everything that is red is colored." The sentence "Everything that is red is colored" recalls our paradigmatic "Everything that is square is rectangular." In the case of the latter sentence, we were able to "analyze the predicate out of the subject": We replaced the subject term "square" with a conjunctive term, "equilateral and rectangular," such that one of its conjuncts is synonymous with the predicate term and the other conjunct is not synonymous with the original subject term. But it would seem to be impossible to find—or even to coin—any conjunctive term which is synonymous with "red" and which is such that one of its two conjuncts is synonymous with "colored" and the other is not synonymous with "red." It is recommended that the reader try to find, or to coin, such a term.

We may be tempted, then, to follow the procedure we took in the case of "All fathers are parents," where, it will be recalled, we replaced the predicate term "parents" by a synonymous disjunctive term, "fathers or mothers," which was such that one of its disjuncts, being synonymous with the subject term "fathers," could be "analyzed out" of the subject. Thus, we might hope to replace the predicate term of "Everything that is red is colored" by a lengthy disjunctive predicate, having for its disjuncts names of each of the colors. In this case, our new sentence might read as follows: "Everything that is red is either red or blue or green or yellow or. . . ." But we will not have replaced the original predicate "colored" by a synonym until we have removed the dots and completed the disjunction. Can we do this? Can we provide a list of colors and say truly, "These colors, red and blue and green and yellow and . . . , are all the colors there are"? And what is even more to the point, if we *can* do this, can we then go on to say that a disjunction of color words, made up from this list of colors, will constitute a *synonym* for "colored"? It would seem not, since one may say without contradiction: "It is possible that a thing may be colored and yet neither red nor blue nor green nor yellow nor. . . . There may be colors that are unknown to us—colors that we would experience if we had a rather different type of sensory apparatus." If such a suggestion is significant and consistent, as it seems to be, then "colored" is not synonymous with any expression that can be formed merely by listing each of the colors. And if this is so, then our lengthy disjunctive predicate will not be one that we have "analyzed out" of the subject, and therefore, we will not have shown that the *a priori* sentence "Everything that is red is colored" is analytic.[24]

It has been suggested that the sentences giving rise to the problem of the synthetic *a priori* are really "postulates about the meanings of words," and therefore, that they do not express what is synthetic *a priori*. But if the suggestion is intended literally, then it would seem to betray the confusion between use and mention that we encountered earlier. A postulate about the meaning of the word "red," for example, or a sentence expressing such a postulate, would presumably mention the word "red." It might read, "The word 'red' may be taken to refer to a certain color," or perhaps, "Let the word 'red' be taken to refer to a certain color." But "Everything that is red is colored," although it uses the words "red" and "colored," doesn't mention them at all. Thus, there would seem to be no clear sense in which it could be said really to be a "meaning postulate" or to refer in any way to words and how they are used.

(2) What Leibniz called the "disparates" furnish us with a second candidate for the synthetic *a priori*. These are closely related to the type of sentence just considered, but involve problems that are essentially different. An example of a sentence concerned with disparates would be our earlier "Being red excludes being blue" or (alternatively put) "Necessarily, nothing that is red is blue." [25] Philosophers have devoted considerable ingenuity to trying to show that "Nothing that is red is blue" can be expressed as a sentence that is analytic, and thus, as a logical truth, but so far as I have been able to determine, all of these attempts have been unsuccessful. Again, it is recommended that the reader try for himself to re-express "Nothing that is red is blue" in such a way that the predicate may be "analyzed out" of the subject in any of the senses described above.

(3) It has also been held, not without plausibility, that certain ethical sentences express what is synthetic *a priori*. Thus, Leibniz, writing on what he called the "supersensible element" in knowledge, said: ". . . But to return to *necessary truths*, it is generally true that we know them only by this natural light, and not at all by the experience of the senses. For the senses can very well make known, in some sort, what is, but they cannot make known what *ought to be* or what

---

[24] Cf. C. H. Langford, "A Proof that Synthetic A Priori Propositions Exist," *Journal of Philosophy*, XLVI (1949), 20–24.

[25] Cf. John Locke, *Essay Concerning Human Understanding*, Book IV, Chap. 1, Sec. 7; G. W. Leibniz, *New Essays Concerning Human Understanding*, Book IV, Chap. 2, Sec. 1; Franz Brentano, *Versuch über die Erkenntnis* (Leipzig: Felix Meiner, 1925), pp. 9–10.

could not be otherwise." [26] Or consider the sentence "Pleasure as such is intrinsically good, or good in itself, whenever and wherever it may occur." If this sentence expresses something that is known to be true, then what it expresses must be synthetic *a priori*. To avoid this conclusion, some philosophers deny that sentences about what is intrinsically good, or good in itself, can be known to be true.[27] An examination of this view would involve us, once again, in the problem of the criterion.

And still other things that we know *a priori* to be true seem to be expressible only in sentences that are synthetic.

[26] Quoted from *The Philosophical Works of Leibniz*, p. 162.
[27] Cf. the discussion of this question in chaps. 5 and 6 in William Frankena, *Ethics*, Prentice-Hall Foundations of Philosophy Series.

part two

DE RE

W. V. O. QUINE

Reference and Modality

1

One of the fundamental principles governing identity is that of *substitutivity*—or, as it might well be called, that of *indiscernibility of identicals*. It provides that, *given a true statement of identity, one of its two terms may be substituted for the other in any true statement and the result will be true*. It is easy to find cases contrary to this principle. For example, the statements:

(1) Giorgione = Barbarelli,

(2) Giorgione was so-called because of his size

are true; however, replacement of the name 'Giorgione' by the name 'Barbarelli' turns (2) into the falsehood:

Barbarelli was so-called because of his size.

Furthermore, the statements:

(3) Cicero = Tully,

(4) 'Cicero' contains six letters

are true, but replacement of the first name by the second turns (4) false. Yet the basis of the principle of substitutivity appears quite solid; whatever can be said about the person Cicero (or Giorgione) should be equally true of the person Tully (or Barbarelli), this being the same person.

* Reprinted by permission of the publishers from Willard Van Orman Quine, *From a Logical Point of View*. Cambridge, Mass.: Harvard University Press, Copyright, 1953, 1961, by the President and Fellows of Harvard College.

In the case of (4), this paradox resolves itself immediately. The fact is that (4) is not a statement about the person Cicero, but simply about the word 'Cicero'. The principle of substitutivity should not be extended to contexts in which the name to be supplanted occurs without referring simply to the object. Failure of substitutivity reveals merely that the occurrence to be supplanted is not *purely referential,* that is, that the statement depends not only on the object but on the form of the name. For it is clear that whatever can be affirmed about the object remains true when we refer to the object by any other name.

An expression which consists of another expression between single quotes constitutes a name of that other expression; and it is clear that the occurrence of that other expression or a part of it, within the context of quotes, is not in general referential. In particular, the occurrence of the personal name within the context of quotes in (4) is not referential, not subject to the substitutivity principle. The personal name occurs there merely as a fragment of a longer name which contains, beside this fragment, the two quotation marks. To make a substitution upon a personal name, within such a context, would be no more justifiable than to make a substitution upon the term 'cat' within the context 'cattle'.

The example (2) is a little more subtle, for it is a statement about a man and not merely about his name. It was the man, not his name, that was called so and so because of his size. Nevertheless, the failure of substitutivity shows that the occurrence of the personal name in (2) is not *purely* referential. It is easy in fact to translate (2) into another statement which contains two occurrences of the name, one purely referential and the other not:

(5) Giorgione was called 'Giorgione' because of his size.

The first occurrence is purely referential. Substitution on the basis of (1) converts (5) into another statement equally true:

Barbarelli was called 'Giorgione' because of his size.

The second occurrence of the personal name is no more referential than any other occurrence within a context of quotes.

It would not be quite accurate to conclude that an occurrence of a name within single quotes is *never* referential. Consider the statements:

(6) 'Giorgione played chess' is true,

(7) 'Giorgione' named a chess player,

each of which is true or false according as the quotationless statement:

(8) Giorgione played chess

is true or false. Our criterion of referential occurrence makes the occurrence of the name 'Giorgione' in (8) referential, and must make the occurrences of 'Giorgione' in (6) and (7) referential by the same token, despite the presence of single quotes in (6) and (7). The point about quotation is not that it must destroy referential occurrence, but that it can (and ordinarily does) destroy referential occurrence. The examples (6) and (7) are exceptional in that the special predicates 'is true' and 'named' have the effect of undoing the single quotes—as is evident on comparison of (6) and (7) with (8).

To get an example of another common type of statement in which names do not occur referentially, consider any person who is called Philip and satisfies the condition:

(9) Philip is unaware that Tully denounced Catiline,

or perhaps the condition:

(10) Philip believes that Tegucigalpa is in Nicaragua.

Substitution on the basis of (3) transforms (9) into the statement:

(11) Philip is unaware that Cicero denounced Catiline,

no doubt false. Substitution on the basis of the true identity:

Tegucigalpa = capital of Honduras

transforms the truth (10) likewise into the falsehood:

(12) Philip believes that the capital of Honduras is in Nicaragua.

We see therefore that the occurrences of the names 'Tully' and 'Tegucigalpa' in (9)–(10) are not purely referential.

In this there is a fundamental contrast between (9), or (10), and:

Crassus heard Tully denounce Catiline.

This statement affirms a relation between three persons, and the persons remain so related independently of the names applied to them. But (9) cannot be considered simply as affirming a relation between three persons, nor (10) a relation between person, city, and country—at least not so long as we interpret our words in such a way as to admit (9) and (10) as true and (11) and (12) as false.

Some readers may wish to construe unawareness and belief as relations between persons and statements, thus writing (9) and (10) in the manner:

(13) Philip is unaware of 'Tully denounced Catiline',

(14) Philip believes 'Tegucigalpa is in Nicaragua',

in order to put within a context of single quotes every not purely referential occurrence of a name. Church[1] argues against this. In so doing he exploits the concept of analyticity, concerning which we have felt misgivings (pp. 23–37 above);* still his argument cannot be set lightly aside, nor are we required here to take a stand on the matter. Suffice it to say that there is certainly no *need* to reconstrue (9)–(10) in the manner (13)–(14). What *is* imperative is to observe merely that the contexts 'is unaware that . . .' and 'believes that . . .' *resemble* the context of the single quotes in this respect: a name may occur referentially in a statement *S* and yet not occur referentially in a longer statement which is formed by embedding *S* in the context 'is unaware that . . .' or 'believes that . . .'. To sum up the situation in a word, we may speak of the contexts 'is unaware that . . .' and 'believes that . . .' as *referentially opaque*. The same is true of the contests 'knows that . . .', 'says that . . .', 'doubts that . . .', 'is surprised that . . .', and so forth. It would be tidy but unnecessary to force all referentially opaque contexts into the quotational mold; alternatively we can recognize quotation as one referentially opaque context among many.

It will next be shown that referential opacity afflicts also the so-called *modal* contexts 'Necessarily . . .' and 'Possibly . . .', at least when those are given the sense of *strict* necessity and possibility as in Lewis's modal logic. According to the strict sense of 'necessarily' and 'possibly', these statements would be regarded as true:

(15) 9 is necessarily greater than 7,

(16) Necessarily if there is life on the Evening Star then there is life on the Evening Star,

(17) The number of planets is possibly less than 7,

and these as false:

(18) The number of planets is necessarily greater than 7,

(19) Necessarily if there is life on the Evening Star then there is life on the Morning Star,

(20) 9 is possibly less than 7.

The general idea of strict modalities is based on the putative notion of *analyticity* as follows: a statement of the form 'Necessarily . . .' is true if and only if the component statement which 'necessarily' governs is

---

[1] A. Church, "On Carnap's Analysis of Statements of Assertion and Belief," *Analysis* (1950).

* [See this volume, pp. 52–65—ed.]

analytic, and a statement of the form 'Possibly . . .' is false if and only if the negation of the component statement which 'possibly' governs is analytic. Thus (15)–(17) could be paraphrased as follows:

(21) '9 > 7' is analytic,

(22) 'If there is life on the Evening Star then there is life on the Evening Star' is analytic,

(23) 'The number of planets is not less than 7' is not analytic,

and correspondingly for (18)–(20).

That the contexts 'necessarily . . .' and 'Possibly . . .' are referentially opaque can now be quickly seen; for substitution on the basis of the true identities:

(24) The number of planets = 9,

(25) The Evening Star = the Morning Star

turns the truths (15)–(17) into the falsehoods (18)–(20).

Note that the fact that (15)–(17) are equivalent to (21)–(23), and the fact that '9' and 'Evening Star' and 'the number of planets' occur within quotations in (21)–(23), would not of themselves have justified us in concluding that '9' and 'Evening Star' and 'the number of planets' occur irreferentially in (15)–(17). To argue thus would be like citing the equivalence of (8) to (6) and (7) as evidence that 'Giorgione' occurs irreferentially in (8). What shows the occurrences of '9', 'Evening Star', and 'the number of planets' to be irreferential in (15)–(17) (and in (18)–(20)) is the fact that substitution by (24)–(25) turns the truths (15)–(17) into falsehoods (and the falsehoods (18)–(20) into truths).

Some, it was remarked, may like to think of (9) and (10) as receiving their more fundamental expression in (13) and (14). In the same spirit, many will like to think of (15)–(17) as receiving their more fundamental expression in (21)–(23). But this again is unnecessary. We would certainly not think of (6) and (7) as somehow more basic than (8), and we need not view (21)–(23) as more basic than (15)–(17). What is important is to appreciate that the contexts 'Necessarily . . .' and 'Possibly . . .' are, like quotation and 'is unaware that . . .' and 'believes that . . .', referentially opaque.

2

The phenomenon of referential opacity has just now been explained by appeal to the behavior of singular terms. But singular terms are eliminable, we know (cf. pp. 7f., 85, 166f.),* by paraphrase. Ultimately the objects referred to in a theory are to be accounted not as the things named by the singular terms, but as the values of the variables of quantification. So, if referential opacity is an infirmity worth worrying about, it must show symptoms in connection with quantification as well as in connection with singular terms. Let us then turn our attention to quantification.

The connection between naming and quantification is implicit in the operation whereby, from 'Socrates is mortal', we infer '($\exists$ x)(x is mortal)', that is, 'Something is mortal'. This is the operation which was spoken of earlier (p. 120)† as *existential generalization,* except that we now have a singular term 'Socrates' where we then had a free variable. The idea behind such inference is that whatever is true of the object named by a given singular term is true of something; and clearly the inference loses its justification when the singular term in question does not happen to name. From:

> There is no such thing as Pegasus,

for example, we do not infer:

> ($\exists x$)(there is no such thing as x),

that is, 'There is something which there is no such thing as', or 'There is something which there is not'.

Such inference is of course equally unwarranted in the case of an irreferential occurrence of any substantive. From (2), existential generalization would lead to:

> ($\exists x$)(x was so-called because of its size),

that is, 'Something was so-called because of its size'. This is clearly meaningless, there being no longer any suitable antecedent for 'so-called'. Note, in contrast, that existential generalization with respect to the purely referential occurrence in (5) yields the sound conclusion:

> ($\exists x$)(x was called 'Giorgione' because of its size),

that is, 'Something was called 'Giorgione' because of its size'.

The logical operation of *universal instantiation* is that whereby we infer from 'Everything is itself', for example, or in symbols '(x)(x = x)', the conclusion that Socrates = Socrates. This and existential generalization are two aspects of a single principle; for instead of saying that '(x)(x = x)' implies 'Socrates = Socrates', we could as well say that the denial 'Socrates $\neq$ Socrates' implies '($\exists$ x)(x $\neq$ x)'. The prin-

---

* [Not reprinted here—ed.]

† [Not reprinted here—ed.]

ciple embodied in these two operations is the link between quantifications and the singular statements that are related to them as instances. Yet it is a principle only by courtesy. It holds only in the case where a term names and, furthermore, occurs referentially. It is simply the logical content of the idea that a given occurrence is referential. The principle is, for this reason, anomalous as an adjunct to the purely logical theory of quantification. Hence the logical importance of the fact that all singular terms, aside from the variables that serve as pronouns in connection with quantifiers, are dispensable and eliminable by paraphrase.

We saw just now how the referentially opaque context (2) fared under existential generalization. Let us see what happens to our other referentially opaque contexts. Applied to the occurrence of the personal name in (4), existential generalization would lead us to:

(26) $(\exists x)($ 'x' contains six letters$)$,

that is:

(27) There is something such that 'it' contains six letters,

or perhaps:

(28) 'Something' contains six letters.

Now the expression:

'x' contains six letters

means simply:

The 24th letter of the alphabet contains six letters.

In (26) the occurrence of the letter within the context of quotes is as irrelevant to the quantifier that precedes it as is the occurrence of the same letter in the context 'six'. (26) consists merely of a falsehood preceded by an irrelevant quantifier. (27) is similar; its part:

'it' contains six letters

is false, and the prefix 'there is something such that' is irrelevant. (28), again, is false—if by 'contains six' we mean 'contains exactly six'.

It is less obvious, and correspondingly more important to recognize, that existential generalization is unwarranted likewise in the case of (9) and (10). Applied to (9), it leads to:

$(\exists x)($Philip is unaware that x denounced Catiline$)$,

that is:

(29) Something is such that Philip is unaware that it denounced Catiline.

What is this object, that denounced Catiline without Philip's having become aware of the fact? Tully, that is, Cicero? But to suppose this would conflict with the fact that (11) is false.

Note that (29) is not to be confused with:

Philip is unaware that $(\exists x)(x$ denounced Catiline$)$,

which, though it happens to be false, is quite straightforward and in no danger of being inferred by existential generalization from (9).

Now the difficulty involved in the apparent consequence (29) of (9) recurs when we try to apply existential generalization to modal statements. The apparent consequences:

(30) $(\exists x)(x$ is necessarily greater than 7$)$,

(31) $(\exists x)($necessarily if there is life on the Evening Star then there is life on $x)$

of (15) and (16) raise the same questions as did (29). What is this number which, according to (30), is necessarily greater than 7? According to (15), from which (30) was inferred, it was 9, that is, the number of planets; but to suppose this would conflict with the fact that (18) is false. In a word, to be necessarily greater than 7 is not a trait of a number, but depends on the manner of referring to the number. Again, what is the thing x whose existence is affirmed in (31)? According to (16), from which (31) was inferred, it was the Evening Star, that is, the Morning Star; but to suppose this would conflict with the fact that (19) is false. Being necessarily or possibly thus and so is in general not a trait of the object concerned, but depends on the manner of referring to the object.

Note that (30) and (31) are not to be confused with:

Necessarily $(\exists x)(x > 7)$,

Necessarily $(\exists x)($if there is life on the Evening Star then there is life on $x)$,

which present no problem of interpretation comparable to that presented by (30) and (31). The difference may be accentuated by a change of example: in a game of a type admitting of no tie it is necessary that some one of the players will win, but there is no one player of whom it may be said to be necessary that he win.

We had seen, in the preceding section, how referential opacity manifests itself in connection with singular terms; and the task which we then set ourselves at the beginning of this section was to see how referential opacity manifests itself in connection rather with variables of quantification. The answer is now apparent: if to a referentially opaque context of a variable we apply a quantifier, with the intention that it govern that variable from outside the referentially opaque context, then what we commonly end up with is unintended sense or nonsense of the type (26)–(31). In a word, we cannot in general properly *quantify into* referentially opaque contexts.

The context of quotation and the further contexts '. . . was so called', 'is unaware that . . .', 'believes that . . .', 'Necessarily . . .', and 'Possibly . . .' were found referentially opaque in the preceding section by consideration of the failure of substitutivity of identity as applied to singular terms. In the present section these contexts have been found referentially opaque by a criterion having to do no longer with singular terms, but with the miscarriage of quantification. The reader may feel, indeed, that in this second criterion we have not really got away from singular terms after all; for the discrediting of the quantifications (29)–(31) turned still on an expository interplay between the singular terms 'Tully' and 'Cicero', '9' and 'the number of planets'. 'Evening Star' and 'Morning Star'. Actually, though, this expository reversion to our old singular terms is avoidable, as may now be illustrated by re-arguing the the meaninglessness of (30) in another way. Whatever is greater than 7 is a number, and any given number *x* greater than 7 can be uniquely determined by any of various conditions, some of which have '$x > 7$' as a necessary consequence and some of which do not. One and the same number *x* is uniquely determined by the condition:

(32) $x = \sqrt{x} + \sqrt{x} + \sqrt{x} \neq \sqrt{x}$

and by the condition:

(33) There are exactly *x* planets,

but (32) has '$x > 7$' as a necessary consequence while (33) does not. *Necessary* greaterness than 7 makes no sense as applied to a *number x*; necessity attaches only to the connection between '$x > 7$' and the particular method (32), as opposed to (33), of specifying *x*.

Similarly, (31) was meaningless because the sort of thing *x* which fulfills the condition:

(34) If there is life on the Evening Star then there is life on *x*,

namely, a physical object, can be uniquely determined by any of various conditions, not all of which have (34) as a necessary consequence. *Necessary* fulfillment of (34) makes no sense as applied to a physical object *x*; necessity attaches, at best, only to the connection between (34) and one or another particular means of specifying *x*.

The importance of recognizing referential opacity is not easily overstressed. We saw in §1 that referential opacity can obstruct substitutivity of identity. We now see that it also can interrupt quantification: quantifiers outside a referentially opaque construction need have no bearing on variables inside it. This again is obvious in the case of quotation, as witness the grotesque example:

$(\exists x)('six'$ contains $'x')$.

3

We see from (30)–(31) how a quantifier applied to a modal sentence may lead simply to nonsense. Nonsense is indeed mere absence of sense, and can always be remedied by arbitrarily assigning some sense. But the important point to observe is that granted an understanding of the modalities (through uncritical acceptance, for the sake of argument, of the underlying notion of analyticity), and given an understanding of quantification ordinarily so called, we do not come out automatically with any meaning for quantified modal sentences such as (30)–(31). This point must be taken into account by anyone who undertakes to work out laws for a quantified modal logic.

The root of the trouble was the referential opacity of modal contexts. But referential opacity depends in part on the ontology accepted, that is, on what objects are admitted as possible objects of reference. This may be seen most readily by reverting for a while to the point of view of §1, where referential opacity was explained in terms of failure of interchangeability of names which name the same object. Suppose now we were to repudiate all objects which, like 9 and the planet Venus, or Evening Star, are nameable by names which fail of interchangeability in modal contexts. To do so would be to sweep away all examples indicative of the opacity of modal contexts.

But what objects would remain in a thus purified universe? An object x must, to survive, meet this condition: if S is a statement containing a referential occurrence of a name of x, and S' is formed from S by substituting any different name of x, then S and S' not only must be alike in truth value as they stand, but must stay alike in truth value even when 'necessarily' or 'possibly' is prefixed. Equivalently: putting one name of x for another in any analytic statement must yield an analytic statement. Equivalently: any two names of x must be synonymous.

Thus the planet Venus as a material object is ruled out by the possession of heteronymous names 'Venus', 'Evening Star', 'Morning Star'. Corresponding to these three names we must, if modal contexts are not to be referentially opaque, recognize three objects rather than one

—perhaps the Venus-concept, the Evening-Star-concept, and the Morning-Star-concept.

Similarly 9, as a unique whole number between 8 and 10, is ruled out by the possession of heteronymous names '9' and 'the number of the planets'. Corresponding to these two names we must, if modal contexts are not to be referentially opaque, recognize two objects rather than one; perhaps the 9-concept and the number-of-planets-concept. These concepts are not numbers, for the one is neither identical with nor less than nor greater than the other.

The requirement that any two names of x be synonymous might be seen as a restriction not on the admissible objects x, but on the admissible vocabulary of singular terms. So much the worse, then, for this way of phrasing the requirement; we have here simply one more manifestation of the superficiality of treating ontological questions from the vantage point of singular terms. The real insight, in danger now of being obscured, was rather this: necessity does not properly apply to the fulfillment of conditions by *objects* (such as the ball of rock which is Venus, or the number which numbers the planets), apart from special ways of specifying them. This point was most conveniently brought out by consideration of singular terms, but it is not abrogated by their elimination. Let us now review the matter from the point of view of quantification rather than singular terms.

From the point of view of quantification, the referential opacity of modal contexts was reflected in the meaninglessness of such quantifications as (30)–(31). The crux of the trouble with (30) is that a number x may be uniquely determined by each of two conditions, for example, (32) and (33), which are not necessarily, that is, analytically, equivalent to each other. But suppose now we were to repudiate all such objects and retain only objects x such that *any two conditions uniquely determining x are analytically equivalent.* All examples such as (30)–(31), illustrative of the referential opacity of modal contexts, would then be swept away. It would come to make sense in general to say that there is an object which, independently of any particular means of specifying it, is necessarily thus and so. It would become legitimate, in short, to quantify into modal contexts.

Our examples suggest no object to quantifying into modal contexts as long as the values of any variables thus quantified are limited to *intensional objects.* This limitation would mean allowing, for purposes of such quantification anyway, not classes but only class-concepts or attributes, it being understood that two open sentences which determine the same class still determine distinct attributes unless they are analytically equivalent. It would mean allowing, for purposes of such quantification, not numbers but only some sort of concepts which are related to the numbers in a many-one way. Further it would mean allowing, for purposes of such quantification, no concrete objects but only what Frege called senses of names, and Carnap[2] and Church have called individual concepts. It is a drawback of such an ontology that the principle of individuation of its entities rests invariably on the putative notion of synonymy, or analyticity.

Actually, even granted these dubious entities, we can quickly see that the expedient of limiting the values of variables to them is after all a mistaken one. It does not relieve the original difficulty over quantifying into modal contexts; on the contrary, examples quite as disturbing as the old ones can be adduced within the realm of intensional objects. For, where A is any intensional object, say an attribute, and 'p' stands for an arbitrary true sentence, clearly

(35) $A = (\imath x)[p \cdot (x = A)]$.

Yet, if the true sentence represented by 'p' is not analytic, then neither is (35), and its sides are no more interchangeable in modal contexts than are 'Evening Star' and 'Morning Star', or '9' and 'the number of the planets'.

Or, to state the point without recourse to singular terms, it is that the requirement lately italicized—"any two conditions uniquely determining x are analytically equivalent"—is not assured merely by taking x as an intensional object. For, think of 'Fx' as any condition uniquely determining x, and think of 'p' as any nonanalytic truth. Then '$p \cdot Fx$' uniquely determines x but is not analytically equivalent to 'Fx', even though x be an intensional object.

It was in my 1943 paper that I first objected to quantifying into modal contexts, and it was in his review of it that Church proposed the remedy of limiting the variables thus quantified to intensional values. This remedy, which I have just now represented as mistaken, seemed all right at the time. Carnap adopted it in an extreme form, limiting the range of his variables to intensional objects throughout his system. He did not indeed describe his procedure thus; he complicated the picture by propounding a curious double interpretation of variables. But I have argued that this complicating device has no essential bearing and is better put aside.

By the time Church came to propound an intensional logic of his own,[3] he perhaps appreciated that quantification into modal contexts

[2] R. Carnap, *Meaning and Necessity* (Chicago: University of Chicago Press, 1947).

[3] A. Church, "A Formulation of the Logic of Sense and Denotation," in *Structure, Method, and Meaning: Essays in Honor of Henry M. Sheffer*, edited by P. Henle, H. Kallen, and S. Langer (New York: Liberal Arts Press, 1951).

could not after all be legitimized simply by limiting the thus quantified variables to intensional values. Anyway his departures are more radical. Instead of a necessity operator attachable to sentences, he has a necessity predicate attachable to complex names of certain intensional objects called propositions. What makes this departure more serious than it sounds is that the constants and variables occurring in a sentence do not recur in Church's name of the corresponding proposition. Thus the interplay, usual in modal logic, between occurrences of expressions outside modal contexts and recurrences of them inside modal contexts, is ill reflected in Church's system. Perhaps we should not call it a system of modal logic; Church generally did not. Anyway let my continuing discussion be understood as relating to model logics only in the narrower sense, where the modal operator attaches to sentences.

Church and Carnap tried—unsuccessfully, I have just argued—to meet my criticism of quantified modal logic by restricting the values of their variables. Arthur Smullyan took the alternative course of challenging my criticism itself. His argument depends on positing a fundamental division of names into proper names and (overt or covert) descriptions, such that proper names which name the same object are always synonymous. (Cf. (38) below.) He observes, quite rightly on these assumptions, that any examples which, like (15)–(20) and (24)–(25), show failure of substitutivity of identity in modal contexts, must exploit some descriptions rather than just proper names. Then he undertakes to adjust matters by propounding, in connection with modal contexts, an alteration of Russell's familiar logic of descriptions. As stressed in the preceding section, however, referential opacity remains to be reckoned with even when descriptions and other singular terms are eliminated altogether.

Nevertheless, the only hope of sustaining quantified modal logic lies in adopting a course that resembles Smullyan's, rather than Church and Carnap, in this way: it must overrule my objection. It must consist in arguing or deciding that quantification into modal contexts makes sense even though any value of the variable of such a quantification be determinable by conditions that are not analytically equivalent to each other. The only hope lies in accepting the situation illustrated by (32) and (33) and insisting, despite it, that the object x in question is necessarily greater than 7. This means adopting an invidious attitude toward certain ways of uniquely specifying x, for example (33), and favoring other ways, for example (32), as somehow better revealing the "essence" of the object. Consequences of (32) can, from such a point of view, be looked upon as necessarily true of the object which is 9 (and is the number of the planets), while some consequences of (33) are rated still as only contingently true of that object.

Evidently this reversion to Aristotelian essentialism (cf. p. 22)* is required if quantification into modal contexts is to be insisted on. An object, of itself and by whatever name or none, must be seen as having some of its traits necessarily and others contingently, despite the fact that the latter traits follow just as analytically from some ways of specifying the object as the former traits do from other ways of specifying it. In fact, we can see pretty directly that any quantified modal logic is bound to show such favoritism among the traits of an object; for surely it will be held, for each thing x, on the one hand that

(36) necessarily $(x = x)$

and on the other hand that

(37) $\sim$ necessarily $[p \cdot (x = x)]$,

where 'p' stands for an arbitrary contingent truth.

Essentialism is abruptly at variance with the idea, favored by Carnap, Lewis, and others, of explaining necessity by analyticity (cf. p. 143).† For the appeal to analyticity can pretend to distinguish essential and accidental traits of an object only relative to how the object is specified, not absolutely. Yet the champion of quantified modal logic must settle for essentialism.

Limiting the values of his variables is neither necessary nor sufficient to justify quantifying the variables into modal contexts. Limiting their values can, however, still have this purpose in conjunction with his essentialism: if he wants to limit his essentialism to special sorts of objects, he must correspondingly limit the values of the variables which he quantifies into modal contexts.

The system presented in Miss Barcan's pioneer papers on quantified modal logic differed from the systems of Carnap and Church in imposing no special limitations on the values of variables. That she was prepared, moreover, to accept the essentialist presuppositions seems rather hinted in her theorem:

(38) $(x)(y)\{(x = y) \supset [\text{necessarily } (x = y)]\}$,

for this is as if to say that some at least (and in fact at most; cf. '$p \cdot Fx$') of the traits that determine an object do so necessarily. The modal logic in Fitch[4] follows Miss Barcan on both points. Note incidentally that (38) follows directly from (36) and a law of substitutivity of identity for variables:

$(x)(y)[x = y \cdot Fx) \supset Fy]$.

---

[4] F. Fitch, *Symbolic Logic* (New York: The Ronald Press Company, 1952).

The upshot of these reflections is meant to be that the way to do quantified modal logic, if at all, is to accept Aristotelian essentialism. To defend Aristotelian essentialism, however, is not part of my plan. Such a philosophy is as unreasonable by my lights as it is by Carnap's or Lewis's. And in conclusion I say, as Carnap and Lewis have not: so much the worse for quantified modal logic. By implication, so much the worse for unquantified modal logic as well; for, if we do not propose to quantify across the necessity operator, the use of that operator ceases to have any clear advantage over merely quoting a sentence and saying that it is analytic.

4

The worries introduced by the logical modalities are introduced also by the admission of attributes (as opposed to classes). The idiom 'the attribute of being thus and so' is referentially opaque, as may be seen, for example, from the fact that the true statement:

(39) The attribute of exceeding 9 = the attribute of exceeding 9

goes over into the falsehood:

The attribute of exceeding the number of the planets = the attribute of exceeding 9

under substitution according to the true identity (24). Moreover, existential generalization of (39) would lead to:

(40) $(\exists x)$(the attribute of exceeding x = the attribute of exceeding 9)

which resists coherent interpretation just as did the existential generalizations (29)–(31) of (9), (15), and (16). Quantification of a sentence which contains the variable of quantification within a context of the form 'the attribute of . . .' is exactly on a par with quantification of a modal sentence.

Attributes, as remarked earlier, are individuated by this principle: two open sentences which determine the same class do not determine the same attribute unless they are analytically equivalent. Now another popular sort of intensional entity is the *proposition*. Propositions are conceived in relation to statements as attributes are conceived in relation to open sentences: two statements determine the same proposition just in case they are analytically equivalent. The foregoing strictures on attributes obviously apply equally to propositions. The truth:

(41) The proposition that $9 > 7$ = the proposition that $9 > 7$

goes over into the falsehood:

The proposition that the number of the planets $> 7 =$ the proposition that $9 > 7$

under substitution according to (24). Existential generalization of (41) yields a result comparable to (29)–(31) and (40).

Most of the logicians, semanticists, and analytical philosophers who discourse freely of attributes, propositions, or logical modalities betray failure to appreciate that they thereby imply a metaphysical position which they themselves would scarcely condone. It is noteworthy that in *Principia Mathematica,* where attributes were nominally admitted as entities, all actual contexts occurring in the course of formal work are such as could be fulfilled as well by classes as by attributes. All actual contexts are *extensional* in the sense of page 30 above.* The authors of *Principia Mathematica* thus adhered in practice to a principle of extensionality which they did not espouse in theory. If their practice had been otherwise, we might have been brought sooner to an appreciation of the urgency of the principle.

We have seen how modal sentences, attribute terms, and proposition terms conflict with the nonessentialist view of the universe. It must be kept in mind that those expressions create such conflict only when they are quantified into, that is, when they are put under a quantifier and themselves contain the variable of quantification. We are familiar with the fact (illustrated by (26) above) that a quotation cannot contain an effectively free variable, reachable by an outside quantifier. If we preserve a similar attitude toward modalities, attribute terms, and proposition terms, we may then make free use of them without any misgivings of the present urgent kind.

What has been said of modality in these pages relates only to strict modality. For other sorts, for example, physical necessity and possibility, the first problem would be to formulate the notions clearly and exactly. Afterward we could investigate whether such modalities, like the strict ones, cannot be quantified into without precipitating an ontological crisis. The question concerns intimately the practical use of language. It concerns, for example, the use of the contrary-to-fact conditional within a quantification; for it is reasonable to suppose that the contrary-to-fact conditional reduces to the form 'Necessarily, if p then q' in some sense of necessity. Upon the contrary-to-fact conditional depends in turn, for example, this definition of solubility in water: To say that an object is soluble in water is to say that it would dissolve if it were in water. In discussions of physics, naturally, we need quantifications containing the clause 'x is soluble in water', or the equivalent in words; but, according to the definition suggested, we should then have to admit within quantifications the expression 'if

* [See this volume, p. 60—ed.]

x were water then *x* would dissolve', that is, 'necessarily if *x* is in water then *x* dissolves'. Yet we do not know whether there is a suitable sense of 'necessarily' into which we can so quantify.

Any way of imbedding statements within statements, whether based on some notion of "necessity" or, for example, on a notion of "probability" as in Reichenbach, must be carefully examined in relation to its susceptibility to quantification. Perhaps the only useful modes of statement composition susceptible to unrestricted quantification are the truth functions. Happily, no other mode of statement composition is needed, at any rate, in mathematics; and mathematics, significantly, is the branch of science whose needs are most clearly understood.

Let us return, for a final sweeping observation, to our first test of referential opacity, namely, failure of substitutivity of identity; and let us suppose that we are dealing with a theory in which (a) *logically* equivalent formulas are interchangeable in all contexts *salva veritate* and (b) the logic of classes is at hand. For such a theory it can be shown that *any* mode of statement composition, other than the truth functions, is referentially opaque. For, let ϕ and ψ be any statements alike in truth value, and let $\Phi(\phi)$ be any true statement containing ϕ as a part. What is to be shown is that $\Phi(\psi)$ will also be true, unless the context represented by 'Φ' is referentially opaque. Now the class named by $\hat{\alpha}\phi$ is either V or Λ, according as ϕ is true or false; for remember that ϕ is a statement, devoid of free α. (If the notation $\hat{\alpha}\phi$ without recurrence of α seems puzzling, read it as $\hat{\alpha}(\alpha = \alpha \cdot \phi)$.) Moreover ϕ is logically equivalent to $\hat{\alpha}\phi = V$. Hence, by (a), since $\Phi(\phi)$ is true, so is $\Phi(\hat{\alpha}\phi = V)$. But $\hat{\alpha}\phi$ and $\hat{\alpha}\psi$ name one and the same class, since ϕ and ψ are alike in truth value. Then, since $\Phi(\hat{\alpha}\phi = V)$ is true, so is $\Phi(\hat{\alpha}\psi = V)$ unless the context represented by 'Φ' is referentially opaque. But if $\Phi(\hat{\alpha}\psi = V)$ is true, then so in turn is $\Phi(\psi)$, by (a).

ALVIN PLANTINGA

De Re et De Dicto

In *Prior Analytics* i, 9 Aristotle makes an interesting observation: "It happens sometimes that the conclusion is necessary when only one premiss is necessary; not, however, either premiss taken at random, but the major premiss." Here Aristotle means to sanction such inferences as

(1) Every human being is necessarily rational.

(2) Every animal in this room is a human being.

∴ (3) Every animal in this room is necessarily rational.

On the other hand, he means to reject inferences of the following sort:

(4) Every rational creature is in Australia.

(5) Every human being is necessarily a rational creature.

∴ (6) Every human being is necessarily in Australia.

Aristotle would presumably accept as sound the inference of (3) from (1) and (2) (granted the truth of 2). But if so, then (3) is not to be read as

(3′) It is necessarily true that every animal in this room is rational;

for (3′) is clearly false. Instead, (3) must be construed, if Aristotle is correct, as the claim that each animal in this room has a certain property—the property of being rational—*necessarily* or *essentially*. That is to say, (3) must be taken as an expression of modality *de re*

* Reprinted from "De Re et De Dicto," *Noûs*, Volume III, No. 3 (September 1969) by Alvin Plantinga by permission of the Wayne State University Press.

rather than modality *de dicto.* And what this means is that (3) is not the assertion that a certain *dictum* or proposition—*every animal in this room is rational*—is necessarily true, but is instead the assertion that each *res* of a certain kind has a certain property *essentially* or *necessarily.*

In *Summa Contra Gentiles* Thomas considers the question whether God's foreknowledge of human action—a foreknowledge that consists, according to Thomas, in God's simply *seeing* the relevant action taking place—is consistent with human freedom. In this connection he inquires into the truth of

(7) What is seen to be sitting is necessarily sitting.

For suppose God sees at t_1 that Theatetus is sitting at t_2: If (7) is true, then presumably Theatetus is necessarily sitting at t_2, in which case this action cannot be freely performed.

Thomas concludes that (7) is true if taken *de dicto* but false if taken *de re;* that is,

(7') It is necessarily true that whatever is seen to be sitting is sitting

is true but

(7'') Whatever is seen to be sitting has the property of sitting essentially

is false. The deterministic argument, however, requires the truth of (7''); and hence that argument fails. Like Aristotle, then, Aquinas appears to believe that modal statements are of two kinds. Some predicate a modality of another statement (modality *de dicto*); but others predicate of an object the necessary or essential possession of a property; and these latter express modality *de re.*

But what is it, according to Aristotle and Aquinas, to say that a certain object has a certain property essentially or necessarily? That, presumably, the object in question *couldn't conceivably have lacked* the property in question; that under no possible circumstances could that object have failed to possess that property. I am thinking of the number 17; what I am thinking of, then, is prime; and *being prime,* furthermore, is a property that it couldn't conceivably have lacked. The world could have turned out quite differently; the number 17 could have lacked many properties that in fact it has—the property of having just been mentioned would be an example. But that it should have lacked the property of being prime is quite impossible. And a statement of modality *de re* asserts of some object that it has some property essentially in this sense.

Furthermore, according to Aquinas, where a given statement of modality *de dicto*—(7'), for example—is true, the corresponding statement of modality *de re*—(7"), in this instance—may be false. We might add that in other such pairs the *de dicto* statement is false but the *de re* statement true; if I'm thinking of the number 17, then

(8) What I'm thinking of is essentially prime

is true, but

(9) The proposition *what I am thinking of is prime* is necessarily true

is false.

The distinction between modality *de re* and modality *de dicto* is not confined to ancient and medieval philosophy. In an unduly neglected paper "External and Internal Relations,"[1] G. E. Moore discusses the idealistic doctrine of internal relations, concluding that it is false or confused or perhaps both. What is presently interesting is that he takes this doctrine to be the claim that all *relational properties* are internal—which claim, he thinks, is just the proposition that every object has each of its relational properties *essentially* in the above sense. The doctrine of internal relations, he says, "implies, in fact, quite generally, that any term which does in fact have a particular relational property, could not have existed without having that property. And in saying this it obviously flies in the face of common sense. It seems quite obvious that in the case of many relational properties which things have, the fact that they have them is a *mere matter of fact*; that the things in question *might* have existed without having them."[2] Now Moore is prepared to concede that objects *do* have *some* of their relational properties essentially. Like Aristotle and Aquinas, therefore, Moore holds that some objects have some of their properties essentially and others non-essentially or accidentally.

One final example: Norman Malcolm believes that the analogical argument for other minds requires the assumption that one must learn what, for example, *pain* is "from his own case." But, he says, "if I were to learn what pain is from perceiving my own pain then I should, necessarily, have learned that pain is something that exists only when I feel pain. For the pain that serves as my paradigm of pain (*i.e.,* my own) has the property of existing only when I feel it. That property is essential, not accidental; it is nonsense to suppose that the pain I feel could exist when I did not feel it. So if I obtain my *conception* of pain from pain that I experience, then it will be a part of my conception

---

[1] G. E. Moore, "External and Internal Relations," in *Philosophical Studies* (Totowa, N. J.: Littlefield, Adams & Company, 1965).

[2] *Ibid.,* p. 289.

of pain that I am the only being that can experience it. For me it will be a *contradiction* to speak of *another's* pain." [3]

This argument appears to require something like the following premiss:

> (10) If I acquire my concept of *C* by experiencing objects and all the objects from which I get this concept have a property *P* essentially, then my concept of *C* is such that the proposition *Whatever is an instance of C has P* is necessarily true.

Is (10) true? To find out, we must know more about what it is for an object to have a property essentially. But initially, at least, it looks as if Malcolm means to join Aristotle, Aquinas, and Moore in support of the thesis that objects typically have both essential and accidental properties; apparently he means to embrace the conception of modality *de re*.

A famous and traditional conception, then, the idea of modality *de re* is accepted, explicitly or implicitly, by some contemporary philosophers as well; nevertheless it has come under heavy attack in recent philosophy. In what follows I shall try to defend the conception against some of these attacks. First, however, we must state more explicitly what it is that is to be defended. Suppose we describe the *de re* thesis as the dual claim that (a) certain objects have some of their properties essentially, and (b) where *P* is a property, *having P essentially* is also a property—or, as we might also put it, where *being F* is a property, so is *being F necessarily*. What is the force of this latter condition? Suppose we define the locution "has sizeability" as follows:

D_1 *x* has sizeability $=$ def. $\lrcorner x \llcorner$ contains more than six letters.

Here the peculiar quotation-like marks around the second occurrence of "*x*" indicate that it is to be supplanted by the result of quoting the singular term that supplants its first occurrence. D_1 is a definitional scheme enabling us to eliminate any sentence or phrase of the form "_____ has sizeability" (where the blank is filled by a name or definite description) in favor of a synonymous sentence or phrase that does not contain the word "sizeability." As such it is unobjectionable; but notice that its range of applicability is severely limited. D_1 gives no hint as to what might be meant by a sentence like "Most of the world's great statesmen have sizeability" or "Your average middle linebacker has sizeability." And accordingly, while it is true that

---

[3] "Wittgenstein's *Philosophical Investigations*," *Philosophical Review*, Vol. LXIII, 1954. Reprinted in Malcolm's *Knowledge and Certainty*, Prentice-Hall, Inc., 1963. The quoted passage is on p. 105 of the latter volume.

(11) Pico della Mirandola has sizeability,

it would be a piece of sheer confusion to conclude

(12) Therefore there is at least one thing that has sizeability;

for as yet these words have been given no semblance of sense. This peculiarity of D_1 is connected with another. To find out whether nine has sizeability we are directed to consider whether "nine" contains more than six letters; since it does not, it is false that nine has sizeability. On the other hand, "the number nine" contains more than six letters; hence the number nine has sizeability.

What this shows, I take it, is that sizeability is not a property—that is, the context "x has sizeability" does not, under the suggested definition, express a property. The proposition *the number nine has sizeability* is true but does not predicate a property of the number nine. For suppose this context *did* express a property: then the number nine would have it, but nine would lack it, a state of affairs conflicting with

(13) Where P is any property and x and y any individuals, x is identical with y only if x has P if and only if y has P.

Like Caesar's wife, this principle (sometimes called the Indiscernibility of Identicals) is entirely above reproach. (Of course the same cannot be said for

(13′) Singular terms denoting the same object can replace each other in anp context *salva veritate,*

a "principle" that must be carefully distinguished from (13) and one that, for most languages, at least, is clearly false.)

(13), then, lays down a condition of propertyhood; any property is had by anything identical with anything that has it. The second clause of the *de re* thesis asserts that P is property only if *having P essentially* is; part of the force of this claim, as we now see, is that if an object x has a property P essentially, then so does anything identical with x. The number nine, for example, is essentially composite; so, therefore, is the number of planets, despite the fact that

(14) The number of planets is composite

is not a necessary truth.

Now the *de re* thesis has been treated with a certain lack of warmth by contemporary philosophers. What are the objections to it? According to William Kneale, the view in question is based on the assumption that

properties may be said to belong to individuals necessarily or contingently, as the case may be, without regard to the ways in which the individuals are selected for attention. It is no doubt true to say that the number 12 is necessarily composite, but it is certainly not correct to say that the number of the apostles is necessarily composite, unless the remark is to be understood as an elliptical statement of relative necessity. And again, it is no doubt correct to say that this at which I am pointing is contingently white, but it is certainly not correct to say that the white paper at which I am looking is contingently white. . . .[4]

The conclusion of this argument, pretty clearly, is that an object does not have a property necessarily *in itself* or *just as an object;* it has it necessarily or contingently, as the case may be, *relative to* certain *descriptions of the object.* "Being necessarily composite," on Kneale's view, is elliptical for something like "Being necessarily composite relative to description D." And hence it does not denote a *property;* it denotes, instead, a three termed *relation* among an object, a description of that object, and a property.

Kneale's argument for this point seems to have something like the following structure:

(15) 12 = the number of apostles.

(16) The number 12 is necessarily composite.

(17) If (16), then if *being necessarily composite* is a property, 12 has it.

(18) The number of the apostles is not necessarily composite.

(19) If (18), then if *being necessarily composite* is a property, the number of the apostles lacks it.

∴ (20) *Being necessarily composite* is not a property.

But *being composite* is certainly a property; hence it is false that where *being F* is a property, so is *being F necessarily*; and hence the *de re* thesis is mistaken.

Now clearly Kneale's argument requires as an additional premiss the Indiscernibility of Identicals—a principle the essentialist will be happy to concede. And if we add this premiss then the argument is apparently valid. But why should we accept (18)? Consider an analogous argument for the unwelcome conclusion that *necessary truth* or *being necessarily true* is not a property that a proposition has in itself or just as a proposition, but only relative to certain descriptions of it:

(21) The proposition that $7 + 5 = 12$ is necessarily true.

(22) The proposition I'm thinking of is not necessarily true.

---

[4] "Modality *De Dicto* and *De Re*," in *Logic, Methodology and Philosophy of Science*, ed. Nagel, Suppes, and Tarski, Stanford Univ. Press, 1962, p. 629.

(23) The proposition that $7 + 5 = 12$ is identical with the proposition I'm thinking of.

∴ (24) *Being necessarily true* is not a property.

This argument is feeble and unconvincing. One immediately objects that if (23) is true then (22) is false. How can we decide about the truth of (22) unless we know *which proposition it is* that I'm thinking of? But isn't the very same answer appropriate with respect to (18) and (15)? If (15) is true, then presumably (18) is false. And so the question becomes acute: why *does* Kneale take (18) to be true? The answer, I believe, is that he is thinking of sentences of the form "x has P necessarily" as defined by or short for corresponding sentences of the form "the proposition x has P is necessarily true."

Quine offers a similar but subtler argument:

Now the difficulty . . . recurs when we try to apply existential generalization to modal statements. The apparent consequence:

(Q30) $(\exists x(x$ is necessarily greater than 7)

of

(Q15) 9 is necessarily greater than 7

raises the same question as did (Q29). What is this number which, according to (Q30), is necessarily greater than 7? According to (Q15), from which (Q30) was inferred, it was 9, that is, the number of planets; but to suppose this would conflict with the fact that

(Q18) The number of planets is necessarily greater than 7

is false. In a word, to be necessarily greater than 7 is not a trait of a number but depends on the manner of referring to the number. . . . Being necessarily or possibly thus and so is in general not a trait of the object concerned, but depends on the manner of referring to the object.[5]

This argument does not wear its structure upon its forehead. But perhaps Quine means to argue (a) that being necessarily greater than 7 is not a trait of a number, and hence (b) that existential generalization is inapplicable to (Q15), so that (Q30) is meaningless or wildly and absurdly false. And presumably we are to construe the argument for (a) as follows:

(25) If *being necessarily greater than 7* is a trait of a number, then for any numbers n and m, if n is necessarily greater than 7 and $m = n$, then m is necessarily greater than 7.

[5] *From a Logical Point of View*, 2nd ed. (New York: Harper & Row, 1963), p. 148. [See this volume, p. 142—ed.]

(26) 9 is necessarily greater than 7.

(27) It is false that the number of planets is necessarily greater than 7.

(28) 9 = the number of planets.

∴ (29) Being necessarily greater than 7 is not a trait of a number.

But why does Quine accept (27)? He apparently infers it from the fact that the proposition *the number of planets is greater than 7* is not necessarily true. This suggests that he takes the context "x is necessarily greater than 7" to be short for or explained by "the proposition *x is greater than 7* is necssarily true." Like Kneale, Quine apparently endorses

D₂ *x* has *P* essentially = def. the proposition *x has P* is necessarily true

as an accurate account of what the partisan of the *de re* thesis means by his characteristic assertions.

Now D₂ is a definitional schema that resembles D₁ in important respects. In particular, its "x" is a schematic letter or place marker, not a full-fledged individual variable. Thus it enables us to replace a sentence like "Socrates has rationality essentially" by a synonymous sentence that does not contain the term "rationality"; but it gives no hint at all as to what that term might mean in such a sentence as "Every animal in this room is essentially rational." And what Quine and Kneale show, furthermore, is that a context like "*x* has rationality essentially," *read in accordance with* D₂, resembles "x has sizeability" in that it does not express a property or trait. So if D₂ is an accurate account of modality *de re*, then indeed Quine and Kneale are correct in holding the *de re* thesis incoherent. But why suppose that it *is?* Proposing to look for cases of modality *de re*, Kneale declares that none exist, since "being necessarily thus and so," he says, expresses a three-termed relation rather than a property of objects. What he offers as argument, however, is that "being necessarily thus and so" read *de dicto*—read in the way D₂ suggests—does not express a property. But of course from this it by no means follows that Aristotle, Aquinas, *et. al.* were mistaken; what follows is that if they were not, then D₂ does not properly define modality *de re*.

But are we not a bit premature? Let us return for a moment to Kneale's argument. Perhaps he does not mean to foist off D₂ on Aristotle and Aquinas; perhaps we are to understand his argument as follows. We have been told that "*x* has *P* essentially" means that it is impossible or inconceivable that *x* should have lacked *P*; that there is no conceivable set of circumstances such that, should they have obtained, *x* would not have had *P*. Well, consider the number 12 and the number of apostles. Perhaps it is impossible that the number 12 should have lacked the property of being composite; but it is certainly possible that the number of apostles should have lacked it; for clearly the number of apostles could have 11, in which case it would not have been composite. Hence *being necessarily composite* is not a property and the *de re* thesis fails.

How could Aristotle and his essentialist confreres respond to this objection? The relevant portion of the argument may perhaps be stated as follows:

(30) The number of apostles could have been 11.

(31) If the number of apostles had been 11, then the number of apostles would have been prime.

Hence

(32) It is possible that the number of apostles should have been prime,

and therefore

(33) The number of apostles does not have the property of being composite essentially.

But one who accepts the *de re* thesis has an easy retort.

The argument is successful only if (33) is construed as the assertion *de re* that a certain number—12, as it happens—lacks the property of being composite essentially. Now (32) can be read *de dicto,* in which case we may put it more explicitly as

(32a) The proposition *the number of apostles is prime* is possible;

it may also be read *de re,* that is, as

(32b) The number that numbers the apostles (that is, the number that *as things in fact stand* numbers the apostles) could have been prime.

The latter, of course, entails (33); the former does not. Hence we must take (32) as (32b). Now consider (30). The same *de re–de dicto* ambiguity is once again present. Read *de dicto* it makes the true (if unexciting) assertion that

(30a) The proposition *there are just 11 apostles* is possible.

Read *de re* however, that is, as

(30b) The number that (as things in fact stand) numbers the apostles could have been 11.

it will be indignantly repudiated by the *de re* modalist; for the number that numbers the apostles is 12 and accordingly couldn't have been 11. We must therefore take (30) as (30a).

This brings us to (31). If (30a) and (31) are to entail (32b), then (31) must be construed as

(31a) If the proposition *the number of apostles is 11* had been true, then the number that (as things in fact stand) numbers the apostles would have been prime.

But surely this is false. For what it says is that if there had been 11 apostles, then the number that in fact *does* number the apostles—the number 12—would have been prime; and this is clearly rubbish. No doubt any vagrant inclination to accept (31a) may be traced to an unremarked penchant for confusing it with

(34) If the proposition *the number of apostles is 11* had been true, then the number that *would have* numbered the apostles would have been prime.

(34), of course, though true, is of no use to Kneale's argument.

This first objection to the *de re* thesis, therefore, appears to be at best inconclusive. Let us therefore turn to a different but related complaint. Quine argues that talk of a difference between necessary and contingent attributes of an object is baffling:

Perhaps I can evoke the appropriate sense of bewilderment as follows. Mathematicians may conceivably be said to be necessarily rational and not necessarily two-legged; and cyclists necessarily two-legged and not necessarily rational. But what of an individual who counts among his eccentricities both mathematics and cycling? Is this concrete individual necessarily rational and contingently two-legged or vice versa? Just insofar as we are talking referentially of the object, with no special bias towards a background grouping of mathematicians as against cyclists or vice versa, there is no semblance of sense in rating some of his attributes as necessary and others as contingent. Some of his attributes count as important and others as unimportant, yes, some as enduring and others as fleeting; but none as necessary or contingent.[6]

Noting the existence of a philosophical tradition in which this distinction *is* made, Quine adds that one attributes it to Aristotle "subject to contradiction by scholars, such being the penalty for attributions to Aristotle." Nonetheless, he says the distinction is "surely indefensible."

Now this passage reveals that Quine's enthusiasm for the distinction between essential and accidental attributes is less than dithyrambic; but how, exactly, are we to understand it? Perhaps as follows. The essentialist, Quine thinks, will presumably accept

(35) Mathematicians are necessarily rational but not necessarily bipedal

and

[6] *Word and Object*, MIT Press, 1960, p. 199.

(36) Cyclists are necessarily bipedal but not necessarily rational.

But now suppose that

(37) Paul J. Swiers is both a cyclist and a mathematician.

From these we may infer both

(38) Swiers is necessarily rational but not necessarily bipedal

and

(39) Swiers is necessarily bipedal but not necessarily rational

which appear to contradict each other twice over.

This argument is unsuccessful as a refutation of the essentialist. For clearly enough the inference of (39) from (36) and (37) is sound only if (36) is read *de re*; but, read *de re*, there is not so much as a ghost of a reason for thinking that the essentialist will accept it. No doubt he will concede the truth of

(40) *All (well-formed) cyclists are bipedal* is necessarily true, but *all cyclists are rational,* is, if true, contingent;

he will accept no obligation, however, to infer that well-formed cyclists all have bipedality essentially and rationality (if at all) accidentally. Read *de dicto,* (36) is true but of no use to the argument; read *de re,* it will be declined (no doubt with thanks) by the essentialist.

Taken as a refutation of the essentialist, therefore, this passage misses the mark; but perhaps we should emphasize its second half and take it instead as an expression of (and attempt to evoke) a sense of puzzlement as to what *de re* modality might conceivably be. A similar expression of bewilderment may be found in *From a Logical Point of View*:

> An object, of itself and by whatever name or none, must be seen as having some of its traits necessarily and others contingently, despite the fact that the latter traits follow just as analytically from some ways of specifying the object as the former traits do from other ways of specifying it.

And

> This means adopting an invidious attitude toward certain ways of uniquely specifying *x* . . . and favoring other ways . . . as somehow better revealing the "essence" of the object.

But "Such a philosophy," he [Quine] says, "is as unreasonable by my lights as it is by Carnap's or Lewis's" (pp. 149–56) . [See this volume, pp. 143–49—ed.]

Quine's contention seems in essence to be this: according to the *de re* thesis a given object must be said to have certain of its properties essentially and others accidentally, despite the fact that the latter follow from certain ways of specifying the object just as the former do from others. So far, fair enough. Snub-nosedness (we may assume) is not one of Socrates' essential attributes; nonetheless it follows (in Quine's sense) from the description "the snub-nosed teacher of Plato." And if we add to the *de re* thesis the statement that objects have among their essential attributes certain non-truistic properties—properties, which, unlike *is red or not red,* do not follow from *every* description—then it will also be true, as Quine suggests, that ways of uniquely specifying an object are not all on the same footing; those from which each of its essential properties follows must be awarded the accolade as best revealing the essence of the object.

But what, exactly, is "unreasonable" about this? And how is it baffling? Is it just that this discrimination among the unique ways of specifying 9 is arbitrary and high-handed? But it is neither, if the *de re* thesis is true. The real depth of Quine's objection, as I understand it, is this: I think he believes that "A's are necessarily B's" *must,* if it means anything at all, mean something like *"All A's are B's* is necessary"; for "necessity resides in the way we talk about things, not in the things we talk about" (*Ways of Paradox,* p. 174). And hence the bafflement in asking, of some specific individual who is both cyclist and mathematician, whether he is essentially rational and contingently two-legged or vice versa. Perhaps the claim is finally, that while we can make a certain rough sense of modality *de dicto,* we can understand modality *de re* only if we can explain it in terms of the former.

It is not easy to see why this should be so. An object has a given property essentially just in case it couldn't conceivably have lacked that property; a proposition is necessarily true just in case it couldn't conceivably have been false. Is the latter more limpid than the former? Is it harder to understand the claim that Socrates could have been a planet than the claim that the proposition *Socrates is a planet* could have been true? No doubt for any property *P* Socrates has, there is a description of Socrates from which it follows; but likewise for any true proposition *p* there is a description of *p* that entails truth. If the former makes nugatory the distinction between essential and accidental propertyhood, the latter pays the same compliment to that between necessary and contingent truth. I therefore do not see that modality *de re* is in principle more obscure than modality *de dicto.* Still, there are those who do or think they do; it would be useful, if possible, to *explain* the *de re* via the *de dicto.* What might such an explanation come to? The following would suffice: a general rule that enabled us to find, for any proposition expressing modality *de re*, an equivalent proposition expressing modality *de dicto*, or, alternatively, that enabled us to replace any sentence containing *de re* expressions by an equivalent sentence containing *de dicto* but no *de re* expressions. Earlier we said that

D_2 *x* has *P* essentially = def. The proposition *x has P* is necessarily true

is incompetent as an account of the *de re* thesis if taken as a definitional scheme with "*x*" as schematic letter rather than variable. Will it serve our present purposes if we write it as

D_2' *x* has *P* essentially if and only if the proposition that *x* has *P* is necessarily true,

now taking "x" as full-fledged individual variable?
No; for in general there will be no such thing, for a given object *x* and property *P*, as *the* proposition that *x* has *P*. Suppose *x* is the object variously denoted by "the tallest conqueror of Everest," "Jim Whittaker," and "the manager of the Recreational Equipment Cooperative." What will be the proposition that *x* has, for example, the property of being 6'7" tall? *The tallest conqueror of Everest is 6'7" tall? Jim Whittaker is 6'7" tall? The manager of the Recreational Equipment Coop is 6'7" tall?* Or perhaps *the object variously denoted by "the conqueror of Everest," "Jim Whittaker" and "the manager of the Recreational Equipment Cooperative" is 6'7"?* Each of these predicates the property in question of the object in question; hence each has as good a claim to the title "*the* proposition that *x* has *P*" as the others; and hence none has a legitimate claim to it. There are *several* "propositions that *x* has *P*"; and accordingly no such thing as *the* proposition that *x* has *P*.

Our problem, then, in attempting to explain the *de re* via the *de dicto*, may be put as follows: suppose we are given an object *x*, a property *P* and the set *S* of propositions that *x* has *P*—that is, the set *S* of singular propositions each of which predicates *P* of *x*. Is it possible to state general directions for picking out some member of *S*—call it the kernel proposition with respect to *x* and *P*—whose *de dicto* modal properties determine whether *x* has *P* essentially? If we can accomplish this, then, perhaps, we can justly claim success in explaining the *de re* via the *de dicto*. We might make a beginning by requiring that the kernel proposition with respect to *x* and *P*—at any rate for those objects *x* with names—be one that is expressed by a sentence whose subject is a proper name of *x*. So we might say that the kernel proposition with respect to Socrates and rationality is the proposition *Socrates has rationality*; and we might be inclined to put forward, more generally,

D₃ The kernel proposition with respect to x and P ("K[x, P]") is the proposition expressed by the result of replacing "x" in "x has P" by a proper name of x

adding

D₄ An object x has a property P essentially if and only if K(x, P) is necessarily true.

Now of course x may share its name with other objects, so that the result of the indicated replacement is a sentence expressing several propositions. We may accommodate this fact by adding that the kernel proposition with respect to x and P must be a member of S—that is, it must be one of the propositions that x has P. (A similar qualification will be understood below in D₅–D₉.) More importantly, we must look into the following matter. It is sometimes held that singular propositions ascribing properties to Socrates—such propositions as *Socrates is a person, Socrates is a non-number* and *Socrates is self-identical*—entail that Socrates exists, that there is such a thing as Socrates. This is not implausible. But if it is true, then D₃ and D₄ will guarantee that Socrates has none of his properties essentially. For *Socrates exists* is certainly contingent, as will be, therefore, any proposition entailing it. K(Socrates, self-identity), accordingly, will be contingent if it entails that Socrates exists; and by D₄ self-identity will not be essential to Socrates. Yet if *anything* is essential to Socrates, surely self-identity is.

But *do* these propositions entail that Socrates exists? Perhaps we can sidestep this question without settling it. For example, we might replace D₄ by

D₅ x has P essentially if and only if K(x, existence) entails K(x, P).[7]

Then Socrates will have self-identity and personhood essentially just in case *Socrates exists* entails *Socrates is self-identical* and *Socrates is a person*; and these latter two need not, of course, be necessary. D₅, however, has its peculiarities. Among them is the fact that if we accept it, and hold that existence is a property, we find ourselves committed to the dubious thesis that everything has the property of existence essentially. No doubt the number 7 can lay legitimate claim to this distinction; the same can scarcely be said, one supposes, for Socrates. Accordingly, suppose we try a different tack: suppose we take the kernel of Socrates and rationality to be the proposition that Socrates *lacks* rationality—that is, the proposition *Socrates has the complement of rationality*. Let us replace D₃ by

[7] This is apparently Moore's course.

D_6 $K(x, P)$ is the proposition expressed by the result of replacing "x" in "x lacks P" by a proper name of x,

revising D_4 to

$D_{4'}$ x has P essentially if and only if $K(x, P)$ is necessarily false.

Now $D_{4'}$ is open to the following objection. The proposition

(41) Socrates is essentially rational

entails

(42) Socrates is rational.

We moved to D_6 and $D_{4'}$ to accommodate the suggestion that (42) is at best *contingently* true, in view of its consequence that Socrates exists. But if (42) is contingent, then so is (41). It is plausible to suppose, however, that

(43) K(Socrates, rationality) is necessarily false

is, if true at all, necessarily true. But if so, then (in view of the fact that no necessary truth is equivalent to one that is merely contingent) (43) cannot be equivalent to (41); $D_{4'}$ is unacceptable.[8] Fortunately, a simple remedy is at hand; we need only add a phrase to the right-hand side of $D_{4'}$ as follows:

$D_{4''}$ x has P essentially if and only if x has P and $K(x, P)$ is necessarily false.

(41), then, is equivalent, according to $D_{4''}$, to

(44) Socrates is rational and K(Socrates, rationality) is necessarily false.

(44) is contingent if its left-hand conjunct is. Furthermore, it no longer matters whether or not *Socrates is rational* entails that Socrates exists. Existence, finally, will not be an essential property of Socrates; for even if attributions of personhood or self-identity to Socrates entail that he exists, attributions of non-existence do not.

A difficulty remains, however. For what about this "P" in D_6? Here we encounter an analogue of an earlier difficulty. If, in D_6, we take "P" as schematic letter, then K(Socrates, Socrates' least significant property) will be

(45) Socrates lacks Socrates' least significant property;

but K(Socrates, snub-nosedness) will be

(46) Socrates lacks snub-nosedness.

[8] Here I am indebted to William Rowe for a helpful comment.

Since (45) but not (46) is necessarily false, we are driven to the un-happy result that Socrates has his least significant property essentially and snub-nosedness accidentally, despite the fact (as we shall assume for purposes of argument) that snub-nosedness *is* his least significant property. If we take "P" as property variable, however, we are no better off; for now there will be no such thing as, for example, K(Soc-rates, personhood). According to D_6, K(x, P) is to be the proposition expressed by the result of replacing "x" in "x lacks P" by a proper name of x; the result of replacing "x" in "x lacks P" by a proper name of Socrates is just "Socrates lacks P," which expresses no proposition at all.

Now we resolved the earlier difficulty over "x" in D_2 by requiring that "x" be replaced by a proper name of x. Can we execute a similar maneuver here? It is not apparent that "snub-nosedness" is a proper name of the property *snub-nosedness*, nor even that properties ordi-narily have proper names at all. Still, expressions like "whiteness," "masculinity," "mean temperedness," and the like, differ from ex-pressions like "Socrates' least important property," "the property I'm thinking of," "the property mentioned on page 37," and the like, in much the way that proper names of individuals differ from definite descriptions of them. Suppose we call expressions like the former "canonical designations." [9] Then perhaps we can resolve the present difficulty by rejecting D_6 in favor of

D_7 K(x, P) is the proposition expressed by the result of replacing "x" and "P" in "x lacks P" by a proper name of x and a canonical designation of P.

We seem to be making perceptible if painful progress. But now another difficulty looms. For of course not nearly every object is named. Indeed, if we make the plausible supposition that no name names un-countably many objects and that the set of names is countable, it fol-lows that there are uncountably many objects without names. And how can $D_{4''}$ and D_7 help us when we wish to find the *de dicto* equiv-alent of a *de re* proposition about an unnamed object? Worse, what shall we say about *general de re* propositions such as

(47) Every real number between 0 and 1 has the property of being less than 2 essentially?

What is the *de dicto* explanation of (47) to look like? Our definitions direct us to

---

[9] I owe this phrase to Richard Cartwright. See his "Some Remarks on Essen-tialism," *Journal of Philosophy*, Vol. LXV, No. 20, p. 631. See also, in this connec-tion, David Kaplan's discussion of *standard names* in "Quantifying In," *Synthese*, Vol. 19, Nos. 1/2, December, 1968, p. 194ff.

(48) For every real number *r* between 0 and 1, K(*r*, being less than 2) is necessarily false.

Will (48) do the trick? It is plausible to suppose not, on the grounds that what we have so far offers no explanation of what the kernel of *r* and *P* for *unnamed r* might be.[10] If we think of D_7 as the specification or definition of a function, perhaps we must concede that the function is defined only for named objects and canonically designated properties. Hence it is not clear that we have any *de dicto* explanation at all for such *de re* propositions as (42).

Now of course if we are interested in a singular *de re* proposition we can always name the object involved. If the set of unnamed objects is uncountable, however, then no matter how enthusiastically we set about naming things, it might be said, there will always remain an uncountable magnitude of unnamed objects;[11] and hence $D_{4''}$ and D_7 are and will remain incapable of producing a *de dicto* equivalent for general propositions whose quantifiers are not severely restricted.

This argument conceals an essential premiss: it is sound only if we add some proposition putting an upper bound on the number of objects we can name at a time. We might suppose, for example, that it is possible to name at most countably many things at once. But is this really obvious? Can't I name all the real numbers in the interval (0, 1) at once? Couldn't I name them all "Charley," for example? If all Koreans are named "Kim," what's to prevent all real numbers being named "Charley"? Now many will find the very idea of naming everything "Charley" utterly bizarre, if not altogether lunatic; and, indeed, there is a queer odor about it. No doubt, furthermore, most of the purposes for which we ordinarily name things would be ill served by such a maneuver, if it is possible at all. But these cavils are not objections. Is there really any reason why I can't name all the real numbers, or indeed, everything whatever in one vast, all-embracing baptism ceremony? I can't see any such reason, and I hereby name everything "Charley." And thus I have rendered $D_{4''}$ and D_7 universally applicable.

In deference to ourtaged sensibilities, however, we should try to surmount the present obstacle in some other way if we can. And I think we can. Let (*x, P*) be any ordered pair whose first member is an object and whose second is a property. Let *S* be the set of all such pairs. We shall say that (*x, P*) is *baptized* if there is a proper name of *x* and a canonical designation of *P*. Cardinality difficulties aside (and those who feel them, may restrict *S* in any way deemed appropriate), we may define a function—the kernel function—on *S* as follows:

[10] Cartwright, *op. cit.,* p. 623.
[11] *Ibid.,* p. 622.

D_8 (a) If (x, P) is baptized, $K(x, P)$ is the proposition expressed by the result of replacing "x" and "P" in "x lacks P" by a proper name of x and a canonical designation of P.

(b) If (x, P) is not baptized, then $K(x, P)$ is the proposition which *would be* expressed by the result of replacing "x" and "P" in "x lacks P" by a proper name of x and a canonical designation of P, if (x, P) *were* baptized.

And if, for some reason, we are troubled by the subjunctive conditional in (b), we may replace it by

(b′) If (x, P) is not baptized, then $K(x, P)$ is determined as follows: baptize (x, P); then $K(x, P)$ is the proposition expressed by the result of respectively replacing "x" and "P" in "x lacks P" by the name assigned x and the canonical designation assigned P.

And now we may reassert $D_{4''}$:

An object x has a property P essentially if and only if x has P and $K(x, P)$ is necessarily false.

A general *de re* proposition such as

(49) All men are rational essentially

may now be explained as equivalent to

(50) For any object x, if x is a man, then x is rational and $K(x,$ rationality$)$ is necessarily false.

So far so good; the existence of unnamed objects seems to constitute no fundamental obstacle. But now one last query arises. I promised earlier to explain the *de re* via the *de dicto*, glossing that reasonably enigmatic phrase as follows: to explain the *de re* via the *de dicto* is to provide a rule enabling us to find, for each *de re* proposition, an equivalent *de dicto* proposition—alternatively, to provide a rule enabling us to eliminate any sentence containing a *de re* expression in favor of an equivalent sentence containing *de dicto* but no *de re* expressions. And it might be claimed that our definitions do not accomplish this task. For suppose they did: what would be the *de dicto* proposition equivalent to

(51) Socrates has rationality essentially?

$D_{4''}$ directs us to

(52) Socrates is rational and $K($Socrates, rationality$)$ is necessarily false.

Now (52) obviously entails

(53) The proposition expressed by the result of replacing "*x*" and "*P*" in "*x* lacks *P*" by a name of Socrates and a canonical designation of rationality is necessarily false.

(53), however, entails the existence of several *linguistic* entities including, for example, "*x*" and "*x* lacks *P*." Hence so does (52). But then the latter is not equivalent to (51), which entails the existence of no linguistic entities whatever. Now we might argue that such linguistic entities are shapes or sequences of shapes, in which case they are abstract objects, so that their existence is necessary and hence entailed by every proposition.[12] But suppose we explore a different response: Is it really true that (52) entails (53)? How could we argue that it does? Well, we *defined* the kernel function that way—that is, the rule of correspondence we gave in linking the members of its domain with their images explicitly picks out and identifies the value of the kernel function for the pair (Socrates, rationality) as the proposition expressed by the result of replacing "*x*" and "*P*" in "*x* lacks *P*" by a proper name of Socrates and a canonical designation of rationality. This is true enough, of course; but how does it show that (52) entails (53)? Is it supposed to show, for example, that the phrase "the kernel of (Socrates, rationality)" is *synonymous with* the phrase "the proposition expressed by the result of replacing '*x*' and '*P*' in '*x* lacks *P*' by a name of Socrates and a canonical designation of rationality"? And hence that (52) and (53) express the very same proposition? But consider a function F, defined on the natural numbers and given by the rule that $F(n) =$ the number denoted by the numeral denoting n. The reasoning that leads us to suppose that (52) entails (53) would lead us to suppose that

(54) F(9) is composite

entails

(55) The number denoted by the numeral that denotes 9 is composite

and hence entails the existence of at least one numeral. Now consider the identity function I defined on the same domain, so that $I(n) = n$. If a function is a set of ordered pairs, then F is the very same function as I, despite the fact that the first rule of correspondence is quite different from the second. And if F is the very same function as I, then can't I give *I* by stating the rule of correspondence given in giving *F*? And if I do, then should we say that

(56) The value of the identity function at 9 is composite

[12] As I was reminded by David Lewis.

entails the existence of some numeral or other? That is a hard saying; who can believe it? Can't we simply *name* a function, and then give the rule of correspondence linking its arguments with its values, without supposing that the name we bestow is covertly synonymous with some definite description constructed from the rule of correspondence? I think we can; but if so, we have no reason to think that (52) entails (53).

Nonetheless difficult questions arise here; and if we can sidestep these questions, so much the better. And perhaps we can do so by giving the kernel function as follows: Let "x" and "y" be individual variables and "P" and "Q" property variables. Restrict the substituend sets of "y" and "Q" to proper names and canonical designations respectively. Then

> D_9 If (x, P) is not baptized, $K(x, P)$ is the proposition y *lacks* Q (where $x = y$ and $P = Q$).
>
> If (x, P) is not baptized, $K(x, P)$ is determined as follows: baptize (x, P); then $K(x, P)$ is the proposition y *lacks* Q (where $x = y$ and $P = Q$).

Unlike D_8, D_9 does not tempt us to suppose that (52) entails (53).

D_4″ together with any of D_7, D_8 and D_9 seems to me a viable explanation of the *de re* via the *de dicto*. A striking feature of these explanations is that they presuppose the following: Take, for a given pair (x, P), the class of sentences that result from the suggested substitutions into "x lacks P." Now consider those members of this class that express a proposition predicating the complement of P of x. These all express the same proposition. I think this is true; but questions of propositional identity are said to be difficult, and the contrary opinion is not unreasonable. One who holds it need not give up hope; he can take $K(x, P)$ to be a class of propositions—the class of propositions expressed by the results of the indicated replacements; and he can add that x has P essentially just in case at least one member of this class is necessarily false.

If the above is successful, we have found a general rule correlating propositions that express modality *de re* with propositions expressing modality *de dicto*, such that for any proposition of the former sort we can find one of the latter equivalent to it. Does this show, then, that modality *de dicto* is somehow more basic or fundamental than modality *de re*, or that an expression of modality *de re* is really a misleading expression of modality *de dicto*? It is not easy to see why we should think so. Every proposition attributing a property to an object (an assertion *de re*, we might say) is equivalent to some proposition ascribing truth to a proposition (an assertion *de dicto*). Does it follow that propositions about propositions are somehow more basic or fundamental than propositions about other objects? Surely not. Similarly here. Nor can I think of any other reason for supposing the one more fundamental than the other.

Interesting questions remain. This account relies heavily on proper names. Is it really as easy as I suggest to name objects? And is it always possible to determine whether a name is proper or a property designation canonical? Perhaps the notion of a proper name itself involves essentialism; perhaps an analysis or philosophical account of the nature of proper names essentially involves essentialist ideas. Suppose this is true; how, exactly, is it relevant to our explanation of the *de re* via the *de dicto*? How close, furthermore, is this explanation to the traditional understanding of essentialism, if indeed history presents something stable and clear enough to be called a traditional understanding? What is the connection, if any, between essential properties and natural kinds? Are there properties that some but not all things have essentially? Obviously so; *being prime* would be an example. Are there properties that some things have essentially but others have accidentally? Certainly: 7 has the property *being prime or prim* essentially; Miss Prudence Alcott, Headmistress of the Queen Victoria School for Young Ladies, has it accidentally. But does each object have an *essence*—that is, an essential property that nothing else has? Would *being Socrates* or *being identical with Socrates* be such a property? *Is* there such a property as *being identical with Socrates*? What sorts of properties does Socrates have essentially anyway? Could he have been an alligator, for example, or an eighteenth century Irish washerwoman? And is there a difference between what Socrates *could have been* and what he *could have become*? Can we see the various divergent philosophical views as to what a *person* is, as divergent claims as to what properties persons have essentially? Exactly how is essentialism related to the idea—set forth at length by Leibniz and prominently featured in recent semantical developments of quantified modal logic—that there are *possible worlds* of which the actual is one, and that objects such as Socrates have different properties in different possible worlds? And how is essentialism related to the "problem of transworld identification" said to arise in such semantical schemes? These are good questions, and good subjects for further study.[13]

[13] I am indebted for advice and criticism to many, including Richard Cartwright, Roderick Chisholm, David Lewis, and William Rowe. I am particularly indebted to David Kaplan—who, however, churlishly declines responsibility for remaining errors and confusions.

ALVIN PLANTINGA

World and Essence

In much traditional philosophy we meet the admonition to distinguish assertions of necessity *de dicto* from assertions of necessity *de re*. Thomas Aquinas, for example, considers whether God's foreknowledge of human behavior is inconsistent with human freedom. Pointing out that such foreknowledge of a given item of behavior simply consists in God's seeing it take place, Thomas asks whether:

(1) Whatever is seen to be sitting at a time t is necessarily sitting at t

is true. For suppose it is, and suppose that Albert the Great is sitting at t. If, at time $t-1$, God has foreknowledge of Albert's sitting at t, then at $t-1$ God sees that Albert sits at t: but if (1) is true, then, so the deterministic argument goes, Albert is necessarily sitting at t, in which case he is not free to stand at t. Thomas replies that (1) is ambiguous; we may take it *de dicto* as:

(2) It is necessarily true that whatever is seen to be sitting is sitting,

or *de re* as

(3) Whatever is seen to be sitting at t has the property of sitting at t *essentially* or *necessarily*.

A true assertion about a proposition, (2) predicates necessary truth of

(4) Whatever is seen to be sitting is sitting.

(3), on the other hand, does no such thing; it predicates of every object of a certain kind—those objects seen to be sitting at t—the essential or necessary possession of a certain property: the property of sitting at t.

* Reprinted from *The Philosophical Review*, Vol. LXXIX (1970), pp. 461–92.
Used by permission of the author and the editors of *The Philosophical Review*.

173

And while (2) is true, says Thomas, (3) is not; but the argument for the inconsistency of divine foreknowledge with human freedom requires the latter as a premise.

A statement of necessity *de re*, therefore, predicates of some object or group of objects the essential possession of some property—or, as we may also put it, such a statement predicates of some object the property of having a certain property essentially. Many philosophers apparently believe that the idea of *de re* modality is shrouded in obscurity, if not an utter mare's nest of confusion. The arguments they give for this conclusion, however, are by no means conclusive.[1] Indeed, I think we can see that the idea of modality *de re* is no more (although no less) obscure than the idea of modality *de dicto;* for I think we can see that any statement of the former type is logically equivalent to some statement of the latter. Suppose we let S be the set of ordered pairs (x, P) where x is an object and P a property; and suppose we say that pair (x, P) is baptized if both x and P have proper names. Ignoring cardinality difficulties for the moment (and those who feel them can restrict S in any way deemed appropriate) we may define a function—call it the kernel function—on S as follows:

(5) (a) If (x, P) is baptized, $K(x, P)$ is the proposition that predicates $\overline{P}$, the complement of P, of x and is expressed by the result of respectively replacing "x" and "P" in "x has the complement of P" by proper names of x and P.

(b) If (x, P) is not baptized, then $K(x, P)$ is the proposition that predicates $\overline{P}$ of x and *would be* expressed by the result of respectively replacing "x" and "P" in "x has the complement of P" by proper names of x and P, if (x, P) *were* baptized.

Then we may add

(6) an object x has a property P essentially just in case x has P and $K(x, P)$ is necessarily false.

(5) and (6) enable us to eliminate any sentence containing *de re* expressions in favor of an equivalent sentence containing no expressions of that sort;

(7) If all men are essentially persons, then some things are essentially rational,

for example, goes over into

(8) If for any object x, x is a man only if $K(x,$ personhood$)$ is necessarily false, then there are some things y such that $K(y,$ rationality$)$ is necessarily false.

[1] See my *"De Dicto et De Re," Noûs,* II (1969), 240–247, 248–258.

(5) and (6) provide an explanation of the *de re* via the *de dicto;* but if the explanation is apt, the former is no more obscure than the latter.

We may approach this matter from a different direction. If we are comfortable with the idea of *states of affairs,* recognizing that some but not all of them obtain, and that some that do not *could have,* we may join Leibniz and logic (the semantics of quantified modal logic, that is) in directing our attention to *possible worlds.* A possible world is a state of affairs of some kind—one which could have obtained if it does not. *Hubert Horatio Humphrey's having run a mile in four minutes,* for example, is a state of affairs that is clearly possible in the relevant sense; *his having had a brother who never had a sibling* is not. Furthermore, a possible world must be what we may call a *fully determinate* state of affairs. *Humphrey's having run a four-minute mile* is a possible state of affairs, as, perhaps, is *Paul X. Zwier's being a good basketball player.* Neither of these, however, is fully determinate in that either of them could have obtained whether or not the other had. A fully determinate state of affairs S, let us say, is one such that for any state of affairs S', either S *includes* S' (that is, could not have obtained unless S' had also obtained) or S *precludes* S' (that is, could not have obtained if S' had obtained). So, for example, *Jim Whittaker's being the first American to reach the summit of Everest* precludes Luther Jerstad's enjoying that distinction and includes Whittaker's having climbed at least one mountain.

We may try a slightly different route to the concept of a possible world if we possess a reasonably firm grasp of the notion of a proposition. Where S is a set of propositions, suppose we say that S is *possible* if it is possible that all of S's members be true; and let us say that q is a consequence of S if S U (not-q) is not possible. A *superproposition,* we shall say, is the union of some set of propositions with the set of its consequences—or, as we may also put it, a set of propositions containing all of its own consequences. Now for each superproposition S there is exactly one state of affairs A such that A obtains if and only if every member of S is true.[2] We have a 1–1 function F, therefore, from superpropositions to states of affairs. Let us say, furthermore, that a *book* is a maximal possible set of propositions—one that is possible and that, for any proposition q, contains either q or its denial not-q. A book, clearly enough, is a superproposition; and a possible world is just the value of F for some book. F-inverse, on the other

---

[2] If we take it that if a state of affairs S includes and is included by a state of affairs S', then S and S' are the same state of affairs. Alternatively, we may introduce the idea of a *super state of affairs* (analogous to a superproposition) and take the range of F to be the set of super states of affairs.

hand, associates a book with each possible world; we might call it *the bookie function*.

Leibniz and logic join further in holding that propositions are properly said to be true or false *in* these possible worlds. A proposition *p* is true in a world *W* if *p* would have been true had *W* been actual; and *the book of W* is the book of which a proposition *p* is a member just in case *p* is true in *W*.[3] The actual world is one of the possible worlds; and the set of true propositions is the set of propositions true in the actual world. Necessarily true propositions are those enjoying the distinction of being true in every world; a possible proposition is true in at least one. Still further, logic and Leibniz hold that individuals, objects, *exist* in these worlds; to say that an object *x* exists in a world *W* is to say that if *W* had been actual, *x* would have existed. Some objects—the number seven, for example—grace every world, but many others are restricted to only some. Socrates, for example, exists in this and some other possible worlds, but not in all; he is a contingent being who exists in fact but need not have. A given individual, furthermore, *has properties in* at least some of these worlds. Again, to say that *x* has property *P* in *W* is to say that if *W* had been actual, *x* would have had *P*. And of course an individual may have in one world a property—snubnosedness, let us say—that he lacks in others.

We now have several plausible options as to what it is for an object to have a property *P* essentially; Socrates has *P* essentially if he has *P* in every world, or has it in every world in which he exists, or—most plausible of all—has *P* in the actual world and has its complement *P̄* in no world. The idea that an object has essential as well as accidental properties, therefore, can be explained and defended. In what follows I shall take its intelligibility for granted and ask some questions about which objects have which properties essentially.

I

Consider first such properties as *having a color if red, being something or other, being self-identical,* and *either having or lacking a maiden aunt.* Clearly everything whatever has these properties; clearly nothing has the complement of any of these properties in any possible world.

---

[3] Here I am taking it for granted that the proposition *Socrates is wise* would have been true or false even if Socrates had not existed. The contrary view—that *Socrates is wise* is neither true nor false in those worlds in which Socrates does not exist— is not unreasonable and can easily be accommodated. Nothing I say below essentially depends upon choosing between these two.

Let us call such properties—properties that enjoy the distinction of being instantiated by every object in every possible world—*trivially essential properties*. While you may concede that indeed every object does have some trivially essential properties, you may think this truth somewhat lackluster. Are there any nontrivial essential properties? Certainly; the number six has the properties of *being an integer, being a number,* and *being an abundant number* essentially; Paul Q. Zwier has none of these properties and a fortiori has none essentially. Well, then, are there properties that some things have essentially and others have, but have accidentally? Surely; *being non-green* is a property seven has essentially and the Taj Mahal accidentally. *Being prime or prim* is an accidental property of Miss Prudence Allworthy, Head-mistress of the Queen Victoria School for Girls; it is essential to seven.

But, you say, these fancy, cooked-up properties—disjunctive or negative as they are—have a peculiar odor. What about Socrates and such properties as being a philosopher, an Athenian, a teacher of Plato? What about having been born in 470 B. C., having lived for some seventy years, and having been executed by the Athenians on a charge of corrupting the youth? Are any of these ordinary meat-and-potatoes properties of Socrates essential to him? I should think not. Surely Socrates could have been born ten years later. Surely he could have lived in Maccedonia, say, instead of Athens. And surely he could have stuck to his stone-cutting, eschewed philosophy, corrupted no youth, and thus escaped the wrath of the Athenians. None of these properties is essential to him.

But what about their disjunction? No doubt Socrates could have lacked *any* of these properties; could he have lacked them *all?* John Searle thinks this suggestion incoherent.

> Though proper names do not normally assert or specify any characteristics, their referring uses nonetheless presuppose that the object to which they purport to refer has certain characteristics. But which ones? Suppose we ask the users of the name "Aristotle" to state what they regard as certain essential and established facts about him. Their answers would be a set of uniquely referring descriptive statements. Now what I am arguing is that the descriptive force of "This is Aristotle" is to assert that a sufficient but so far unspecified number of these statements are true of this object. Therefore, referring uses of "Aristotle" presuppose the existence of an object of whom a sufficient but so far unspecified number of these state-ments are true. To use a proper name referringly is to presuppose the truth of certain uniquely referring descriptive statements, but it is not ordinarily to assert these statements or even to indicate which exactly are presupposed.[4]

---

[4] "Proper Names," *Mind*, LXVII (1958), 171. Henceforth, page references to this article will be given in the text.

So there are what we might call "identity criteria" associated with a name such as "Aristotle" or "Socrates"; these are what the users of the name regard as essential and established facts about him. Suppose we take these criteria to be properties of Socrates rather than facts about him. Then among them we should certainly find such properties as *having been born about 470 B.C., having married Xantippe, being a Greek philosopher, being the teacher of Plato, having been executed by the Athenians on a charge of corrupting the youth,* and the like. The disjunction of these properties, Searle says (and this is the point at present relevant), is essential to its owner:

> It is a contingent fact that Aristotle ever went into pedagogy (though I am suggesting it is a necessary fact that Aristotle has the logical sum, inclusive disjunction, of properties commonly atrributed to him; any individual not having at least some of these properties could not be Aristotle) [p. 172].

If $S_1, S_2, \ldots, S_n$, are the identity criteria associated with the name "Socrates," therefore, then Socrates has the disjunction of these properties essentially. But why so, exactly? Searle does not explicitly say, no doubt because the focus of his piece is not on just this point. One possibility is this: we might be tempted to believe that if the S_i are the identity criteria for "Socrates," then to suppose that Socrates could have lacked most of these properties is tantamount to thinking it possible that the man who has most of the S_i does not have most of them —tantamount, that is, to endorsing

(9) Possibly, the man who has most $S_1, S_2 \ldots, S_n$ lacks most of $S_1, S_2, \ldots, S_n$.

But (9) appears to be false and indeed necessarily false;[5] hence Socrates could not have lacked the disjunction of the S_i. To yield to this temptation, however, is to commit the error of confusing (9), a false *de dicto* assertion, with the assertion *de re* that

(10) The person who has most of the S_i might conceivably have lacked most of them.

(9), indeed, is necessarily false; that (10) is false does not follow. Suppose all I know about Paul B. Zwier is that he is the redheaded mathematician seated in the third row. *Being redheaded, being a mathematician,* and *being seated in the third row* are, then, presumably, my identity criteria for the name "Paul B. Zwier"; it scarcely follows that Zwier is essentially redheaded or that he could not have been standing or seated elsewhere, or that "Paul B. Zwier is not a mathematician" expresses a necessary falsehood. These properties are ones

---

[5] If we suppose, as I do, that a modal statement—one predicating necessity or possibility of some statement—is either necessarily true or necessarily false.

that I may use to get you to see about whom it is I am talking; if I say, "My, isn't Paul B. Zwier distinguished-looking!" and you say, "Who?" these characteristics are the ones I cite. They enable my interlocutor to identify the subject of my remarks; that these properties are essential to him does not follow.

Searle recognizes this objection and replies as follows:

> But is the argument convincing? Suppose most or even all of our present factual knowledge of Aristotle proved to be true of no one at all, or of several people living in scattered countries and in different centuries? Would we not say for this reason that Aristotle did not exist after all, and that the name, though it has a conventional sense, refers to no one at all? On the above account [i.e., the one according to which the S_i serve merely to identify the subject for discussion], if anyone said that Aristotle did not exist, this must simply be another way of saying that "Aristotle" denoted no objects, and nothing more; but if anyone did say that Aristotle did not exist he might mean much more than simply that the name does not denote anyone [p. 168].

And further:

> We say of Cerberus and Zeus that neither of them ever existed, without meaning that no object ever bore these names, but only that certain kinds (descriptions) of objects never existed and bore these names [p. 169].

I am not clear as to the exact structure of this argument; I do not see just how it bears on the suggestion it is designed to refute. What is fairly clear, however, is that it is to be construed as an argument for the conclusion that

(11) Socrates lacks most (or all) of the S_i

is necessarily false, where the S_i are the identity criteria for "Socrates." But the prospects for this argument are not initially promising. Different people associate different identity criteria with the same name, even when using it to name the same person (no doubt the criteria mentioned above for "Paul B. Zwier" are not the ones his wife associates with that name). Indeed, at different times the same person may associate different criteria with the same name; are we to suppose that the properties essential to Aristotle vary thus from time to time and person to person? Nevertheless, suppose we take a closer look at the argument. How, exactly, does it go? Perhaps we can fill it out as follows. The S_i are the identity criteria for "Socrates." In (11) we have a referring use of this name; this use, therefore, presupposes the existence of an object that has a sufficient number of the S_i. (11), therefore, entails

(12) Someone has enough of the S_i.

But surely it is necessarily true that

(13) If anyone has enough of the S_i, Socrates does.

So if (11) is true, it follows that Socrates has enough of the S_i—that is, that (11) is false; (11) therefore, is necessarily false.

But why suppose that (11) entails (12)? That is, why suppose that if S_1, S_2, . . ., S_n are the identity criteria for the name "Socrates"— the properties we employ to locate and identify Socrates—then "Socrates lacks enough of the S_i" must express a proposition entailing that someone or other *has* enough of them? Perhaps the argument goes as follows. If we discovered that no one had enough of the S_i, we should say (and say quite properly) that there never was any such person as Socrates—that he did not exist.

(14) No one had enough of the S_i,

therefore, entails

(15) Socrates did not exist.

(11), on the other hand—the assertion that Socrates had the complement of most of the S_i—entails

(16) There really was such a person as Socrates—that is, Socrates did exist.

(16) is inconsistent with (15); it is also inconsistent, therefore, with (14); (11), too, therefore, is inconsistent with (14) and entails its denial —namely (12).

But is it really true that (14) entails (15)? Why so? The answer, according to Searle, is that (14) and (15) make the same assertion; (15), despite appearances, is not a singular statement predicating a property of Socrates but a general statement to the effect that no one has enough of S_1, S_2, . . ., S_n (p. 172). And, of course, on this view the statement "Socrates does (did) exist" and its variants do not predicate of Socrates the dubious property of existence; they assert instead that some object does (or did) have enough of the S_i.

But why should we think *that* true? Suppose, says Searle, we discovered that no one had enough of the S_i: then what we should normally say is not "Oddly enough, as it turns out, Socrates did not have enough of the S_i: no one did"; what we should say is that Socrates never really existed. Is this correct? I think it is. Suppose all we know about Homer is that he was the blind bard of Chios who was born about 835 B.C. and composed the *Iliad* and *Odyssey*, so that these properties are the identity criteria associated with the name "Homer." Now imagine that a historian says, "I have discovered that no one had those properties; Homer himself had 20–20 vision, never lived in Chios, and did not compose either the *Iliad* or the *Odyssey*; they were class projects in Xenophon's School for Rhetoric." We should be justifiably perplexed. If he goes on to add, "Furthermore, his name wasn't Homer—it was Alfred E. Neuman—and actually he was an illiterate thirteenth-century French peasant," we should no doubt think him crazed with strong drink. In discovering that no one had these properties, what he discovered is a fact we should ordinarily put by saying "Homer never really existed"; and his further allegations allegedly about Homer are utterly unintelligible. By "Homer" we mean to refer to the man who had the above properties; in answer to the question "Who was Homer?" these are the properties we should mention. If he tells us, therefore, that Homer *lacks* all these properties, we no longer have any idea whom he is talking about.[6]

So

(17) No one had (enough of) $H_1, H_2 \ldots, H_n$.

entails what we should ordinarily express by saying

(18) Homer never existed.

But the way to show that Homer really did exist, conversely, is to show that there really was a person who had most of the above properties; so (18) also entails (17). A pair of classicists might have a dispute as to whether Homer really existed. It would be incorrect to represent them as each referring to the same person—the one who had $H_1, H_2 \ldots, H_n$—one of them attributing to him the property of existence and the other the property of nonexistence; and this is so even if existence and nonexistence are properly thought of as properties. Searle is right in taking that dispute to be instead about whether enough of these properties are instantiated by a single person.

Ordinarily, then, when someone says, "Socrates really existed," he is to be understood as affirming that some one person had enough of $S_1, S_2, \ldots, S_n$. But of course he could be affirming something quite different; out of sheer whimsy, if for no other reason, he could be referring to the man who satisfies the identity criteria associated with "Socrates" and predicating existence of him. The fact that people do not ordinarily do this scarcely shows that it cannot be done. A man might point to the Taj Mahal and say, "That really exists." [7] If he did, he would be right, though his assertion might be pointless or foolish. Bemused by Cartesian meditations, De Gaulle might say, "I really do exist." Nor would he then be saying that enough of the identity criteria associated with some word ("De Gaulle"? "I" in some

---

[6] I do not mean to deny, of course, that the pressure of historical discovery could cause a change in the identity criteria for "Homer."

[7] See G. E. Moore, "Is Existence a Predicate?," *Philosophical Papers* (London, 1959).

particular use?) are satisfied by someone; he might be talking about himself and saying of himself that he really exists. Furthermore, the sentence "Socrates does not exist" ordinarily expresses the proposition that no one has enough of the S_i; but it can also be used to express a proposition predicating of Socrates the complement of the property of existence. This proposition is false. Perhaps, furthermore, no one can believe it; for suppose someone did: how could he answer the question "Whom do you mean by 'Socrates'? Which person is it of whom you are predicating nonexistence?" It is nonetheless a perfectly good proposition.

Now suppose we rehearse Searle's argument.

(11) Socrates lacks most of the S_i

was said to entail

(12) Someone has most of the S_i.

But necessarily

(13) If anyone has the S_i, Socrates does

from which it follows that (11) entails its own denial. Why does (11) entail (12)? Clearly (11) entails

(16) Socrates does (did) exist.

But (16) is the contradictory of

(15) Socrates did not exist;

since the latter is equivalent to

(14) No one has (had) enough of the S_i,

the former must be equivalent to the contradictory of (14)—namely, (12). (11), therefore, entails (16), which is equivalent to (12); so (11) entails (12).

But (16), as we have seen, turned out to be ambiguous between (12) and a proposition predicating existence of Socrates. This argument turns on that ambiguity. For it is plausible to suppose that (11) entails the latter (presumably any world in which Socrates has the complement of most of the S_i is a world in which he has the property of existing); but we have no reason at all for thinking that it entails the former.

What we have seen so far is that

(16) Socrates does exist

and

(15) Socrates does not exist

normally express statements to the effect that a sufficient number of $S_1, S_2, \ldots, S_n$ are (are not) instantiated by the same person; but each of them can also be used to express a proposition predicating existence (nonexistence) of Socrates. Let us call these latter propositions (15′) and (16′). It is important to see the difference between the primed and unprimed items here. Let us say that a subset A of $(S_1, S_2, \ldots, S_n)$ is *sufficient* just in case the fact that each member of A is instantiated by the same person is sufficient for the truth of (16); and let S be the set of sufficient sets. Call the property a thing has if it has each property in some member of S a *sufficient* property. Then if the disjunction of the sufficient properties is not essential to Socrates, it is possible that (15) be true when (15′) is false. That is, if it is possible that Socrates should have lacked each sufficient property, then (15) does not entail (15′). And indeed this is possible. Socrates could have been born ten years earlier and in Thebes, let us say, instead of Athens. Furthermore, he could have been a carpenter all his life instead of a philosopher. He could have lived in Macedonia and never even visited Athens. Had these things transpired (and if no one else had had any sufficient property), then (15) but not (15′) would have been true. Similarly, it is conceivable that Socrates should never have existed and that someone else—Xenophon, let us say—should have had most of $S_1, S_2, \ldots, S_n$. Had this transpired, (15) but not (15′) would have been false.

The old saw has it that Homer did not write the *Iliad* and the *Odyssey:* they were written by another man with the same name. Although this has a ring of paradox, it is in fact conceivable; there is a possible world in which the person denoted by "Homer" in this world (supposing for the moment that there is only one) does not exist and in which someone else writes the *Iliad* and the *Odyssey.*

II

Searle is wrong, I believe, in thinking the disjunction of the S_i essential to Socrates. But then what properties does he have essentially? Of course he has such trivially essential properties as *the property of having some properties* and *the property of being unmarried if a bachelor.* He also has essentially some properties not had by everything: *being a non-number* and *being possibly conscious* are examples. But these are properties he shares with other persons. Are there properties Socrates has essentially and shares with some but not all other persons? Certainly; *being Socrates* or *being identical with Socrates* is essential to Socrates; *being identical with Socrates or Plato,* therefore, is a property essential to Socrates and one he shares with Plato. This property is had essentially by anything that has it. *Being Socrates or Greek,* on the other hand, is one Socrates shares with many other persons and one he and he alone has essentially.

Socrates, therefore, has essential properties. Some of these he has in solitary splendor and others he shares. Among the latter are some that he shares with everything, some that he shares with persons but not other things, and still others that he shares with some but not all other persons. Some of these properties, furthermore, are essential to whatever has them while others are not. But does he have, in addition to his essential properties, an *essence* or *haecceity*—a property essential to him that entails each of his essential properties and that nothing distinct from him has in any world? [8] It is true of Socrates (and of no one else) that he is Socrates, that he is identical with Socrates. Socrates, therefore, has the property of *Socrates-identity.* And if a property is essential to Socrates just in case he has it and there is no world in which he has its complement, then surely *Socrates-identity* is essential to him. Furthermore, this property entails each of his essential properties; there is no possible world in which there exists an object that has *Socrates-identity* but lacks a property Socrates has in every world in which he exists. But does it meet the other condition? Is it not possible that something distinct from Socrates should have been identical with him? Is there no possible world such that, had it obtained, something that in *this* world is distinct from Socrates would have been identical with him? And is it not possible that something in fact identical with Socrates should have been distinct from him? In this world Cicero is identical with Tully; is there no possible world in which this is not so? Hesperus is in fact identical with Phosphorus; is there no possible world in which, in the hauntingly beautiful words of an ancient ballad, Hesperus and Phosphorus are entities distinct?

I think not. Cicero is in fact Tully. Cicero, furthermore, has the property of being identical with Cicero; and in no world does Cicero have the complement of that property. Cicero, therefore, has *Cicero-diversity in no possible world.* But if an object *x* has a property *P*, then so does anything identical with it; like Calpurnia, this principle (sometimes called the Indiscernibility of Identicals) is entirely above reproach. Tully, therefore, has *Cicero-diversity in no possible world.*

Socrates-identity, therefore, is essential to anything identical with Socrates. But this does not suffice to show that this property is an *essence* of Socrates. For *that* we must argue that nothing distinct from Socrates could have had *Socrates-identity*—that is, we must argue that an object distinct from Socrates in this world nowhere has *Socrates-*

[8] Where a property *P* entails a property *Q* if there is no world in which there exists an object that has *P* but not *Q*.

identity. This (together with the previous conclusion) follows from the more general principle that

> (19) If *x* and *y* are identical in any world, then there is no world in which they are diverse.[9]

Is (19) true? I think we can see that it is. Recall that a possible world is a state of affairs that could have obtained if it does not. Here "could have" expresses, broadly speaking, logical or metaphysical possibility. Now are there states of affairs that *in fact* could have obtained, but would have lacked the property of possibly obtaining had things been different in some way? That is, are there states of affairs that in *this* world have the property of obtaining in some world or other, but in *other* worlds lack that property? Where it is metaphysical or logical possibility that is at stake, I think we can see that there are no such worlds. Similarly, we may ask: are there states of affairs that are *in fact* impossible, but would have been possible had things been different? That is, are there states of affairs that in fact have the property of obtaining in no possible world, but in some possible world have the property of obtaining in some possible world or other? Again, the answer is that there are no such worlds. Consider, therefore,

> (20) If a state of affairs *S* is possible in at least one world *W*, then *S* is possible in every world.

This principle may be false where it is causal or natural possibility that is at stake; for logical or metaphysical possibility, it seems clearly true. In semantical developments of modal logic we meet the idea that a possible world *W* is possible *relative to* some but not necessarily all possible worlds,[10] where a world *W* is *possible relative to* a world *W'* if *W* would have been possible had *W'* obtained. As an obvious corollary of (20) we have

> (20') Where *W* and *W'* are any possible worlds, *W* is possible relative to *W'*.

Given the truth of (20), however, we can easily show that (19) is true. For let *x* and *y* be any objects and *W* any world in which *x* is identical with *y*. In *W*, *x* has *x-identity* (that is, the property a thing

---

[9] Where the variables "*x*" and "*y*" range over objects that exist in the actual world.

[10] See, e.g., Saul Kripke's "Some Semantical Considerations on Modal Logic," *Acta Philosophia Fennica* (1963). To accept (20'), of course, is to stipulate that *R*, the alternativeness relation Kripke mentions, is an equivalence relation; the resulting semantics yields as valid the characteristic axiom of Lewis' S_5, according to which a proposition is necessarily possible if possible.

has just in case it is identical with x); and clearly there is no world possible with respect to W in which x has x-*diversity*. By (20′), therefore, it follows that there is no world at all in which x has x-*diversity*; in W, therefore, x has the property of being nowhere x-diverse. Now by the Indiscernibility of Identicals, y also has this property in W; that is, in W y has the property of being nowhere x-diverse. Therefore, y's *being x-diverse* is an impossible state of affairs in W; accordingly, by (20) it is impossible in every world; hence, there is no world in which x and y are diverse. (19), therefore, is true. But then *Socrates-identity* is an essence of Socrates (and of anything identical with him); for (19) guarantees that anything distinct from Socrates in this or any world is nowhere identical with him.

Socrates, therefore, has an essence as well as essential properties. But here the following objection may arise. In arguing that Socrates has an essence I made free reference to such alleged properties as *being identical with Socrates in no world, being everywhere distinct from Socrates,* and the like. And is there even the slightest reason for supposing that there *are* any such properties as these? Indeed, is there any reason to suppose that "being identical with Socrates" names a property? Well, is there any reason to suppose that it does not? I cannot think of any, nor have I heard any that are at all impressive. To be sure, one hears expressions of a sort of nebulous discomfort; when asked to believe that there is such a property as *being identical with Socrates,* philosophers often adopt an air of wise and cautious skepticism. But this does not constitute an objection. Surely it is true of Socrates that he is Socrates and that he is identical with Socrates. If these are true of him, then *being Socrates* and *being identical with Socrates* characterize him; they are among his properties or attributes. Similarly for the property of being nowhere Socrates-diverse: a thing has the property of being Socrates-diverse in a given world W if that thing would have been diverse from Socrates had W obtained; it has the property of being nowhere Socrates-diverse if there is no possible world in which it is Socrates-diverse. So these are perfectly good properties. But in fact the argument does not really depend upon our willingness to say that *Socrates-identity* is a property. We may instead note merely that *that he is identical with Socrates* is true of Socrates, that *that he is diverse from Socrates in some world* is not true of Socrates in any world, and that anything true of Socrates is true of anything identical with him.

But if we propose to explain Socrates' essence and his essential properties by means of properties he has in every world in which he exists, then do we not encounter a problem about identifying Socrates across possible worlds? What about the celebrated Problem of Trans-

World Identification?[11] Well, what, exactly, *is* the problem? David Kaplan puts it as follows.

I'll let you peek in at this other world through my Jules Verne-o-scope. Carefully examine each individual, check his finger prints, etc. The problem is: which one, if any, is Bobby Dylan? That is, which one is our Bobby Dylan—of course he may be somewhat changed, just as he will be in our world in a few years. But in that possible world which ours will pass into in say 30 years, someone may ask "Whatever happened to Bobby Dylan?" and set out to locate him. Our problem is similarly to locate him in G (if he exists there.)[12]

But have we really found a problem? Here, perhaps, there is less than meets the eye. For what, exactly, is our problem supposed to be? We are given a world W distinct from the actual world, an individual x that exists in the actual world, and asked how to determine whether x exists in W and if so which thing in W is x. We might like to know, for example, whether Raquel Welch exists in W; and (supposing that she does) which thing in W *is* Raquel Welch. But the answer to the first question is easy; Raquel Welch exists in W if and only if Raquel Welch would have existed had W been actual. Or to put the matter bibliographically, she exists in W if and only if W's book contains the proposition *Raquel Welch exists*. Granted, we may not know enough about W to know whether its book *does* contain that proposition; we may be told only that W is some world in which, let us say, Socrates exists. Whether we can determine if W's book contains this proposition depends upon how W is specified; but surely that constitutes no problem for the enterprise of explaining Socrates' essence in terms of properties he has in every world he graces.

Similarly with the second question. Consider a world—call it RW_f —in which Raquel Welch exists and weighs 185 pounds, everything else being as much like the actual world as is consistent with that fact. Which individual, in RW_f, is Raquel Welch? That is, which of the persons who would have existed, had RW_f been actual, would have been such that, if *the actual world* had obtained, she would have been Raquel Welch? The answer, clearly, is Raquel Welch. But such an

---

[11] See R. Chisholm, "Identify through Possible Worlds: Some Questions," *Nous*, I (1967), 1–8; J. Hintikka, "Individuals, Possible Worlds and Epistemic Logic," *Nous*, I (1967), 33–63; D. Kaplan, "Trans-World Identifications" (presented to an APA symposium, Chicago, 1967, but unpublished); L. Linsky, "Reference, Essentialism and Modality," *Journal of Philosophy*, LXVI (1969), 687–700; R. Purtill, "About Identity through Possible Worlds," *Nous*, II (1968); and R. Thomason, "Modal Logic and Metaphysics," in *The Logical Way of Doing Things*, ed. by K. Lambert (New Haven, 1968).

[12] Kaplan, *op. cit.*, p. 7.

easy answer may lead us to suspect that we have misidentified the question. Perhaps we are to think of it as follows. How shall we determine which of the individuals we see (through the Verne-o-scope, perhaps) sporting in RW_f is Raquel Welch? (Can you be serious in suggesting she is that unappetizing mass of blubber over there?) Put more soberly, perhaps the question is as follows. We are given a world RW_f in which we know that Raquel Welch exists. We are given further that RW_f contains an individual that uniquely meets condition C_1, one that meets condition C_2, and the like. Now which of these is Miss Welch? Is it the individual meeting C_1, or is it some other? To have the answer we must audit the book of RW_f; does it contain, for example, the proposition *Raquel Welch meets C_1?* If so, then it is the person who meets C_1 that is Raquel Welch. Of course our information about RW_f may be limited; we may be told only that *Raquel Welch exists* and *Raquel Welch weighs 185 pounds* are in its book; we may not know, for any other (logically independent) proposition predicating a property of her, whether or not it is in the book. Then, of course, we may be unable to tell whether the thing that meets condition C_1 in RW_f is or is not identical with Raquel Welch.

This is indeed a fact; but where is the problem? (We need not step outside the actual world to find cases where identification requires more knowledge than we possess.) Is the suggestion, perhaps, that for all we can tell there is *no* world (distinct from the actual) in which Raquel Welch exists? But to make this suggestion is to imply that there is no book containing both *Raquel Welch exists* and at least one false proposition. That is, it is to suggest that the conjunction of *Raquel Welch exists* with any false proposition *p*—for example, *Paul I. Zwier is a good tennis player*—is necessarily false; and hence that *Raquel Welch exists* entails every true proposition. Obviously the assets of Raquel Welch are many and impressive; nonetheless they scarcely extend as far as all that.

I therefore do not see that the Problem of Trans-World Identification (if indeed it is a problem) threatens the enterprise of explaining the essence of Socrates in terms of properties he has in every world in which he exists. But what about the following difficulty? If (as I suggested above) for any object x, the property of x-identity (the property a thing has just in case it is identical with x) is essential to x, then the property of being identical with the teacher of Plato is essential to the teacher of Plato. Furthermore, *being identical with the teacher of Plato* is essential to anything identical with the teacher of Plato—Socrates, for example. Hence, *identity with the teacher of* Plato is essential to Socrates. But surely

(21) If a property P is essential to an object x, then any property entailed by P is also essential to x

where, we recall, a property P entails a property Q if there is no world in which there exists an object that has P but not Q. Now whatever has the property of *being the teacher of Plato* in a given world surely has the property of *being a teacher* in that world. But the former property is essential to Socrates; so, therefore, is the latter. And yet this is absurd; the property of being a teacher is not essential to Socrates. (Even if you do not think that is absurd, we can show by an easy generalization of this argument that any property Socrates has is essential to him—and *that* is patently absurd.) What has gone wrong? (21) certainly has the ring of truth. Must we conclude after all that such alleged properties as *being identical with the teacher of Plato* are a snare and a delusion?

That would be hasty, I think. Consider a world W in which Socrates exists but does not teach Plato; let us suppose that in W Xenophon is the only teacher Plato ever had. Now in W Socrates is not identical with the teacher of Plato—that is, Socrates is not identical with the person who *in W* is Plato's only teacher. He is, however, identical with the person who *in the actual world* is the only teacher of Plato. Here a certain misunderstanding may arise. If W had transpired, then W would have been the actual world—so is it not true that in W it is *Xenophon*, not Socrates, who has the property of being the person who is the only teacher of Plato in the actual world? *Being actual* is a peculiar property; this is a property that in any given world is had by that world and that world only. Accordingly in W it is Xenophon who is the teacher of Plato in the actual world. We may forestall this *contretemps* as follows. Suppose we give a name to the actual world—the one that does in fact obtain; suppose we name it "Kronos." Then this property of being identical with the teacher of Plato—the property Socrates has essentially according to the above argument—is the property of being identical with the person who in fact, in the actual world, is the teacher of Plato. It is the property of being identical with the person who *in Kronos* is the teacher of Plato. But *that* property— *identity with the person who in Kronos is the teacher of Plato*—does not entail *being a teacher*. For a thing might have that property in some world distinct from Kronos—a world in which Socrates teaches no one, for example—without having, in that world, the property of being a teacher.

But now still another query confronts us. Consider the well-known facts that Cicero is identical with Tully and that Hesperus is the very same thing as Phosphorus. Do not these facts respectively represent (for many of us, at least) historical and astronomical *discovery*? And hence are not the counterfacts *Hesperus and Phosphorus are entities distinct* and *Tully is diverse from Cicero*, though counterfacts indeed, *contingently* counterfactual? Historical and astronomical science have been known to reverse themselves; might we not sometime come to discover that Cicero and Tully were really two distinct persons and that Hesperus is not identical with Phosphorus? But if so, then how can it be true that *being identical with Phosphorus* is an essence of Hesperus, so that *Hesperus is diverse from Phosphorus* is necessarily false?

The argument here implicit takes for granted that the discovery of necessary truth is not the proper business of the historian and astronomer. But this is at best dubious. I discover that Ephialtes was a traitor; I know that it is Kronos that is actual; accordingly, I also discover that Kronos includes the state of affairs consisting in Ephialtes' being a traitor. This last, of course, is necessarily true; but couldn't a historian (*qua*, as they say, *historian*) discover it, too? It is hard to believe that historians and astronomers are subject to a general prohibition against the discovery of necessary truth. Their views, if properly come by, are a posteriori; that they are also contingent does not follow.

On the other hand, when I discovered that Kronos contained *Ephialtes' being a traitor,* I also discovered something contingent. Is there something similar in the case of Venus? Exactly what was it that the ancient Babylonians discovered? Was it that the planet Hesperus has the property of being identical with Phosphorus? But *identity with Phosphorus* is in fact the very same property as *identity with Hesperus;* no doubt the Babylonians knew all along that Hesperus has *Hesperus-identity;* and hence they knew all along that Hesperus has *Phosphorus-identity.* Just what was it the Babylonians believed before the Discovery, and how did this discovery fit into the total economy of their belief? Perhaps we can put it like this. The Babylonians probably believed what can be expressed by pointing in the evening to the western sky, to Venus, and saying *"This* is not identical with" (long pause) *"that"* (pointing to the eastern sky, to Venus, the following morning). If so, then they believed of Hesperus and *Phosphorus-identity* that the latter does not characterize the former; since *Phosphorus-identity* is the same property as *Hesperus-identity,* they believed of *Hesperus-identity* that it does not characterize Hesperus. No doubt the Babylonians would have disputed this allegation; but of course one can easily be mistaken about whether one holds a belief of this kind. And the quality of their intellectual life was improved by the Discovery in that thereafter they no longer believed of Hesperus that it lacked the property of Hesperus-identity. Of course we can scarcely represent this improvement as a matter of discovering that Hesperus *had Hesperus-identity;* they already knew that. Their tragedy was that they knew that, and also believed its contradictory; the Discovery consisted in part of correcting this deplorable state of affairs.

Still, this is at best a partial account of what they discovered. For they also believed that there is a heavenly body that appears first in the evening, and another, distinct from the first, that disappears last in the morning. This is a contingent proposition; and part of what they discovered is that it is false. Or, to put things just a little differently, suppose the identity criteria for "Hesperus"—such properties as *appearing just after sundown, appearing before any other star or planet, being brighter than any other star or planet that appears in the evening*—are H_1, H_2, . . ., H_n; and suppose the identity criteria for "Phosphorus" are P_1, P_2, . . ., P_n. Then what the Babylonians discovered is that the same heavenly body satisfies both the P_i and the H_i. They discovered that the planet that satisfies the P_i also satisfies the H_i. And of course this is a contingent fact; there are possible worlds in which the thing that in fact has the distinction of satisfying both sets of criteria satisfies only one or neither. The Babylonian discovery, therefore, was a complex affair; but there is nothing in it to suggest that *being identical with Phosphorus* is not essential to Hesperus.

III

Socrates, therefore, has an essence—being *Socrates* or *Socrateity*. This essence entails each of his essential properties. And among these we have so far found (in addition to trivially essential properties) such items as *being Socrates or Greek, being a non-number,* and *being possibly conscious*. But what about the property of having (or, to beg no questions, being) a body? Could Socrates have been disembodied? Or could he have had a body of quite a different sort? Could he have been an alligator, for example? That depends. We might think of an alligator as a composite typically consisting in a large, powerful body animated by an unimpressive mind with a nasty disposition. If we do, shall we say that any mind-alligator-body composite is an alligator, or must the mind be of a special relatively dull sort? If the first alternative is correct, then I think Socrates could have been an alligator (or at any rate its personal or mental component); for I think he could have had an alligator body. We have no difficulty in understanding Kafka's story about the man who wakes up one morning to discover that he now has the body of a beetle; and in fact the state of affairs depicted there is entirely possible. In the same way I can imagine myself awakening one morning and discovering, no doubt to my chagrin, that I had become the owner of an alligator body. I should then give up mountain climbing for swimming and skin diving. Socrates, therefore, could have had an alligator body; if this is sufficient for his having been an alligator, then Socrates could have been an alligator.

On the other hand, we might think, with Descartes, that an alligator is a material object of some sort—perhaps an elaborate machine made of flesh and bone. Suppose that is what an alligator is; could Socrates have been one? Descartes has a famous argument for the conclusion that he is not a material object:

> I am therefore, precisely speaking, only a thinking thing, that is, a mind (*mens sive animus*), understanding, or reason—terms whose signification was before unknown to me. I am, however, a real thing, and really existent; but what thing? The answer was, a thinking thing. The question now arises, am I aught besides? I will stimulate my imagination with a view to discover whether I am not still something more than a thinking being. Now it is plain I am not the assemblage of members called the human body; I am not a thin and penetrating air diffused through all these members, or wind, or flame, or vapour, or breath, or any of all the things I can imagine; for I supposed that all these were not, and, without changing the supposition, I find that I still feel assured of my existence.[13]

How shall we construe this argument? I think Descartes means to reason as follows: it is at present possible both that I exist and that there are no material objects—that is,

(23) Possibly, I exist and there are no material objects.

But if so, then

(24) I am not a material object.

But is the premise of this argument true? I think it is. The proposition that there are no material objects does not entail, it seems to me, that I do not exist. Furthermore, Descartes could have employed a weaker premise here:

(23′) Possibly, I exist and no material object is my body.

But even if these premises are true, the argument is at the best unduly inexplicit. We might well argue from

(25) Possibly, I exist and no brothers-in-law exist

to

(26) I am not a brother-in-law.

What follows from (23) is not (24) but only its possibility:

(27) Possibly, I am not a material object.

What the argument shows, therefore, is that even if human beings are in fact physical objects, they are only contingently so. But some-

---

[13] Descartes, *Meditations*, Meditation I.

thing else of interest follows from the possibility of (23) and (23′); it follows that there are worlds in which I exist and not only *am* not a body, but do not *have* a body. *Being embodied,* therefore, is not essential to human persons. Here we might be inclined to object that

(28) All human persons have bodies

is necessarily true. Perhaps it is and perhaps it is not; in neither case does it follow that human persons are essentially embodied. What follows is only that, if they are not, then *being a human person* is not essential to human persons, just as *being a brother-in-law* is not essential to brothers-in-law. The property of being a human person (as opposed to that of being a divine person or an angelic person or a person *simpliciter*) may entail the possession of a body; it may be that whatever, in a given world, has the property of being a human person has a body in that world. It does not follow that Socrates, who is in fact a human person, has the property of having a body in every world he graces.

As it stands, therefore, Descartes's argument does not establish that he is not a body or a material object. But perhaps his argument can be strengthened. G. H. von Wright suggests the following principle:

> If a property can be significantly predicated of the individuals of a certain universe of discourse then either the property is necessarily present in some or all of the individuals and necessarily absent in the rest or else the property is possibly but not necessarily (that is, contingently) present in some or all individuals and possibly but not necessarily (contingently) absent in the rest.[14]

We might restate and compress this principle as follows:

(29) Any property *P* had essentially by anything is had essentially by everything that has it.

Is (29) true? We have already seen that it is not; *being prime or prim, being Socrates or Greek* constitute counterexamples. Still, the principle might hold for a large range of properties, and it is plausible to suppose that it holds for the property of being a material object as well as for the complement of that property. It seems to me impossible that there should be an object that in some possible world is a material object and in others is not. That is to say, where "*M*" names the property of being a material object and "$\overline{M}$" names its complement,

(30) Anything that has *M* or $\overline{M}$, has *M* essentially or has $\overline{M}$ essentially.

And armed with this principle, we can refurbish Descartes's argument. For if I am not essentially a material object, then by (30) I am not one

[14] G. H. von Wright, *An Essay in Modal Logic* (Amsterdam, 1951), p. 27.

at all. And hence Descartes is right in holding that he is not a material object. But if I do not have the property of being a material object, I have its complement, and by another application of the same principle it follows that I have its complement essentially. Descartes, therefore, is correct; he is an immaterial object and, indeed, is such an object in every world in which he exists. What Descartes's argument establishes is that persons are essentially immaterial; Socrates, therefore, could have been an alligator only if alligators are not material objects.

IV

Socrates' essence, accordingly, contains or entails trivially essential properties, the property of being immaterial, the property of being Socrates or Greek, and the like. But aren't these—except perhaps for immateriality—pretty drab properties? What about such everyday properties as qualities of character and personality—being a saint or a sinner, wise or foolish, admirable or the reverse; are none of these essential to him? I think the answer is that none are. But if the essence of Socrates has no more content than this, isn't it a pretty thin, lackluster thing, scarcely worth talking about? Perhaps; but it is hard to see that this is legitimate cause for complaint. If indeed Socrates' essence is pretty slim, the essentialist can scarcely be expected to pretend otherwise. To complain about this is like scolding the weatherman for the lack of sunshine. Still it must be conceded that the present conception of essence might seem a bit thin by comparison, for example, with that of Leibniz:

> This being so, we are able to say that this is the nature of an individual substance or of a complete being, namely, to afford a conception so complete that the concept shall be sufficient for the understanding of it and for the deduction of all the predicates of which the substance is or may become the subject. Thus the quality of king, which belonged to Alexander the Great, an abstraction from the subject, is not sufficiently determined to constitute an individual, and does not contain the other qualities of the same subject, nor everything which the idea of this prince includes. God, however, seeing the individual concept, or haecceity, of Alexander, sees there at the same time the basis and the reason of all the predicates which can be truly uttered regarding him; for instance, that he will conquer Darius and Porus, even to the point of knowing *a priori* (and not by experience) whether he died a natural death or by poison—facts which we can learn only through history.[15]

[15] Leibniz, *Discourse on Metaphysics* (La Salle, Ind., 1945), pp. 13-14.

Might *seem* a bit thin, I say; in fact it is not thin at all. And while what Leibniz says sounds wildly extravagant if not plainly outrageous, it, or something like it, is the sober truth.

Return to the property of being snubnosed. This is a property Socrates has in this world and lacks in others. Consider, by contrast, the property of being snubnosed in this world, in Kronos. Socrates has this property, and has it essentially. This is perhaps obvious enough, but we can argue for it as follows. What must be shown is that (*a*) Socrates has the property of being snubnosed in Kronos in the actual world, and (*b*) there is no world in which Socrates has the complement of this property. (*a*) is clearly true. Now Kronos includes the state of affairs—call it "*B*"—consisting in Socrates' being snubnosed: that is, the state of affairs consisting in *Kronos' obtaining and B's failing to obtain* is impossible. By (20), therefore, this is impossible in every world; hence, Kronos includes *B* in every world. But clearly Socrates exists in a given world *W* in which Kronos includes *B* only if, in that world, he has the property of being snubnosed in Kronos. Accordingly, Socrates has this property in every world in which he exists; hence, there is no world in which he has its complement.

We may also put the matter bibliographically. It suffices to show that Kronos' book contains *Socrates is snubnosed* in every world. But it is evident, I take it, that

(31) For any proposition *P* and book *B*, *B* contains *p* if and only if *p* is a consequence of *B*

is necessarily true. Now clearly *Socrates is snubnosed* is a consequence of Kronos' book: Kronos' book *U* (*it is false that Socrates is snubnosed*) is an impossible set. By (20), therefore, this set is impossible in every world—that is, *Socrates is snubnosed* is a consequence of Kronos' book in every world. Hence Kronos' book contains that proposition in every world.

The property of being snubnosed in Kronos, therefore, is essential to Socrates. And (presuming that in fact Socrates was the only teacher Plato ever had) while there are worlds and objects distinct from Socrates such that the latter *teach Plato* in the former, there is no such object that in some world has the property of *teaching Plato in Kronos*. The property of teaching Plato in Kronos, therefore, entails the property of being Socrates; accordingly, this property is an essence of Socrates. Clearly we can find as many more essences of Socrates as we wish. Take any property he alone has—*being married to Xantippe*, for example, or *being the shortest Greek philosopher* or *being A. E. Taylor's favorite philosopher*. For any such property *P*, *having P in Kronos* is an essence of Socrates. Take, more generally, any property

P and world W such that in W Socrates alone has P; the property of having P in W will be an essence of Socrates.

According to Leibniz, "God, however, seeing the individual concept, or haecceity, of Alexander, sees there at the same time the basis and the reason of all the predicates which can be truly uttered regarding him." Arnauld was shocked and scandalized when he read this suggestion—no doubt in part because of the bad cold he claimed he had when he received the *Discourse* from Count von Hessen Rheinfels. But in fact what Leibniz says, or something similar, is correct. We can see that this is so if we take a closer look at the notion of *essence,* or *individual concept,* or *haecceity.* An essence E of Socrates, as we have seen above, is a property that meets three conditions. First of all, it is essential to Socrates. Secondly, for any property P, if Socrates has P essentially, then E entails P. And finally, the complement of E is essential to every object distinct from Socrates. Suppose we investigate some of the consequences of this definition. We might note, first, that for any world W, either Socrates exists in W or Socrates does not exist in W. Take any world W, that is; either Socrates would have existed, had W obtained, or Socrates would not have existed had W obtained. And that he exists in W, if he does, is, by the argument above, a matter of his essence; for any world W, either *exists in W* is essential to Socrates or *does not exist in W* is. Accordingly, if E is an essence of Socrates, then for any world W, either E entails *exists in W* or E entails *does not exist in W.*

Secondly, notice that for any property P and world W in which Socrates exists, either Socrates has P in W or Socrates has $\bar{P}$ in W. This, too, is a matter of his essence; so for any such world and property, any essence of Socrates either entails *has P in W* or entails *has $\bar{P}$ in W.* But what about those worlds in which Socrates does *not* exist? Does he have properties in *those* worlds? Take, for example, the property of being snubnosed, and let W be any world in which Socrates does not exist. Are we to suppose that if W had obtained, Socrates would have had the property of being snubnosed? Or that if W had obtained, he would have had the complement of that property? I should think that neither of these is true; had W obtained, Socrates would have had neither snubnosedness nor its complement. I am inclined to think that Socrates has no properties at all in those worlds in which he does not exist. We cannot say, therefore, that if E is an essence of Socrates, then for just any world W and property P, either E entails *the property of having P in W* or E entails *the property of having $\bar{P}$ in W;* Socrates has neither P nor $\bar{P}$ in a world where he does not exist. Still, in *this* world, in Kronos, Socrates has, for any world W and property P, either

the property of having P in W or *the property of not having P in W.*
For either

(32) If W had obtained, Socrates would have had P

or

(33) If W had obtained, Socrates would not have had P.

More generally, an essence of Socrates will entail, for any property P
and world W, either the property of having P in W or the property of
not having P in W.

An essence E of Socrates, therefore, meets three conditions: (a) for
any world W, E entails *exists in W* or *does not exist in W;* (b) for any
world W such that E entails *exists in W,* E also entails, for any property P, *has P in W* or *has P̄ in W,* and (c) for any world W and property P, E entails *has P in W* or *does not have P in W.* In addition, of
course, E is essential to Socrates and its complement is essential to everything distinct from him. We might therefore characterize an essence,
or haecceity, or individual concept as follows:

(34) E is an *individual concept,* or *essence,* or *haecceity* if and only if (a)
    has E essentially is instantiated in some world, (b) for any world W
    and property P, E entails *has P in W* or *does not have P in W,* (c)
    for any world W, E entails *exists in W* or *does not exist in W,* (d) for
    any world W such that E entails *exists in W,* E also entails, for any
    property P, *has P in W* or *has P̄ in W,* and (e) in no world is there
    an object x that has E and an object y distinct from x that has E in
    some world or other.

But if existence is a property, clause (c) will be redundant in that it is
entailed by (b). Furthermore, it is necessarily true that an object x
exists only if it has, for any property P, either P or P̄; hence clause
(d) is also redundant. Still further, (e) is redundant. For let W be
any world in which there exists an object x that has E. Now clearly
enough it is not possible that two distinct objects share all their properties; in W, therefore, there is no object distinct from x that has E.
But further, W contains no object y distinct from x that has E in
some world W'. For suppose it does. E then entails *exists in W';* hence
both x and y exist in W'. But in W' there is at most one object that
has E; hence in W' x is identical with y. Accordingly in W, y is diverse
from x but possibly identical with x; and this is impossible.

Shorn of redundancy, our present characterization goes as follows:

(35) E is an essence if and only if (a) *has E essentially* is instantiated in

some world or other, and (b) for any world W and property P, E entails *has P in W* or *does not have P in W*.[16]

By way of conclusion, then, let us return to Leibniz and his claims about God and Alexander. What we see is that he was right, or nearly right. God has a complete knowledge of Alexander's essence; hence for any property P and world W, God knows whether or not Alexander has P in W. He knows, furthermore, that it is Kronos that has the distinction of being the actual world. From these two items he can read off all the properties—accidental as well as essential—that Alexander does in fact have. So what we have here is surely no paucity of content; an essence is as rich and full-bodied as anyone could reasonably desire.

APPENDIX

Can we make a further simplification in our account of essencehood? Yes. Suppose we say that a property P is *world-indexed* if there is a world W and a property Q such that P is equivalent to the property of *having Q in W* or to its complement—the property of *not having Q in W*. *Being snubnosed in Kronos*, for example, is a world-indexed property. Let us say further that a property Q is *large* if for every world-indexed property P, either Q entails P or Q entails $\bar{P}$. *Being Socrates* or *Socrateity*, as we have seen, is a large property. Now where Q is a large property, there may be a large property P distinct from Q that *coincides with Q on world-indexed properties*—that is, a property that, for each world-indexed property R, entails R if and only if Q entails R. *Being Socrates*, for example, and *being Socrates and snubnosed* are distinct large properties that coincide on world-indexed properties. Accordingly, let us say that a property is *encaptic* if it is large, and is entailed by every property that coincides with it on world-indexed properties. Roughly, we may think of an encaptic property as a property equivalent to some conjunctive property Q each conjunct of which is a world-indexed property, and such that for each world-indexed property P, either P or $\bar{P}$ is a conjunct of Q. We should note that an encaptic property may entail properties that are not world-indexed; if an encaptic property Q entails *has P in W* for every world W for which it entails *exists in W*, then Q entails W. So, for example, *Socrateity* entails the property of being possibly conscious and the property of not being a number, neither of which is world-indexed. (Of course, any such non world-indexed property entailed by an encaptic property Q will be essential to whatever instantiates Q.) Given these definitions, then, we may say that

---

[16] See appendix.

(36) An essence is an encaptic property that is instantiated in some world or other.

I think we can see that (35) and (36) equivalently characterize the idea of essence. Let us note first that any instantiated encaptic property meets the conditions for essencehood laid down by (35). Obviously, any such property will entail, for any world-indexed property P, either P or $\bar{P}$. But further, whatever instantiates an encaptic property Q has Q essentially. For let W be any world in which there exists an object x that has Q, and let W^* be any world in which x exists. What must be shown is that x has Q in W^*. It suffices to show that in W^* x has every world-indexed property entailed by Q. But an interesting peculiarity of world-indexed properties, as we have seen, is that nothing in any world has any such property accidentally. Accordingly since in W x has each world-indexed property entailed by Q, x has each such property in W^* as well; and hence x has Q in W^*.

On the other hand, any property that meets conditions (a) and (b) of (35) is an encaptic property that is somewhere instantiated. Obviously, if E is any such property, E is instantiated in some world. But it is also encaptic. E entails, for any world-indexed property P, has P or has $\bar{P}$. Accordingly, E entails some encaptic property Q. Let W^* be any world in which there is an object x that has Q. E, as we know, is essentially instantiated; so there is a world W' in which there exists an object y that has E and has it in every world in which it exists. Now Q (and hence E) entails *exists in* W^*; accordingly y exists in W^*, has E in W^*, and has Q in W^*. Now clearly there is no world in which two distinct objects share an encaptic property; if, for every property P, x has P in W if and only if y has P in W, then x is identical with y. In the present case, therefore, x and y are identical in W^*, since each has Q there. But y has E in W^*; hence so does x. Accordingly, Q *but not E* is not instantiated in W^*; hence E both entails and is entailed by Q, and is itself, therefore, encaptic.

Bibliography

~~~~~~

An excellent bibliography centered around the *de dicto* modalities may be found in SUMNER and WOODS, *Necessary Truth: A Book of Readings* (New York: Random House, Inc. 1969). PAP and EDWARDS, *A Modern Introduction to Philosophy*, revised edition (New York: The Free Press, 1965) also contains a helpful bibliography. (See the bibliography at the close of section "Apriori Knowledge.") PAP's work, *Semantics and Necessary Truth* (New Haven, Conn.: Yale University Press, 1958) may also be recommended. Also of great interest to those with some background in logic is QUINE's *Philosophy of Logic* (Englewood Cliffs, N.J.: Prentice-Hall, Inc., 1970).

The following works may be recommended for those interested in the formal aspects of the *de re* modalities:

CARNAP, R., "Modalities and Quantification," *Journal of Symbolic Logic,* II (1946), 33–64.

HINTIKKA, J., "Modality and Quantification," *Theoria*, No. 27 (1961), 119–28.

———, "The Modes of Modality," *Acta Philosophica Fennica*, No. 16 (1963), 65–82.

HUGHES, G., and M. CRESSWELL, *An Introduction to Modal Logic.* London: Methuen & Co., Ltd., 1968.

KANGER, S., *Provability in Logic.* Stockholm: Almquist and Wiksill, 1957.

KRIPKE, S., "A Completeness Theorem in Modal Logic," *Journal of Symbolic Logic,* No. 24 (1959), 1–14.

————, "Semantical Considerations on Modal Logic," *Acta Philosophica Fennica,* No. 16 (1963), 83–94.

MONTAGUE, R., "Logical Necessity, Physical Necessity, Ethics, and Quantifiers," *Inquiry,* No. 4 (1960), 259–69.

————, "Pragmatics," in *Contemporary Philosophy,* edited by R. Klibansky, pp. 102–22. Florence: La Nuova Italia Editrice, 1968.

THOMASON, R., "Modal Logic and Metaphysics," in *The Logical Way of Doing Things,* edited by K. Lambert, pp. 119–46. New Haven, Conn.: Yale University Press, 1969.

The following discussions of *de re* modalities are less formal on the whole than those mentioned above:

CARNAP, R., *Meaning and Necessity.* Chicago: University of Chicago Press, 1956.

CARTWRIGHT, R., "Some Remarks on Essentialism," *The Journal of Philosophy,* LXV (1968), 615–26.

CHISHOLM, R., "Identity Through Possible Worlds: Some Questions," *Noûs,* I (1967), 1–8.

FITCH, F., "The Problem of the Morning Star and the Evening Star," revised edition reprinted in Copi and Gould, *Contemporary Readings in Logical Theory,* pp. 273–78. New York: The Macmillan Company, 1967.

FØLLESDAL, D., "Quine on Modality," *Synthese,* No. 19 (1968), 147–57.

KANGER, S., "The Morning Star Paradox," *Theoria,* No. 23 (1957), 133–34.

————, "A Note on Quantification and Modalities," *Theoria,* No. 23 (1957), 133–34.

KNEALE, W., "Modality De Dicto and De Re," in *Logic, Methodology and Philosophy of Science,* edited by Nagel, Suppes, and Tarski, pp. 622–33. Stanford, Calif.: Stanford University Press, 1962.

LEWIS, D., "Anselm and Actuality," *Noûs,* IV (1970), 175–88.

————, "Counterpart Theory and Quantified Modal Logic," *The Journal of Philosophy,* LXV (1968), 113–26.

LINSKY, L., "Reference, Essentialism, and Modality," *The Journal of Philosophy,* LXVI (1969), 687–700.

PURTILL, R., "About Identity Through Possible Worlds," *Noûs,* II (1968), 87–89.

QUINE, W., "The Problem of Interpreting Modal Logic," *The Journal of Symbolic Logic,* No. 12 (1947), 43–48.

————, "Three Grades of Modal Involvement," reprinted in *The Ways of Paradox and Other Essays,* pp. 156–74. New York: Random House, Inc., 1966.

SMULLYAN, A., "Modality and Description," *The Journal of Symbolic Logic,* No. 13 (1948), 31–37.

THOMASON, R., and R. STALNAKER, "Modality and Reference," *Noûs,* II (1968), 359–72.